"Rock It Come Over"

Author Olive Lewin listening to Queenie
who is holding a sick child

"Rock It Come Over"

The Folk Music of Jamaica

With special reference to Kumina
and the work of Mrs Imogene "Queenie" Kennedy

Olive Lewin

THE UNIVERSITY OF THE WEST INDIES PRESS
Barbados • Jamaica • Trinidad and Tobago

University of the West Indies Press
1A Aqueduct Flats Mona
Kingston 7 Jamaica

04 03 02 01 00   5 4 3 2 1

CATALOGUING IN PUBLICATION DATA
Lewin, Olive
"Rock it come over": The folk music of Jamaica with
special reference to Kumina and the work of
Mrs Imogene "Queenie" Kennedy / Olive Lewin.
p. : ill. ; cm
Includes bibliographical references and index.
ISBN: 976-640-028-8
1. Folk music – Jamaica – African
influences. 2. Kennedy, Imogene
"Queenie". 3. Kumina (cult) – Jamaica.
4. Music – Jamaica – African influences.
I. Title

ML3565.L58 2000   781.62 dc-20

Set in Palatino 10.3/15–16 pt
Book and cover design by Alan Ross
Page composition by Donavan Grant

Printed in Canada

To
my mother and father,
and to
Johanna, Gillian and Jason

JAMAICA – ITS PARISHES
Location of main cults in 1987

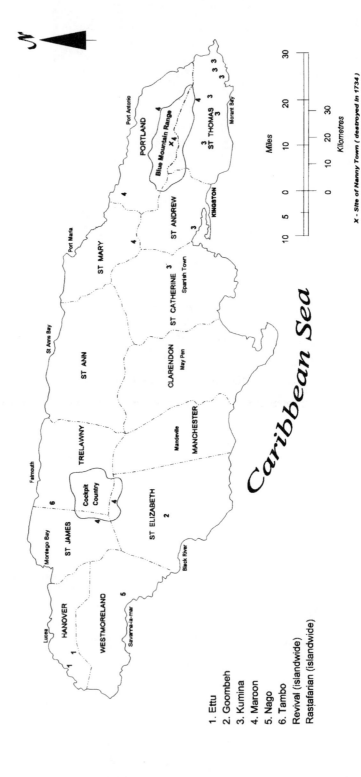

1. Ettu
2. Goombeh
3. Kumina
4. Maroon
5. Nago
6. Tambo

Revival (islandwide)
Rastafarian (islandwide)

X - Site of Nanny Town (destroyed in 1734)

Contents

Illustrations

Foreword

Jamaica is one of the few countries which have made the transition from a folk-based musical culture to a popular international music form. As the focus shifts from the traditional to the popular, so do public attention and recognition. Special steps have to be taken in such cases to preserve the treasury of folk heritage.

Several positive steps have been taken in Jamaica to record its musical heritage. The Jamaica Festival provides a platform for annual performance of the arts in which folk music is well represented in song and dance. What is more, the performances are largely school presentations, ensuring that the music is nurtured for each succeeding generation.

More important to the future is a record of the past. That immense responsibility was assigned by me officially to Dr Olive Lewin more than thirty years ago during my tenure as the minister responsible for culture. Dr Lewin was eminently suitable for a programme to collect our folk music in recordings and for transcribing many works to sheet music. Her qualifications as an accomplished teacher of music and pianist in her own right were a sound background to carry out this historical assignment.

Because we were very largely breaking new ground, much of the collection had to be carried out in the field, particularly in the rural areas where the retention of traditional music is stronger.

Olive Lewin went beyond the original scope of her assignment which was to collect the large number of mento songs and the ring play tunes performed as games among children and adults in folk society. The African retentions which still exist in some areas of Jamaica, as expressed in musical dance and song, came to her attention: Tambo, Ettu, Nago, and Goombeh. Dr Lewin researched these relatively unfamiliar areas of folk culture, adding them to the collection. Of special interest were the legendary Maroons and the Kumina cult, both Afrocentric groups where, for special reasons, survival of African traditions were highest.

"Rock It Come Over" will be a valuable, authoritative addition to the literature on Jamaican music. Moreover, it will add much to a better understanding of the linkage of traditional music to the immensely popular forms of Jamaican music which have achieved worldwide recognition over the past forty years.

E.P.G. Seaga

Introduction

In the 1970s I, along with several colleagues at the Smithsonian Institution, collaborated with Olive Lewin and Jamaican tradition bearers, including Queenie Imogene Kennedy, on two Festivals of American Folklife held in Washington, DC, on the National Mall of the United States. The collaboration we undertook was guided by a principle of collegiality with Jamaican cultural workers and grassroots tradition bearers. Our goal was to foreground the ways of knowing and ways of doing of grassroots cultural communities.

Achieving collegial relations of respect and shared authority is especially challenging when professional cultural workers initiate projects with community-based cultural bearers whose immediate social life, work and expressive practices emanate from their own agency and in response to the inner workings and expectations of their local and national, and increasingly transnational, communities. The collegial goal is never fully realized because festival projects presented far away from the local community or home country invariably impose a hierarchy of decision making and therein assumptive work behaviours among the cultural workers who provide overall direction for the endeavour. The process of festival development and collaboration with community cultural representatives is further complicated by negotiations with national governments and private-sector funders who have their own views about who and what cultural expressions should represent their nation at the prestigious Smithsonian Institution in the revered and sometimes dreaded United States of America.

Despite inherent obstacles in festival planning and presentation, full collegiality, respect, trust, and honourable representations of the life and values of both tradition bearers and cultural workers can be achieved if cultural workers are committed, disciplined, and socially and educationally prepared. Throughout her personal and professional life, Olive Lewin has striven to consistently live and to publicly communicate and educate about values and cultural expression that reflect the integrity of grassroots communities and the integrity of cultural workers, from varied socioeconomic, cultural, and racial backgrounds, who have also demonstrated commitment to such communities.

In contrast to cultural work with grassroots communities and festivals that simply present traditional performance groups without context or as quaint, even exotic, aspects of life in rural and "foreign" places, Olive Lewin's professional collaboration with Jamaican tradition bearers has always been consistent with the philosophy of the Smithsonian Institution Center for Folklife Programs and Cultural Studies: "to join high quality scholarship with strong community service and educational outreach". The two Festival programmes developed with Olive were based on research and presentation of Jamaican traditional music, religious rituals and dance, crafts, and organized discussions between tradition bearers and public audiences about the views, values, aspirations, and aesthetic standards and intellectual perspective that undergird and motivate their cultural expressions. Collaboration on these programmes reflected Olive Lewin's abiding commitment to tradition bearers of folk music and expressive forms that "embodies the ideas and beliefs of people at or near the base of the socioeconomic pyramid and/or relates to their point of view about their daily activities recounted faithfully from their points of view".

Although this book focuses largely on Olive Lewin's development as musician, teacher and cultural programmer, the underlying philosophy, values, concepts and methodologies extend well beyond an individual voice and profile. The content of this book is of critical importance in considering and figuring out the next phase that nations, especially developing nations, might formulate in development of cultural policies at the start of the twenty-first century. Academic research methodologies, weighty theoretical constructs, and politicized ideological perspectives that national policy makers usually rely upon to formulate and vet cultural development strategies and address vexing cultural and social issues are less likely to be viable. Top-down, government-formulated cultural policies are too often bereft of knowledge and cultural sensitivities required for mediation and accommodation of distinct, and increasingly violent, conflicting linguistic, religious, class and aesthetic values. Status-quo approaches generally fail to consider the respect and integrity that Olive Lewin accords to expressive forms that undergird the social life of Jamaican working people in cities and rural areas. Her informal and formal education led her to approach traditional folklife as foundational dimensions which would inspire and inform an authentic national Jamaican arts culture and avoid being "forever limited to imitation". The elaboration of Olive Lewin's life work in this book provides avenues of passion, commitment and personal and professional practice critical to discerning the way forward for cult workers and cult policy makers at the end of a century.

At the dawn of the new millennium, Jamaica and all other nations, especially in the developing world, are snared in a web of stretched and strained relations and tensions about national and transnational values, individual and social obligations and urban and grassroots-based cultural expressions. The foreboding spread of a global market economy, and the concomitant emergence of an imperious market and media-induced culture, force developed and developing nations alike to review and revise national cultural policies at home and in international relations.

Where will national governments and locally based cultural workers and institutions turn for guidance to sustain national cultural integrity while taking advantage of the positive attributes of cosmopolitan culture? The historical complexities and contemporary consequences of slavery, colonialism, anti-colonial struggle and the present-day sociology of race, class, and gender all play havoc with neatly defined notions of identity. Adoption of and/or over-reliance on universal class-based notions of national cultural identity impedes creative, substantive national development based in the social and cultural terrain in which the actual lives of common citizens are rooted. Olive Lewin's straightforward but unpretentious autobiographical charting of her personal development and professional cultural work is instructional as it opens windows into how middle-class upbringing and privileged relations with government can embrace defining grassroots dimensions of Jamaican national culture and negotiate the ideological prejudices of would-be Afro-Saxons and preachy leftists who romanticize the masses.

The contributions of contemporaries and forerunners among Jamaican grassroots cultural workers (Louise Bennett, Ivy Baxter, Edward Seaga, Rex Nettleford, among others) are each in their own way informed by a cultural focus infrequently attributed by others to folk tradition bearers whose perseverance through the vicissitudes of slavery, post-emancipation neocolonial cultural allures and post-independence struggles for national identity are the groundwork for what is distinct in national cultural values and practices. The demands of national development and professional aspirations have motivated and/or forced many of us like Olive to toil to master, even savour, the foundations and intricacies of Eurocentric cultures and epistemologies. But many of us throughout the developing world and developing communities were not as fortunate as Olive to have parents who consciously and consistently instilled awareness, understanding and appreciation of grassroots tradition bearers whose religious views, aesthetic traditions, oral literatures, occupational cultures and family values have been the bases, sometimes wholesome and sometimes contradictory, for national and class development, pride and shame, economic and spiritual nourishment.

I have no doubt that Olive Lewin will not see herself in the grander scheme of things I suggest this book opens up to us; nor will she fully concur with the portrait I offer of her life and values. I am confident, however, that she will glow, albeit inside, and smile faintly, when praise is given to the Memory Bank project she developed to motivate grassroots and upper-class communities to preserve the grassroots folkways of Jamaica for future generations and future iterations of national identity.

Of the readers, this book asks, and deserves answers to, the questions: What songs do you sing? What cultural questions will you leave behind? What memories can build a future?

James Early
The Smithsonian Institution

This book presents an account of work done since 1966 and of lifelong contact with the heart of Jamaica and the keepers of her traditional music, with its base of wisdom and its surrounding lore. Nine of those years were devoted exclusively to fieldwork, observing, listening to and recording the memories of elderly Jamaicans. Since then, much time has been spent on primary and secondary research, documentation and dissemination.

The music and lore assembled here relate to the years from slavery in the early sixteenth century through full emancipation in 1838 to the later twentieth century.

Making this heritage material and its context known in Jamaica and further afield can, I believe, increase the artistic repertoire of the wider world as well as improve communication practices and human understanding at many levels on our shrinking planet.

The past twenty-five years have allowed me to take note of the salutory effect that knowledge of this music has on Jamaicans in school, church, theatre and community settings at home and among those dispersed throughout the world. Many have come to recognize that, contrary to predominant assumptions, slavery was not our origin, a shameful one, but rather a phase in the journey of our ancestors towards the Creator's "mercy seat". It is an experience that we have shared with many races.

Elderly, and mostly unlettered, Jamaicans also have been assured of the unique contribution that they can make to the understanding and development of Jamaica. Could not this tapping of traditional experiential wisdom be undertaken worldwide?

I grew up with well-centred and culturally enlightened parents in a small Jamaican village. Life there taught me to respect and love the music, stories and words of wisdom that surrounded me. I also learned to treasure the people who gave them to us and who were part of our everyday environment.

On this solid foundation, I have been able to build with the academic tools provided by my education here and abroad.

Lend me the stone strength
Of the past, and I
Will lend you
The wings of the future.

–Robinson Jeffers

Acknowledgments

Hundreds of persons helped to make this book possible. There are some from whose work and wisdom I have benefited yet never met. It was nineteenth century plantation owners who made my secondary education possible by the bequests they left for educational purposes.

More Jamaicans than I can count told me stories and proverbs, taught me games and sang for me from childhood through to the writing of this book. Many shared cherished personal and family memories and documents as well as ideas that for decades fuelled and sustained my interest. Scores more, family – especially Monica and David Atkinson – teachers, friends, and strangers too, at home and abroad, filled many and varied needs with humbling generosity and enthusiasm. They believed in the importance of heritage awareness. Some of them became pivotal sharers in my life's work.

Informants have been central to my enlightenment. Foremost have been Bishop Kapo Reynolds, intuitive artist and Revival Shepherd; Count Ossie, pioneer Rastafarian musician; Mrs Phyllis Williams, Ettu savante; Miss Mary Turner, Bruckins expert; Mr Benjie Reid, Tambo master drummer; retired Colonel C.L.G. Harris of the Maroons; Mrs Marie Rennock of the Eastern Maroons; and Mrs 'Queenie' Kennedy, Kumina informant extraordinaire. For over thirty years, the Jamaican Folk Singers have strengthened me by their dedication, criticism and cameraderie. We have had a very special relationship. Leonie Forbes and my daughter Johanna merit particular mention: Leonie for her years of patience in coping with various tasks and miles and miles of typing, and for prodding me whenever my energies flagged; Johanna for helping me in so many ways, especially by willingly sharing her mother with work that many others feared would jeopardize our family life.

The inspiration and confidence of academic and professional colleagues have been crucial. Chief among them are Klaus Wachsmann, Charles Seeger, Maude Karpeles, Fela Sowande, Edward Ploman and members of the International Council for Traditional Music. The contribution of John Blacking of Queen's University, Belfast, is inestimable. He insisted on my completing, at all costs, the thesis which forms the basis of this book. He was always there for advice and, when necessary, bullying of the most charming kind.

Above all, my parents encouraged constant curiosity and questioning, provided insight, stimulation and an unattainable example. Words cannot describe the sacrifices that they made for their own children and for the many children who were brought into their ever-extending family.

My deepest gratitude goes out to all these persons and to Liz Hearne and Maurice Gordon who worked with me in preparing the original thesis for publication. I share with all of them any good that may flow from this book.

I

Introduction

1

The Making of a Musician

Many factors influenced my pursuit of music as a profession. The first was family background, then my formal and informal education and cultural influences. Later came concern about the lack of scholarly work and proper documentation of Jamaica's rich musical heritage, my own work in the field, and, finally, my research of Jamaican traditional music.

My first informal education undoubtedly came from my mother. This is not surprising but it was unusually intense because I was a sickly child and had a lot of attention at home. The sound of my mother humming as she went about her domestic chores bolstered the emotional security that I craved to an inordinate extent. She was a saintly woman. Throughout my life I never heard her say anything unkind, though she had strong views and would promptly remove herself from any setting of which she did not approve. We children thought twice about what we said in front of her. An ungracious word would cause tears to well up in her eyes.

She was also a very caring teacher, but her home and family always came first. When she had to be away from home, it was on paid helpers that I depended. These too exerted great influence on me. They and their families had very little of this world's goods, yet they were amazingly generous-hearted and treated me as if I were their own child. I frequently fell asleep with the sound of Jamaican stories or songs in my ears. My mother also constantly brought the sounds of our environment to my attention: bird song; a cow calling her calf; tree frogs; the conch being blown on an estate four miles away to announce work time, lunch time, and the end of the work day; the person passing by and throwing words at someone who had displeased him or her, the solo voice of a man berating a neighbour. There would also be the sounds of death ceremonies, Revival meetings, and the Salvation Army band at the school gate. My father's rehearsals with the church choir in excerpts from Handel and Mozart, Haydn and Elgar told us that it was Thursday. Towards the end of each year came the sound of the Jonkunnu rehearsals, then, at Christmas, the processions along the street. My mother not only drew my attention to these sounds but encouraged me to entertain her by repeating them when we were alone together. This obviously trained me to listen carefully and to observe too, because I would be expected to include the movement and mime aspects of any performances or activity that she requested. It was a priceless education.

I was particularly fortunate in having parents who were also knowledgeable and enlightened. My father was an historian, trained in Jamaica, the United States and Britain. His overseas education deepened his understanding of the history of Jamaica, its significance and the importance of history in living form. Every stone, tree or marking on a rock had for him its own silent memories. When questioned about them, he gave me not just a reply, but a story or the promise of a story. Sometimes it even became an exciting enquiry, a journey in which we could participate. He had more than a passing knowledge of Latin and Greek and was a stickler for "good English", both written and spoken. He also knew Swahili and had lived in East Africa, visited Nigeria and had met Aggrey of Africa, whose dream of human cooperation regardless of colour and allusion to playing on both black and white keys to make good music so appealed to us. He showed us that Paul Bogle who was hanged for leading Jamaica's 1865 uprising against distressing working and living conditions was not a rabble-rouser but a freedom fighter: a man willing to sacrifice his life for a cause in which he believed. We were made aware of being part of a wider world, and surrounded by enriching interest and excitement in things seen and unseen.

Living in the country and then winning a scholarship to a rural boarding school kept me close to the Jamaica that I loved and needed, the peasantry with their sincerity, wit, and wealth of stories and songs. Our English headmistress was close to things Scottish, and this helped. She loved that country's music and told us of Scotland's special cooking, ceremonies and songs. I learnt that it was not only Jamaicans who had dialects.

We learnt folk songs from other countries, enjoyed them and found in them reinforcement of our innate belief in the folk-ways of Jamaica.

My Father and Schoolmaster

Formal education started at the school where my father was headmaster and my mother a member of the staff. In those days, children were supposed to go to school from the age of seven to fifteen. There was a thirst for learning and I can recall several parents bringing their little children by the hand and begging my father to discipline them in whatever way he thought fit, "Only see that they learn, Teacher, because if I walk on the floor, my child must walk on the shelf." In spite of the government stipulation about age, children were usually taken to school at five years of age. Parents would swear that the child was seven and apologize for not being able to produce the "age paper" as they called the birth certificate. When the child was fifteen by school records, the parents would produce the birth certificate showing that the child was only thirteen. In this way an extra two years of schooling was gained. This was a frequent and, I would say, accepted form of deception.

The school was a small wooden structure with no partitions, built to accommodate 152 children. On that same floor, slaves had once been sold. I have always thought it a sign of the speed with which we have developed that in just over a hundred years my father, born in that same village, became headmaster, then manager of the school and a member of the Parish School Board.

An Exciting Curriculum

The building was also used for Anglican church services. We, therefore, had a harmonium which was usually locked and covered during the week, but available for special events. Otherwise, a family piano would be borrowed, tuned and used for the concerts that dotted the school year. Some were given by the school. Our senior boys sang rousing music like the "Soldiers' Chorus" from Faust, and the girls revelled in singing Brahms' "Lullaby" and other ladylike songs. Voices combined for hymns or anthems in two to four parts, as well as for "Ye Mariners of England", "Land of Hope and Glory" and other British national songs that had to be prepared for the King's Birthday and Empire Day each year.

Music was an integral part of the school curriculum. We all not only sang but also learnt tonic sol-fa and had to be able to sight-sing from the blackboard or from hand signs given by my father. We had regular visiting violinists and singers, and the military band playing foot-tapping (never hip-swinging) arrangements of Jamaican folk songs. Occasionally we also had the thrill of having our church choir accompanied by the military band in performances of popular standards such as the Hallelujah Chorus. We were members of 4H Clubs and agricultural societies. We gardened and were encouraged to play games like "Jane and Louisa" and "In an' Out the Window". The boys specialized in marbles, using nichol seeds which they could pick in the wooded areas nearby or cushu (cashew) pot which was similar to marbles but was played with cashew nuts flicked by the thumb into specially dug holes in the school yard. Cricket, played with balls made of string, rubber and rags, and bats made from coconut boughs, was a perennial favourite.

We had a thorough grounding not only in the three Rs but in the history and geography of Jamaica. There was nature study, and we watched as beans sprouted and tadpoles became frogs. We made a model of the world and with a flashlight my father would show us why there was night and day, why there were the seasons and how the tilt of the world's axis affected it all. At times a student would be called upon to hold a ball which would be the moon so that we could see how the moon reflected the light of the sun and how eclipses occurred. Certain lessons were taught by rhythm. My father would tap on a desk with a long wooden pointer and we were expected to recognize the rhythm and join in. These rhythms related to Jamaican exports, imports, agricultural products and railway stations. Kingston, Gregory Park, Grange Lane, Spanish Town, Hartlands, Bushy Park, Old Harbour, May Pen and so on became:

My father laid great emphasis on language arts. Spelling was learnt not by rote, but rather by attention to the derivation of words, and the accenting of syllables. He was one of Jamaica's most highly respected teachers. Many parents crossed the island with children for whom they had special ambition, bringing them to live in the district, sometimes sharing our own rooms, so that he could teach them.

Teachers – All Able and Committed

The school was always overcrowded. This was eased by having classes under trees in the school yard. We learnt to protect our noses from the clouds of dust that rose from the road every time a plantation vehicle passed. Private cars were mercifully few. Our teachers, many untrained, were brilliant and thorough, always managing to hold our attention, even out of doors. In those days, higher education was not available for poor black children. There were, however, scholarships. Three hundred of us would sit a scholarship examination and one would win funding for a secondary school place.

People were amazed that in spite of his success my father did not allow us to do homework. We were expected to be one hundred percent attentive during lessons and to ask questions to ensure that we understood what was happening. He would even trick us into answering incorrectly if we appeared inattentive. We were forced to think, and to think for ourselves. Nothing was done primarily for an examination. Mathematics taught us to think logically. English helped us to express our ideas: dictation and letter writing were skills that would be needed in later life. After school we were told to fill our lungs with oxygen so that our brains could be nourished by good red blood. After supper we sat together reading. Children of the family and boarders were encouraged to read classics or books within our capabilities, like biographies of saints, *Wuthering Heights*, *Black Beauty*, or to read at random and look at the pictures and captions in *Cassell's Books of Knowledge*. Anything that puzzled or was not understood had to be referred to my father. We became very conversant with the *Encyclopaedia Britannica*.

Punishment was an accepted part of a child's life. My father abhorred corporal punishment but we sometimes thought it would have been better if he had given us a few good slaps instead of the hours of lecturing and reasoning which antisocial behaviour earned us. He punished severely if anyone told a lie. No matter how serious the misdemeanour, it was always better to tell the truth. Good manners were implanted and strictly enforced when necessary. The boys were expected to be gentlemen, and the girls, no matter how young, ladies.

Education for Children of Slaves Provided by Owners of Slaves

It is perhaps ironic that my higher education came as a result of Trusts established by slave owners. It was the English-born Raines Waites (1650–1699) who, by his will, left money to establish a Trust to build and maintain the first primary schools for the children of the poor in Vere. Many of Jamaica's leading citizens and scholars received their higher education as a result of this Trust.

My elder sister and I were sent to Hampton, a small boarding school for girls tucked away in the hills of St Elizabeth far, we thought, from everywhere. Separated from home and mother, I really suffered for the first two or three terms, especially as it was not a school which poor black children were expected to attend. We were teased mercilessly, but thanks to our wonderful English headmistress, who was colour blind and loving to all of us, I eventually settled down. This also was partly due to the fact that I learnt that working hard made time fly.

Before breakfast at seven-thirty, we practised music and went to drill classes as directed by the timetable, then had lessons until lunchtime followed by one hour's rest period of absolute silence, which meant absence of any sort of communication. After rest, there was an hour of prep-study and assignments, tea, and two hours for games; a shower and supper were followed by more study and preparation. Before bedtime there were stories and music for the younger children.

As we grew older, we would be allowed to read, to sing or to listen to recordings of symphonic, chamber, choral, solo, vocal or instrumental works by Beethoven, Mendelssohn, Schubert and other composers in the headmistress's study. The school was unusual, not only because of its size and staff/pupil ratio – ninety girls and twelve members of staff – but because, as early as the 1930s, it had a well-equipped science laboratory and art studio. Academic subjects were taught, but only as part of a far more general education. This included working at crafts, gardening and a very wide programme of games and sporting activities which, however, emphasized sportsmanship rather than competition. There were thirteen pianos for school use, a grand piano in the hall, though instrumental lessons, elocution, Greek dancing and drama were electives and cost extra. Every class had a singing period. There was a school choir and a string orchestra. These were some of the reasons my father insisted on sending us to Hampton. He had been told that it was not a school for black people. He promptly searched for the documents of the Trust and saw that Munro and Dickenson, planters and slave owners, had left money for the education of the poor. He was satisfied that his children qualified. My sister and I learnt to excel and more than held our own in academic subjects, music and games. If we were presumed inferior because of the colour of our skins, we had to show that any misunderstandings about inferiority were quite incorrect.

External Influences

We were privileged to have artists of international standing perform at Hampton, the pianist Benno Moiseivitch was one. In addition, a small group of students would be allowed to go to Kingston to listen to visiting artists of stature. We heard, for example, Paul Robeson, Marian Anderson, Arthur Rubenstein, Jascha Heifitz and Yehudi Menuhin, among others. Many touring performers found it convenient to pause in Jamaica as they moved from North to South America.

We sat examinations for the Royal Drawing Society. We were proud that one of our art teachers, who also taught us games, later became the first principal of the school established by Menuhin in Hampstead. Music examinations set by Royal Schools of Music were also encouraged, both theory and practical, mainly violin and piano. One year I was given a bursary by the Associated Board for the standard of my work. My teacher very generously exchanged the bursary for her violin which, of course, was much more costly.

Further Training

In 1943 I won the West Indies Scholarship to the Royal Academy of Music. World War II was raging at the time, so all scholarship winners had to wait for peace in 1945 before leaving for Britain. It was there that the neglect of our indigenous music first struck me with great force. I realized that composers such as Bach, Handel, Mozart and Beethoven, whom we had learnt to revere, were human beings and products of their time and their environment. I heard live performances of European folk music for the first time, Scottish songs, Scandinavian fiddlers, German chorales, Russian choruses, and it was not difficult to make the connection between them and the musical giants of Europe.

I was the only black student at the Royal Academy of Music and the object of much interest. My professors were first-rate and very helpful. It seemed clear that I would need to get all the qualifications I could in order to be able to stand up to international standards and be recognized.

I was, therefore, happy when my two-year scholarship was extended to three and then four years. It was a great strain on my parents but they never complained and I never asked for more money than they sent.

Arriving in England in the days of rationing had prepared me for frugal living. If tea and soup were all I could afford for a few days in order to buy a book or a metronome, I did it gladly. With the help of my professors, I was able to gain Licentiates of the Royal Academy of Music in piano performance as well as in teaching, violin teaching and in harmony, counterpoint and composition. For the last, the subject of my thesis was Russian music. This gave me insight into the journey from folk to art music. From the Royal College of Music, I gained the Associate of the RCM diploma for piano performance.

In my spare time I went to dance and drama classes and even appeared in a West End play. I thoroughly enjoyed performing on BBC radio and for student and community events.

I had gained the Licentiates of the Royal Schools of Music (piano performing) in Jamaica in 1944. Later they were followed by the Licentiateship and the Fellowship from Trinity College for piano and the Licentiate of the Royal Schools of Music in singing. I considered that I was then prepared to tackle my career as a musician. I was equally determined to work towards the understanding, study and appreciation of Jamaica's music. This was absolutely vital since without knowing our own styles we would never be able to produce Jamaican art music and would be forever limited to imitation.

The Route to Research Into Jamaica's Musical Heritage

On returning to Jamaica in 1949, I first taught at Hampton, then in Kingston as a studio teacher and later at another school until 1955 when I returned to England, mainly to prepare for the concert stage. This was hard work. In order to pay for my lessons I had to teach and accompany dancing classes. The latter proved very useful because it exposed me to another art as taught at the Cone Ripman school and Royal Academy of

Dance. Later I became what was known as a peripatetic music teacher for the Middlesex County Council, specializing in school music and violin classes. Highlights of this period were performances on BBC and Independent Television and two piano recitals in the Royal Festival Hall. On returning to Jamaica, I was glad to be asked to teach at Mico College, my father's alma mater. It would also be a point from which I could influence music education islandwide through graduate teachers.

It was difficult, however, to get most in-service teachers to change direction and include Jamaican songs in their classes or to concentrate on music-making rather than pedagogy. The stigma of centuries was hard to erase. At that time, students who chose to concentrate on music education had to pass a music theory examination. That, of course, did not motivate them to help children enjoy music. The graduates left college with a repertoire of songs that they had been taught how to teach and this was easy, even if one was not creative. In the six years of my tenure there, with the enlightened support of the principal, Mr Glen Owen, I succeeded in redirecting energies toward teaching children to make music, which they did with enthusiasm. Through the use of songs and music games I was also able to enrich other areas of the curriculum, for example, by helping pre-schoolers to learn to count and to enjoy usually dry subjects such as English grammar.

The changes were moving ahead too slowly, so I decided to resign and concentrate on community development through music, an area which had become an increasingly absorbing hobby. It was at this point that, at the direction of the Minister of Development and Welfare, I was asked to research Jamaica's musical heritage.

Government-Supported Folk Music Research

As Folk Music Research Officer, appointed by the Government in 1966, I was responsible for carrying out research and documenting Jamaica's musical heritage. The contract was for three years, but the work continued uninterrupted for nine. The Minister then in charge, Edward Seaga, had been keen on handing over his own field tapes on Jamaican cults to someone who would continue the work, concentrating on aspects of music and dance in our heritage. A post was established at the Jamaica School of Music, although this was not the ideal arrangement since that institution was not research oriented but geared instead towards teaching and studies relating to performing arts.

At the time this was, perhaps, the only practicable arrangement that could be made although there was a lot of confusion in the minds of some of those responsible for the administration of the project. I was later told that they had not really seen the need for the new department and had not intended to be helpful. This lack of perception surfaced in many ways, some trivial, others serious, ranging from unwillingness to listen to tapes of the unfamiliar music to the misuse of material which had been lent out. However, I felt that the project had its greatest support and understanding from the Minister and that this would make it possible to withstand all the buffetings that were already beginning to escalate.

Critics and Detractors

Jamaican ears had grown accustomed to hearing only a handful of our traditional songs (usually in a titillating night club or tourist setting). Songs that seemed strange to these ears would be identified as "obviously not Jamaican, possibly African". Songs that had clear-cut melodies and neatly balanced phrases were "obviously English". One of those that was identified by these critics as being English was "Missa Potta".

Missa Potta

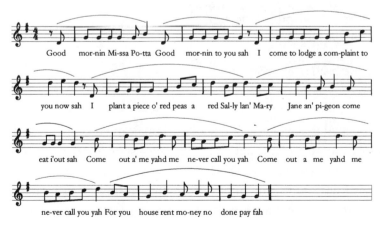

Good mornin, Missa Potta,
Good mornin to you, sah
I come to lodge a complaint to you now, sah.
I plant a piece o' red peas
A red Sally lan',
Mary Jane an' pigeon come eat i'out, sah.
Come out a' me yahd, me never call you yah
Come out a' me yahd, me never call you yah
For you house rent money no done pay fah.

After I had presented this song on a school broadcast radio programme not under Music but under Social Studies, there were many scathing comments: "It was obviously a European melody, probably learnt at school, claimed and given new words." Fortunately, some time later, a group of rural Jamaicans agreed to illustrate songs being presented on a television programme for the Jamaica Information Service.

One was asked to sing the song and another to do the actions that were associated with it. They fitted beautifully. It had manifestly been part of their everyday life, knocking "Cooper Lantern" rhythm while cleaning floors with coconut brushes and singing the song:

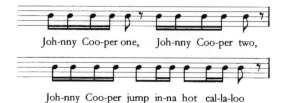

Joh-nny Coo-per one, Joh-nny Coo-per two,

Joh-nny Coo-per jump in-na hot cal-la-loo

Johnny Cooper one, Johnny Cooper two,
Johnny Cooper jump inna hot callaloo.

It so happened that Monica Whyte of the Jamaican Folk Singers had come from Westmoreland, the parish of the song's source, and had been part of the tenant farming setting. Her family rented plots of land to small farmers who paid not in cash, but in produce. The woman mentioned in the song had not been able to pay her rent to Mr Potter in peas as arranged. She came with the excuse that Mary Jane and pigeons had stolen her peas. Notice the linking of Mary Jane with the pigeons as a typical Jamaican way of belittling an adversary. The landlord, or landmaster as they used to be more frequently called, was not impressed. He told her to "Come out a' me yahd", for he wanted rent, not excuses. The television programme demonstrated for all that the song was a genuine part of Jamaican heritage.

The struggle, however, continued. I asked the Minister to find someone who could do the work better, since I could not possibly be right and so many others wrong. He refused. Finally, when members of one of the most precious traditional groups (the only one that had kept a particular postemancipation celebration alive) were injured in a traffic accident, it came home to me how easily we could be cut off from whole areas of our cultural heritage. No one seemed to care beyond helping to find alternative transportation for the people. In my distress, I contacted the Minister. He immediately grasped the gravity of the situation and told me how I could try to obtain funds and other assistance for them.

From Field to Family Bungalow

The research, nevertheless, became increasingly exciting and absorbing. In 1967 I gathered a few friends together and after consulting Ivy Baxter, Jamaica's premier pioneer in dance research, discussed with them the possibility of our meeting regularly to sing Jamaican folk songs. They were as enthusiastic as I was, especially as some of them also had valuable childhood memories and experiences in folklore. We decided to sing together in a home setting twice a week, on Wednesday nights and Saturday afternoons. This has continued to the present day. Someone called us the Jamaican Folk Singers and the name stuck.

We not only sang but also went into the field, re-established links with childhood friends, with people who had worked in schools and at home, who had been farmers and sugar workers in the various areas from which we came. This led to phase two of my work in Jamaican research. From expecting to seek out and document material, I found my role had changed to being a participant. Invitations flooded my desk, to attend a death ceremony, a Tea Meeting, a Revival Table, to go and see the making of the masks for that year's Jonkunnu Christmas parades.

At about this time I resigned from the staff of the Jamaica School of Music and accepted a post to create and administer a programme of activities in community development under Art and Culture. Participation in islandwide traditional events was easy, and fitted well into the work of my new substantive post. It was also possible to introduce young people to interesting and important, though humble, senior citizens in their own areas and establish links that gave them first-hand experience of traditional wisdom and arts. How exciting it was to hand over the teaching of songs and dances to the real keepers of our culture. They revelled in being appreciated and consulted. Young people saw them in a new light.

As contact increased, so did invitations and opportunities to learn and become involved in village, backyard and family gatherings, festivities and funerals, work and play. Gradually my role was again changing. As we shared experiences and solved problems together, I became friend and counsellor. Little did they know how much they were enriching my life and affecting my world view.

Acceptance and Accession

Phase two melted into phase three. I became the only non-Maroon initiated into the Moore Town Maroon Community. There were no more secrets between us, but I had to be even more careful than before about recognizing and respecting their confidences. The Rastafarians asked the Jamaican Folk Singers to sing at the funeral of Count Ozzie, their revered pioneer in music. We were invited to participate in important Revival ceremonies, Kumina rituals, death ceremonies, evenings of traditional rural entertainment. Help was requested in all types of personal as well as communal matters. The Singers and I were accepted as friends, and there is no friend like a grassroots Jamaican. As the saying goes, they will "go to jail for you". Having earned this type of relationship, one must constantly nurture and maintain it.

The research, transformed, filtered into many areas of Jamaican life: formal and non-formal education, church activities, theatre, entertainment for audiences of home folk and visitors, international cultural exchanges, publications, creative writing, music composition, media programmes.

In 1981, a Memory Bank was established to collect and document the memories and artifacts of our senior citizens with a view to creating a data bank at our National Library for proper storage as well as accession. Centenarians and even younger senior citizens interviewed contribute priceless oral history, heritage material and information. When they repeat what their parents and grandparents told them, they give us new insights into life in pre-Emancipation Jamaica and the plantation era. After proper steps have been taken to protect and organize the material deposited in the Bank, it is intended to make it available for study and use at home as well as abroad. We hoped that some of the time-tested appropriate technology of these senior citizens might be used to improve the quality of life here and in the wider world, even in this age of high technology.

Research Methods

The research methods I used in gathering the materials which form the foundation of this book are based primarily on the techniques and characteristics of several projects undertaken between 1966 and 1986. These projects evolved alongside the development of local research into Jamaica's traditional culture. At times, therefore, the methods might appear simple and unorthodox, but together they have uncovered a rich pool of material with continuity and focus. Since I was personally involved with each of these projects, my own data-gathering techniques developed along with each project and its resources.

A period following the nine years of concentrated field research was spent in teaching, sharing and using the results of this research in various programmes of national development and international cultural exchange.

The first project began in 1966 when the Jamaica School of Music started its Folk Music Research Project. The objectives were to collect and document the folk music of Jamaica, ensuring authenticity and objectivity. I used a reel-to-reel tape recorder at the beginning. But there were times when this machine was inappropriate or unacceptable, in which case I would make written notes, transcribing words, melody, harmonization, instrumentation, style and context. During the period, music relating to Kumina, Revival, Death Ceremonies, Rastafarianism, seasonal celebrations and community festivities was collected.

In due course I became acquainted and worked with Ettu, Tambo, Goombey, Bruckins, and Nago groups. In 1967, I visited Guyana to gain knowledge of Arawak Indians. They had been the first Jamaicans and, though now described as being extinct in Jamaica, still live in groups in the Guyanese interior.

I accepted the decisions and, therefore, the criteria of the people in various communities who identified culture bearers and specialists. Out of this grew the recognition of folk music as that which has been accepted and passed on for generations through the work of, or guided by, culture bearers, or created anonymously chiefly for communal use. It embodies the ideas and beliefs of people at or near the base of the socioeconomic pyramid and can relate to their daily activities faithfully from their points of view. The words and wording were usually mine, but the essence is theirs. Over the years, my understanding of their proverbial and symbolic language increased just as my ability to comprehend their use of English and Creole grew. Close observation of body language also improved.

It should be noted that in the Jamaican situation a lot of music other than folk songs is orally transmitted and even operatic and oratorio choruses are largely learnt by rote. This has meant that problems of identification have sometimes surfaced. In the case of "Evening Time", which is widely accepted and used as a folk song, the lyrics and music exist in print as the work of Louise Bennett and Barbara Ferland, respectively. Other songs, such as "Dip an' Fall Back" and "Win the Sweepstake" (see chapter 5) are called folk songs islandwide. However, they may not be true folk songs as they were in the repertoire of itinerant singers who wrote many of their own songs and may well have composed these. Jamaicans have had many unpleasant experiences relating to the music recognized on the island as authentic Jamaican folk music but copyrighted elsewhere. Since gaining independence in 1962, the country has had to establish means of retaining its links with international copyright conventions and copyright laws.

The collection of folk music led to interest in other aspects of life in Jamaica. Among them were language, belief systems, world view and religious practices. The embryonic Jamaica School of Music Project began to take on wider objectives and created a network of contacts throughout the island.

The next project was a Community Cultural Programme carried on by the Social Development Commission from 1974 to 1978. An outreach and dissemination project, it was an attempt to integrate traditional culture and techniques with the schedule of community centres and groups. Although it was not a data-gathering exercise, it put me in touch with a wide range of people such as young rural Rastafarians, people in prisons and senior citizens practising traditional arts and crafts. The use and, in some cases, the abuse of traditional cultural resources had to be viewed in practical terms. Although at this time there was an attempt by some of the young radicals in government to politicize culture in order to use it as a channel to the grassroots, a great deal was accomplished in the area of establishing links with sources.

The 1981 Memory Bank Project, which has continued through to the present, has become a national campaign to collect oral history. UNESCO contributed funds to assist with workshops and documentation and to provide some basic equipment. The United Nations University made a modest investment in specific research areas, and the government provided the office and administrative and support services. This enabled us to sustain a network of volunteer interviewers using cassette tape recorders that improved the collection. We were also able to videotape a few of the more important traditional ceremonies.

The data-gathering and documentation procedures at the Memory Bank consisted of:

1. Collection of music and oral histories by volunteers (who received basic training in interviewing techniques and thematic priorities).
2. Cataloguing of material (preliminary).
3. Transcription of material.

Working out the procedures for the Project provided me with a good opportunity to consider the integration of cultural research material into national policy objectives and activities. Memory Bank was also used as a pilot project and nucleus for other similar projects in the Caribbean.

The data-gathering aspect of the research consisted of:

- reel-to-reel tapes
- cassette audiotapes
- videotapes
- notes
- participatory observation
- computer for basic inventory of most recent material.

Two other important factors related to the research were: performances by groups such as the Jamaican Folk Singers, inspired by their forerunners which include the Cudjoe Minstrels, the Jamma Rhythmers and the Frats Quintet, and the influence and assistance of overseas researchers. The Folk Singers began in 1967 and performed, in many cases, to middle-class or urban audiences that had never been exposed to folk music, as well as to rural audiences that had never heard music from other rural areas of the country. By integrating research material into real-life situations, I was able to generate interest rather than relegate the music to academic vaults. Similar use of folk material was also made by other non-governmental groups, among them Ivy Baxter and her dancers, Neville Black, Eddie Thomas and Alma Mock Yen, each with a dance group, and the National Dance Theatre Company of Jamaica (NDTC). All have used folk movement and music for dance theatre. Both the Folk Singers and the NDTC have provided examples of the practical use of cultural research in developing countries by providing authentic sources for the artistic manifestations of indigenous culture.

The long, tedious and often lonely process of researching folk music and cultural traditions cannot be neatly arranged into academic classifications. It becomes a vocation and a part of the researcher's personal development. I must, therefore, give credit to certain overseas specialists who, knowing the likely problems, gave encouragement and advice in the early years. They included: Maud Karpeles, Alan Merriam, Willard Rhodes, Fela Sowande, Frank Gillis, Charles Seeger and Klaus Wachsmann. There was also the close association with the International Folk Music Council (IFMC), now the International Council for Traditional Music (ICTM), that kept me in touch with developments in other parts of the world.

My research methods have been based on personal experiences and a rather isolated approach to fieldwork – since it was left to me to motivate myself. This is certainly not an exceptional situation, but it was difficult at times since there were very few local researchers in this area with whom I could exchange views and discoveries.

2

Slavery: Old Souls in a New World

ost of the Africans who were transported to Jamaica as slaves came from West and Central Africa. They were brought across the Atlantic under shamefully inhuman conditions to toil for strange masters in an alien society. Some slave owners and hired administrators were unduly harsh in their determination to get as much work as possible out of each slave. Some, we are told, were more humane.

In no circumstances could slavery have been pleasant. However, unlike the slaves who were taken to North America, those who came to the Caribbean would at least have had environmental conditions similar to those of the countries left behind. The conditioning of Africans brought to the Caribbean would not have been as severe as for those taken to North America. This must have had certain implications for character building, especially where the conditioning had been in progress for generations. Transplanting to the Caribbean, therefore, was climatically less traumatic than that of the North American slaves.

> For the traditional African, a discourse involves as likely participants not only those of his fellow human beings who are in his immediate vicinity or within reach, but also his gods and goddesses, his ancestors and heroes, the departed members of his society, the forces of the elements, the spirits of nature and 'Mother Earth' [Sowande 1974: 84].

In the Jamaican environment, African forebears would have found it possible to feel the presence of their gods and spirits, re-establish vital links with them and give succeeding generations the opportunity to experience a measure of cultural continuity. The colonial masters were primarily interested in amassing wealth, and used the slaves to that end. No effort was made to expose the workers and their children to any form of education nor to allow them time for any pursuits that were not in the interest of the masters or related to their varied tasks.

The results of this neglect were not entirely negative, since it led to disregard rather than destruction of the subject peoples' cultural mores at deeper levels. There must, however, have been serious conflicts created in the minds of the workers with regard to the spiritual values (or lack of them) of the masters.

> It is sometimes imagined that the main drive to the economic activity of tribal people is their immediate desire to satisfy their material wants. But it would be untrue to interpret their economic organization as a simple response to their requirement of food, clothing, shelter, and the like. In the first place, it is a socialized and not an individual response. The values which they put upon their food do not consist simply in its capacity to satisfy hunger but in the use they can make of it to express their obligations to their relatives-in-law, their chiefs, their ancestors; to show their hospitality; to display their wealth; to initiate or marry off their sons. The value that is put on a canoe is not measured only in terms of the capacity of the vessel to carry goods and passengers nor of the fish that are caught from it, but also by the way in which it is a symbol of craftmanship in wood, an object of artistic carving and decoration, a reminder of traditional voyages, and even the resting place or embodiment of a god. The value of a cow does not simply consist in its yield of milk and the uses to which its flesh hide and horns can be put, nor in what it will fetch at a sale, but also in its role as part of a marriage portion, as a ritual sacrifice, and as a token of social status. The whole economic system of the people is run with its complex set of values in mind. From this, it is seen then, in the second place, that many of the wants upon which their economic life is based are of an immaterial kind [Firth 1958: 64–65].

Even now, older Jamaicans who have clung to the old values through oral traditions look upon the earth as "mother", some still referring to her as "Mother Clay".

It seems reasonable to presume that, in keeping with this, they saw the land as the asset that, if cherished and cared for and cooperated with, would literally take care of human beings in return. From it, food and water came. On it depended animals, including human beings, for sustenance. Homes were built on and out of it. It was the means of communicating physically. In order to draw out, however, something must be put in; there should not be a feeling of constantly taking and taking nor should anyone take more than was needed. One cow could be killed to feed family and neighbours, not one hundred slaughtered for financial gain. Contrast this with the attitude of slave owners, whose main aim was to get as much as possible out of the earth with no real consideration for putting anything back; no thought, like the slave, of paying homage to the world of nature and appeasing it if disturbed, as in digging a grave or laying the foundations of a building. The slave offered libations. The slave owner had no qualms about having even the most magnificent cotton tree felled without a word of thanks or explanation to the spirit of that tree though his ancient forebears would have thought differently. Before carrying out such an order, the African immigrant, and later his Jamaican descendant, would sing and make peace with the life, the spirit, in that tree about to be destroyed. A song used in that context by Jamaican sawyers up to the 1940s was: "A noh me a bahss say" ("Don't blame me, it's the boss's order").

Considering how many such situations must have arisen, it is conceivable, therefore, that the deep inner conflicts caused spiritual and mental suffering.

The colonial masters, often through their absentee landlords, viewed the plantations in the colonies primarily as an economic venture with the land as part of the raw material, in much the same way that they saw the slaves. It was Albert Schweitzer's opinion that the devastating effect of World War I on victor, vanquished and neutral alike was due not to the war but to "the spiritually denuded atmosphere which caused that war in the first place". Slavery could be seen in similar terms.

The slaves, however, lived in a world where all living things were part of a spiritual whole, part of the great mystery of creation and, under certain conditions, were used to further the evolution of others. According to Sowande, "Yoruba tradition teaches us in accordance with the sayings of our high priest Orumila that human beings become gods! That every god in our pantheon was once a human being who was deified after his death because of his wisdom and his manner of life" [Sowande 1974: 78].

In his *Seven Sermons to the Dead*, Carl Jung wrote:

Numberless gods await the human state.
Numberless gods have been men.
Man shareth in the nature of the gods,
He cometh from the gods and goeth unto God.
[Jung 1967: 25]

Arising out of this is the other equally vital awareness of the responsibility of man to life, to all life, and the recognition that nothing created is without life. From this springs that reverence for life about which Albert Schweitzer spoke: "It is from a fundamental idea about our relation to all that lives, as such, that it must flow in the future, as from a spring which can never dry up and never become a swamp. That spring is reverence for life" [Schweitzer 1949: 81, 92].

Philosophy took over as the guide and substance, rather than economics. In this connection, the slave seems nearer to Shakespeare's character who saw "sermons in stones" at a time when he was bereft of all earthly goods. The philosophical concord of ideas between advanced Western thinkers and the lowly slave is remarkable and even touching. There is a startling parallel between Schweitzer's "spring which can never dry up" and Miss Becky Blackwood's lullaby, "Milky water never dry, you get it dung a fountain" (pp. 64–65). As Seneca said, "The best ideas are common property." Complete lack of formal education does not preclude wisdom and knowledge. Nature allows for no vacuum. Everyday Jamaican life teems with examples of this.

An incident in 1963 must suffice to show how far the knowledge of ordinary people can outstrip information. At the time, I was teaching at

Mico Teachers' Training College. No hurricane had struck Jamaica since the devastating Hurricane Charlie of 1951. Now 1963 brought the dreaded news that Hurricane Flora was approaching.

Everyone at the college was sent home with instructions to keep a battery-operated radio at hand for the latest bulletins and to make full preparations for the approaching storm. When I reached home, I found that the radio was on but my helper was working as if blissfully ignorant of the impending catastrophe. She listened respectfully as I told her to go home, taking whatever her family might need to weather the storm. An hour later she was still at work. I repeated my advice more than once and explained that Flora was being tracked by satellite, observed by American weather stations and constantly monitored by our own meteorologists. She must leave at once.

She listened patiently, but finally the time came to put me straight. "No breeze going to blow," she said firmly. I was flabbergasted at her stubborn "stupidity". She calmly continued, "If hurricane was coming, is not so the hens would be behaving." I gave up.

Gradually the bulletins began to prove her right. The hurricane changed course and veered away from Jamaica. Some northern parts of the island had high winds and flood rains. Kingston experienced torrential rains, but "no breeze blow".

The slaves must have brought stores of knowledge and attitudes to knowledge from their countries of origin. These helped them through periods of suffering, and became important to varying degrees, depending on the magnitude of their sufferings. The same attitudes have also continued to help their descendants to come to terms with life and its problems. It is interesting to note that long before the ways of the Europeans began to be fed to the slave, the slave was influencing Europeans through their children. The lullabies, stories, proverbs and sayings used by black nannies, as well as their attitudes to life in its many aspects, must have had some, even if only a minute, effect on their infant charges. Pity this influence was all too soon removed and counteracted as soon as the children left the nursery.

By the early nineteenth century, slavery in Jamaica seemed doomed:

Violent protest against slavery in the form of riot or rebellion had been
endemic in eighteenth-century Jamaica . . . The abolition of the slave trade
in 1808 and the stabilization of areas of settlement produced more settled
conditions; the negro villages were no longer dominated by immigrant
Africans, and a creole slave society emerged [Reckord 1969: 25].

Anti-slavery agitation in England helped to foment disturbances in
the 1820s. In April 1831 a campaign for the immediate abolition of slavery
was launched in the House of Commons. Despite advice from the Colonial
Office to quiet "signs of unrest", the Jamaican plantocracy rather
provoked it by openly opposing all efforts to even mitigate the system.

The slaves listened, and watched. Rumours ran rife among them.
They ranged from imminent freedom, to plans by the bakra people (Ibo,
bakra: he who governs) to keep the women and children in slavery and
shoot the men.

Religious groups, which had multiplied as a result of the work of the
mission churches, mingled traditional African beliefs with Christianity.
They not only reflected the religious interests of the slaves but also came
near to satisfying their emotional needs and their hopes for early
emancipation. "Freed from the supervision of the missionary and his
emphasis on conformity and obedience, the slaves were also able to
express their political interest and to use religion as a sanction for their
hopes" [Reckord 1969: 25].

By late 1831 the unrest had reached such a level that Sam Sharpe, a
Jamaican Baptist Deacon, planned for mass passive resistance by the
slaves in western Jamaica and their refusal to work after the Christmas
holiday until their masters acknowledged their freedom and offered them
wages. Sharpe was a powerful charismatic speaker. Though his
arguments were mainly religious, he generated great political fervour in
his large audiences. Added to this was the widespread belief among the
slaves that slavery had already ended but their freedom was being
withheld by the owners, and that a Baptist pastor due to return from

England at Christmas would bring their free-paper. The missionaries realized that their congregations saw them as Christian allies. They warned against violence: "If you have any love of Jesus Christ, your religion, to your masters, to their kind friends in England who have given money to help you build this Chapel, be not led away by wicked men." So pleaded William Knibb at the opening of the Baptist Chapel in St James on December 27, 1831.

The planters got word of the slaves' plans so were prepared when a trash house on a hill at Kensington Estate, St James, was set on fire that same evening. Martial law was declared and the ill-armed slaves, unskilled in the ways of war, were soon outmatched. By January, the armed rebellion had virtually ended.

The rebellion quashed, the slaves were intimidated into returning to work by various harsh and brutal measures. The troubles did not cease. On the one hand, rebels burned, looted, defied; on the other, landowners wreaked vengeance for their humiliation and loss of property. Ruthless and hasty military courts martial, destruction of negro villages, slave courts (after the lifting of martial law) and the settling of private grievances cost the slaves dearly in life and what little property they possessed. Bleby states that on the gallows erected in Montego Bay three or four condemned men were hanged at a time: "The bodies remained stiffening in the breeze till the court martial had provided another batch of victims . . . [the hangman] would ascend a ladder with his knife, sever the ropes by which the poor creatures were suspended and let them fall to the ground" [Bleby 1853: 26–27].

Another batch of victims, he records, would soon be provided, all the bodies remaining in a heap until "workhouse negroes came in the evening with carts and took them away to cast them into a pit dug for the purpose, a little distance out of town."

Life could never again be the same for slave or slave owner. It has been repeatedly stated that though there was widespread destruction, it was protest against a system, not an anti-white crusade.

Bleby states that during the rebellion there were two crimes of violence against white individuals. This, in spite of the fact that the slaves so greatly outnumbered the plantocracy. H. M. Waddell's quotation from a Presbyterian missionary is worthy of note: "Had the masters when they got the upper hand been as forbearing, as tender of their slaves' lives as their slaves had been of theirs, it would have been to their lasting honour and to the permanent advantage of the colony" [Waddell 1963: 280].

The missionaries, mainly Baptist and Wesleyan, were seen as allies of the slaves in their march to freedom. Chapels were destroyed, some missionaries were tried for direct complicity, and preaching was outlawed. The church sent delegates to join in the emancipation campaign in England where it was being carried on both in and outside Parliament. However, credit for the demise of slavery must also be given to the rebel slaves in spite of their immediate defeat.

Emancipation and Indenture

Emancipation came in 1834, and was celebrated by church services and joyful festivities. The apprenticeship system which it heralded brought hardship to the newly freed slaves and the coloured population, but the transition to wage labour, "full free", in 1838 was comparatively smooth.

Many of the emancipated slaves were worse off after abolition than during their bondage. The "masters" now needed to take no responsibility for their workers' welfare, and so life, though supposedly being lived at a more human level, was in fact in some ways more difficult. Labourers were still beholden to the plantation owners who clung to old habits and expressions touching the inferiority of the darker people. These attitudes continued to be handed down through the plantation system. Such attitudes die hard, and it is possible that many more years must still go by before this stigma dies; to quote Oppenheimer [1917: 42], "Imperial dynasties have been overthrown in a single day, but generations go to the changing of a single social law."

War dung a Monklan'

War dung a Monk-lan'   War dung a Mo-ran Bay   War dung a Chi-gga foot De

Queen ne-va know War war war oh War oh hea-vy War oh Sol-diers from New-cas-tle

come dung a Monk-lan Wit' gun an' sword fe kill si-nna oh War war war oh War oh

heavy war oh

War dung a Monklan'
War dung a Moran' Bay
War dung a Chigga Foot
De Queen nevva know.

Refrain: War, war, war Oh,
War Oh, heavy war Oh

Soldiers from Newcastle
Come dung a Monklan'
Wit' gun an sword
Fe kill sinna Oh.

Refrain: War, war, war Oh,
War, oh, heavy war Oh.

Note that "De Queen nevva know" indicates the unlawful situation, and "sinna" refers to the rebels.

The planters became increasingly interested in recruiting immigrant labour. European indenture was not a success so hundreds of Asians and Africans were brought to swell the Jamaican labour force. The post-slavery African "arrivants" settled mainly in St Thomas in eastern Jamaica.

By the 1860s, economic conditions had deteriorated for Jamaican workers and small farmers. High unemployment, heavy taxation and hardships resulting from a serious drought precipitated what has been called the Morant Bay Rebellion of 1865. Once again punishment was swift and brutal. Martial law was imposed and the leaders, including Paul Bogle, were summarily hanged.The uprising is remembered in a traditional worksong inspired by the tragic aftermath of the uprising. (see pp. 30–31).

After Emancipation, Jamaica had continued to enjoy a limited form of representative government, based on wealth and land ownership, although the Assembly's legislation had to be approved in Westminster. This was replaced after the Morant Bay uprising by full Crown Colony government. The next century saw much political and labour unrest, with leaders critical of British government and bureaucracy emerging among coloured and black Jamaicans. Two of these leaders from the late nineteenth and early twentieth century were Alexander Bedward and Marcus Garvey, hailed as "Black Moses".

Alexander Bedward

Alexander Bedward was the shepherd of a large and very trusting Revival church during the late 1890s and the early twentieth century. He spoke to the poor and forlorn, promising escape, not to Africa but to heaven where their troubles would be over. If their faith was strong enough, they would be able to fly to that heaven. He himself would lead them. Faithful, expectant followers sold all and at the appointed time gathered by a tree in August Town from which Bedward was supposed to fly. It ended in disaster with Bedward falling injured and his followers even poorer. He was admitted to Bellevue Mental Asylum where he died years later, in 1930. His church still exists near the University of the West Indies in a suburb of Kingston.

Middle-class Jamaicans never took Bedward seriously and scoffed at his preaching and his flock. He had, however, been a very successful healer and an inspiring preacher, and this is how his church remembers him.

A mento dance song lightheartedly recalls his work as healer and baptizer of hundreds in the Hope River.

Dip dem Bedward

Dip dem Bedward, dip dem
Dip dem in the healin' stream,
Dip dem sweet but not too deep
Dip dem fe cure bad feelin'.
An' me always go up a Augus' Town,
But me never go up a Mona
One day I was invited
By a ole man dem call Jonah.

When me go up a Mona, me see
Bredda Bedward standin',

'Im tek Sister Mary, pull im han'
An' dip her in de healin' stream

Some come from de north wid dem face full a wart
Fe go dip in a de healin' stream.
Some come from de south wid dem big yabba mout'
Fe go dip inna de healin' stream.

Marcus Garvey and the Ancestral Home

Disillusioned by being blacklisted after failing in an attempt to organize a printers' strike in Kingston in 1907–1908, the young Garvey left Jamaica and travelled extensively in South and Central America. He was shocked at the negro's lot wherever he went. He subsequently lived in the United Kingdom (1912–1914) before returning to Jamaica and founding the Universal Negro Improvement Association (UNIA) "for the general upliftment of the negro peoples of the world". Jamaica did not offer him the scope he wished, so he emigrated to the USA in 1916. There he captured the imagination and the allegiance of millions of Americans and an enormous following in Central America, Africa, the Caribbean and even Europe. His racial nationalism included a black God and black religion. The New African Orthodox Church was established in the United States of America in 1921.

Racial pride, spiritual redemption and return to the ancestral promised land (One Aim, One God, One Destiny) were thus interlocking tenets of Garveyism [Eaton 1975: 21].

In 1925 he was imprisoned on questionable charges of mail fraud and tax evasion, and then expelled from the USA in 1927. Back in Jamaica, Garvey continued to work towards furthering his plans which, according to his widow Amy Jacques Garvey [1963: 262], were built around three fundamentals:

1. Uniting the people of the West Indies, the coloured population of the USA and Africans at home into one brotherhood for betterment and upliftment.

2. The redemption of Africa from the exploitation of her lands and labour.

3. African nationalism – nationhood being the only organized system by which a people can achieve self-expression and self-determination in a well-ordered world society.

He experienced all sorts of hindrances and problems. It became increasingly difficult for him to function in Jamaica and in 1934 he left the island for England. His fortunes did not improve, though he made successful visits to Canada, the USA and Caribbean countries.

Garvey died in London in 1940. More than twenty-two years later, after gaining independence, Jamaica declared him a national hero. His body was exhumed and brought home for an elaborate ceremonial reburial in our National Heroes Park.

Garvey still has very loyal supporters in the UNIA in Jamaica, and has been a much-quoted inspiration to the Rastafarians, yet even now he has not become as messianic a figure in his own island as he had been in the USA.

The Legacy of Colonialism

Jamaica was a British colony for over three hundred years until Independence was achieved in 1962. This fact has not only affected Jamaica's history and culture but it has also had sociological, psychological and educational effects, some of them negative. Cultural manifestations such as language, religion, methods of socialization and the creative arts have been greatly influenced, as the ideas and values of Britain were imposed through both formal and informal education. One negative result of this has been the development of a belief in the superiority of cultural expressions of other societies, particularly those of the former colonizers, and the inferiority of the indigenous traditions.

Another effect of the colonial experience which has both negative and positive consequences for the social and cultural life of the country, is the social structure that emerged out of the colonial situation, a structure largely based on factors of ethnicity and colour and, in turn, wealth and education, although today much of the old structure is fast disappearing. The traditional structure was Caucasians at the top with a middle class consisting of Caucasians, African-Europeans, and educated blacks. The lowest class, and the largest, consisted of urban and rural black manual labourers who were usually poor and lacking in formal education. It was they who practised and preserved, even to the present, many of the cultural traditions of their ancestors, as can be seen in their attitudes to religion, language, folklore, music, marriage and family life.

The negative effect has been the relegation of blacks with their cultural expressions to the lowest position of the social structure. The positive effect is that the social outcast status has allowed this group to retain and preserve the vibrant and indigenous heritage that has perhaps sustained and strengthened its members. In spite of attempts to suppress some of their cultural forms, this group somehow managed to protect and preserve them. With growing official sanction of many cultural practices that were once looked down upon, not only are the negative historical, sociological, and psychological effects of colonialism being countered but Jamaica's national cultural identity is also now being increasingly accepted by more of her people as being valuable and worthy of pride.

Many African-Jamaicans, particularly the youth whose social position and education took them closer to European customs and values, are now demanding that the wide gaps in information on Jamaica's African heritage be filled. Many Rastafarians go further by rejecting Jamaicanness, seeing themselves as forced exiles from Africa.

One of the most notable manifestations of the changes taking place is the acceptance and increased use of what Frederic Cassidy calls "Jamaica Talk". The official language of Jamaica is Standard English, which is read and spoken by most educated Jamaicans, but the language of the majority of Jamaicans, particularly those from the lower socioeconomic groups, is Jamaican Creole.

Professor Cassidy distinguishes between Standard English and Creole/"Folk" language as follows:

Standard here means what it does in England: the language of the educated, accepted for public usage and superseding local or regional differences. "Folk" language here refers to the usages of the Jamaican communality of country and city: cultivators, labourers, small artisans, domestic servants and so on, with little formal education beyond the 'Three Rs'; "Folk speech" is that which they use among themselves [Cassidy 1961: vii].

This "folk" language also comes easily to the lips of most other Jamaicans. It is also soon understood, in its less broad forms, by even short-term expatriates who wish to integrate with Jamaican society and relate to more than life on the surface.

Frederic Cassidy was well placed to write on Jamaican language with authority. The son of a mother "to whom Jamaica was home" and a father "whose second home it became", he had an excellent formal education. He also immersed himself in the Jamaican vernacular, therefore gaining a thorough knowledge of Jamaican Creole from the inside. This creole language with a base of English has been influenced by the various other peoples who have settled in Jamaica since about the eighth century A.D.: Arawak Indians, Spanish and Portuguese, French, Dutch, East Indians, Chinese and Africans. The last has exerted "the largest and most profound" influence, not only on vocabulary, but on inflection, grammar and pronunciation.

We shall later see how important the use of this language, forged out of the need for a common mode of communication among those who were brought to Jamaica from diverse language backgrounds, became in the life and music of plantation labourers. The following figures quoted by Cassidy from *The New Act of Assembly of Jamaica* (1789) indicate how many tribal languages were brought to Jamaica in less than twenty years by slaves imported by four companies during 1764 and from 1779 to 1788:

Annamoboe	8,510	(Gold Coast)
Bonny	8,203	(Niger Delta)
Gold Coast	2,164	(Gold Coast)
Calabar	2,688	(South Nigeria)

Windward Coast	2,679	(Liberia)
Whydah	2,436	(Dahomey)
Angola	1,894	(Angola)
Old Calabar	1,667	(South Nigeria)
Benin	1,319	(South Nigeria)
Pawpaw	131	(Dahomey)
Gambia	95	(Gambia)
(Unidentified	6,039)	

[Cassidy 1961: 16]

No living language remains static, but there has been more than normal change in the Jamaican vernacular since the middle of this century. This has been mainly due to conscious efforts by the Rastafarians to assert their independence of thought by the use of new words, imagery, much of it Biblical, and the adaptation of existing expressions.

Since adult suffrage in 1944, Jamaica has been fortunate in having some political leaders who, no matter how diametrically opposed ideologically and otherwise, have valued traditional culture, encouraged the development of the arts, and seen Jamaica's cultural heritage as the foundation of national development. It is encouraging that links with ancestral sources have been maintained while at the same time, and within the limits of our resources, increasing advantage is being taken of modern technology. The result is a cultural variety as rich and resonant as the hills that greeted Christopher Columbus in 1494.

3

Conflicting Concepts
of Wealth

Wealth at Any Price

From the sixteenth century until emancipation in 1834, the Jamaican society was one in which a small ruling class was bent on extracting as much as possible from the island. The slave-plantation system was the only one that applied in Jamaica until 1834 when the paid worker's lot depended on the benevolence or otherwise of the property owner. The slave-supported system meant wringing as much as possible from the enslaved workers' bodies in labour and in offspring. Eventually, these workers outnumbered their owners, sometimes by more than eight to one. A census taken in 1791 showed the population to be 290,000 made up as follows: 30,000 Europeans, 10,000 free people of colour and freed blacks, 250,000 black slaves. It can, therefore, be understood how threatening the ruling class found the situation and explains the consequent oppressive measures instituted to protect the property owners.

Many studies have been made of Jamaican social systems, expressing widely divergent views. They all examine the emergence of a colour-class system which, as late as 1953, could be summed up by Fernando Henriques in his *Family and Colour in Jamaica* as being "dependent upon the almost complete acceptance by each group of the superiority of the white and the inferiority of the black". One author, however, Adam Kuper, considers that "Jamaican studies have too often failed to achieve the necessary distancing from Jamaican folk models and values, which are seldom properly understood as a system of action in their own right" [Kuper 1976: 1]. He also stated in the same work: "Social and economic historians have provided valuable studies of the slave society and of the immediate post-emancipation period but, unfortunately, they have left a serious gap in our understanding of the years of direct colonial rule from 1865 to 1944" [Kuper 1976: 3].

The statement has important implications for this study, since the fieldwork gleaned memories that mainly cover just that period. Information given to Seaga by an old woman in St Thomas relating to the shooting of a follower of Bogle, leader of the 1865 Morant Bay uprising and subsequently National Hero, pinpoints the date. We note too that the Great Revival, out of which Jamaican Revival cults grew, took place near the mid nineteenth century, as did the arrival of African indentured labourers who brought Kumina to Jamaica and have kept it alive to the present day. The memories of the older informants also go back to that period when they are quoting parents and grandparents.

In theory, the harsher conditions became, the more necessary it was for our enslaved ancestors to ensure that they did not allow themselves to be impeded on their spiritual journey through this and other lives towards perfection, God's throne or the "mercy seat". This attitude has persisted into recent times. It has surfaced in exhortations and counselling by persons such as Kapo (Revival), Brother Everald Brown (Rastafarian) and Imogene Kennedy (Kumina) when urging their listeners to cope positively with even the most perplexing problems of today, since they cannot be as difficult as those faced by their ancestors. The ancestors sang "Chris' is coming an' me no wan' no condemnation". It was necessary to cleanse the spirit as well as to keep in touch with the Life at the source and be in harmony with all its manifestations. Fortunately, this was possible without the knowledge or approval of the masters. Overt means like drumming might be and were, in fact, outlawed. Memories were another matter. Recently, as a drummer chanted "Gi' me back mi history an' mi culture" at a national function, a Kumina leader sitting nearby asked, "How them take it? . . . Me have fe me." (I have mine.)

Rhythms could be reproduced by feet and hands. Contact could even be made in silence or in secrecy but important social aspects would be missing. One result of the suppression was that people learned to be wary. They had to be ready to retreat in order to protect forms of expression that were too precious to be put at risk. This attitude has persisted to the present. No longer is it fear of punishment that causes the retreat: today it is prying eyes and ears, tape recorders and cameras that must be treated with caution; unsympathetic attitudes, harsh criticism and virulent attacks from compatriots must be carefully noted and assessed. This is not surprising since perceptive people know that it is often curiosity and commercialism rather than genuine interest that motivates enquiries, that it is easier for many to dismiss the wisdom of centuries and judge by appearances than to listen and to learn.

Music to the Rescue

The music that is most alive today is that which has been carefully and at times secretly guarded. Because of its deep significance, it has sometimes survived in spite of being outside the law. If descended upon, those who have cherished it simply pull back and show the surface only. Such is the nature of the music that it is meaningless without its surrounding and supporting lore, and so the loss to the practitioners is minimal. This has had a twofold effect:

1. Much misinformation and many misinterpretations have been published and passed on in good faith by those who have not had the time (meeting deadlines and other requirements for grants, etc.) to establish the necessary rapport, confidence and meaningful dialogue with sources.
2. Those with serious interest have had to work hard and long, not just listening to the people who produce the relevant material but also learning about them and their way of life, and striving to see life through their eyes.

Colonial policies caused Jamaicans not only to be ignorant of their African past but also to despise sounds, sights and ideas that did not synchronize with those of the ruling powers. Children were taught songs and stories from European countries thousands of miles away and cultures as far remote. They were beautiful and interesting, but were presented as though nothing else worthy of notice existed. No mention of hibiscus, orchid or orange blossom, doctor bird or firefly. Even after an educational system was introduced in the nineteenth century, Jamaican children were taught far more about the "mother country" than about their own island, a situation which lasted well into the middle of the twentieth century.

The "lower classes" might have heard their parents or grandparents sing: "Docta bud a cunning bud, hard bud fe dead", but never would the strains have been allowed to intrude further than the middle-class back verandah, let alone into the classroom. It was as though there had never been any African, Caribbean or even Jamaican cultural heritage or creativity. Whatever was hinted at was certainly beyond the limits of polite society. It was absolutely taboo to use Jamaican vernacular, the main language of most Jamaicans. Scottish and Yorkshire speech styles in which "gin a body meet a body" and "on Ilkla moor baht 'at" were permitted, but certainly not "Dis long time gal me never see you, come mek me hol' you hand." This alone effectively separated those aspiring to "higher things", or a "good education" from most of Jamaica's own music.

Recognition of Jamaica's Traditional Music

In spite of neglect and outright rejection by certain levels of society, the traditional music of Jamaica survived. It was interwoven with all aspects of everyday life, it made communication with the gods and spirits possible and generated and maintained feelings of belonging and self-worth. However, the middle and upper echelons of society, exposed as they were to the Eurocentric influences of their education and the effects of colonial rule, were unaware of the cultural wealth of the music of the people. It is ironic but not surprising that visiting English and American scholars such as Walter Jekyll, Martha Beckwith and Helen Roberts first took the trouble to research and document aspects of Jamaica's cultural heritage. Serious and of great integrity, they brought new perspectives to old practices. Without their work, much of Jamaica's traditional music and oral history might well have been irretrievably lost.

Walter Jekyll: A Visitor who Stayed a Lifetime

The Folk-Lore Society for Collecting and Printing Relics and Popular Antiquities was established in England in 1878. In 1907, David Nutt of London published for this Society *Jamaican Song and Story*, subtitled *Anancy Stories, Digging Songs, Ring Tunes and Dancing Tunes*, collected and edited by Walter Jekyll. The book includes a lengthy introduction by Alice Werner whose comments are mainly linguistic, comparing and making linkages between Jamaican stories and song texts with African, English and occasionally Asian prototypes. The author's preface states, "The stories and tunes of this book are taken down from the mouths of men and boys in my employ" by "slow dictation".

English-born Jekyll first settled in the mountains near Kingston but later lived in Hanover in the west where his grave can be seen in a Lucea churchyard. His book, in his own words, is "as a whole a tribute to my love for Jamaica and its dusky inhabitants, with their winning ways and their many good qualities, among which is to be reckoned that supreme virtue, cheerfulness".

Jekyll was well aware of the difficulties of a newcomer wishing to really understand the Jamaican vernacular, and made a great effort to do so. In writing of one ring tune, he quite openly admits that he at first misunderstood the words "dude" and "dudess" transcribing them as "dood" and "doodess" and considered them to be "nonsense words suggested by the repetition of do, do, do". Further enquiries showed that the song was about a "beau man". The American term "dude" and its female counterpart "dudess" here take the place of the "gal" and "boy" commonly used in the Jamaican context. Judging by the information gleaned from his employees, Jekyll must have been kind, trusted and able to put his performers at ease. This, no doubt, contributed to some of his misconceptions, for instance, as regards slave owners. In notes relating to an Anancy song, he states:

> This story refers to the time of slavery. It is almost indisputable that in certain cases, when a slave was in a weak state owing to incurable illness or old age, he was carried out and left to die. To his pitiful remonstrants 'Massa me no dead yet' the overseer made no reply, but went on with his directions to the bearers, 'Carry him go along.' This kind of barbarity was not practised by owners living in Jamaica. By them the slaves were well treated and such a thing would have been impossible. But when the masters went away they left the control in the hands of overseers, men of low caste who had neither scruples nor conscience [Jekyll 1907: 51].

Jekyll says of a dancing tune that it has an "infectious quality about it and its sections are sung over and over and interchanged". He adds that after repeating the song "as often as they do" one feels "stealing over you that kind of intoxication which the Dancing Dervishes experience".

Jamaican Song and Story contains 108 songs, tunes and texts with very well researched explanatory notes. There is the occasional error, as in describing duckunoo, a kind of starchy boiled dessert, as being a kind of mango, and sweet-mout', as "greedy" instead of flattering or mealy mouthed.

The accentuation of some of Jekyll's melody transcriptions is open to question, but this is a problem with which we all contend, and he himself was well aware of it. In his introduction he says:

> With regard to the tunes, they gain a peculiar and almost indescribable lilt from a peculiarity in the time-organization of the Negro. If you ask him to beat the time with his foot, he does it perfectly, regularly, but just where the white man does not do it. We beat with the time; he beats against it. To make my meaning quite plain, take common measure. His first beat in the bar will be exactly midway between our first and second beats. The effect of this peculiarity in their singing is, that there is commonly a feeling of syncopation about it. The Americans call it Rag-time [Jekyll 1907: 6].

This is an interesting, early and accurate description of the rhythmic layers that are a salient feature of sub-Saharan African music. Although Jekyll's interest extended beyond music to Jamaican folklore, it was by his considerable knowledge as a musician that he made the most valuable contribution to this all too neglected field of scholarship.

In addition to Jekyll's own work, the book contains short appendices by C. S. Myers, on "Traces of African Melody in Jamaica", and by Lucy Broadwood, on "English Airs and Motifs in Jamaica".

Myers prefaces her contribution by pointing out that "knowledge of African music is scantier than that of almost any other kind of primitive music". She notes the "unwarrantable assumptions" made that the versions brought from Africa were written by travellers with "correct musical ears" and that European notation can express "those delicate shades of pitch and time in which the characteristics of primitive music so essentially consist". She also complains that the most erroneous notions have been expressed as to the "nature of African music", and adds that her intention is to emphasize the prevailing ignorance of African music and to point the way to further study [Myers 1907: 278–85].

Lucy Broadwood cites many links with folk music of the British Isles, for example, Jamaica's "Tacoma and Witch Girl" (see below) with "The Keys of Heaven" and "Madam, I Will Gie to You". She also associates various Jamaican dance tunes with Scottish and English ones.

If You'll Only Be My True Lover
(from "Tacoma and Witch Girl")

Tacoma Sings

I will make you have a pre-sent of a nice silk dress just to wear on your back for to

let the peo-ple see   If you'll only be my   true lov-er   If you'll only be my   true lov-er

Gid replies

No, no dear not for   all your silk dress   I will ne-ver be your   true lov-er

I will ne-ver be your   true lo-ver

I will make you have a present of a nice silk dress
Just to wear on your back for to let the people see
If you'll only be my true lover. (x2)
No, no, dear, not for all your silk dress,
I will never be your true lover. (x2)

Broadwood errs, however, by presuming that:

> By far the greater part of these Jamaican tunes and song words seem to be reminiscences or imitations of European sailors' 'chanties' of the modern class; or of trivial British nursery-jingles adapted, as all such jingles become adapted. Except in the cases specified below, I have not found one Jamaican tune which is entirely like any one English or European tune that I happen to know. But unrecorded folk tunes are essentially fluid, and pass through endless transformations. In all countries any one traditional ballad may be sung to dozens of distinct traditional tunes, each of these again having variants. It is therefore quite possible that versions of some of the older-sounding Jamaican airs are being sung unrecorded at this moment in the British Islands or elsewhere [Broadwood 1907: 285].

Martha Beckwith's Work: A Valuable Point of Departure

Martha Beckwith collected Jamaican folklore in July 1919 and May 1924. Her work was published by the American Folk-Lore Society in 1928 in *Jamaican Folklore*, a book of some 350 pages. It is full of interesting information based on notes which were taken "directly from the country people themselves and represent, as faithfully as such transcription is possible, the true art of the African population of that island". At the time of her research, black Jamaicans would hardly have seen themselves as "the African population" but Beckwith's book is, nevertheless, a valuable source of information and material presented under the headings: Folk Games in Jamaica; Christmas Mummings in Jamaica; Jamaican Proverbs; and Notes on Ethnobotany.

There are many misconceptions and misspellings due quite understandably to the author's lack of familiarity with Jamaican pronunciation and imagery, as well as her informants' probable attempts to help her by anglicizing their speech. This does not detract from the fact that Beckwith's work was painstaking and amazingly wide-ranging, considering how short were her periods of research. She enhances her text with photographs, illustrations and over one hundred music samples.

The song texts and music manuscripts for Beckwith's collection were prepared by Helen Roberts, then Research Assistant in Anthropology at the Yale University Institute of Psychology. Beckwith pays tribute to her "quick and accurate ear", so she presumably transcribed the music direct from performances. It is no wonder that Jamaicans are uneasy with the accentuation, rhythmic patterns and words in some of the songs. For example, no one has been found who sings, "Carry me half a hoe, come gie me a'." The "a" should read "yah", meaning "here". A common exclamation, "Wah-i" often appears as "why". The transcription of a widely known stone-pounding game collected in Browns Town and which, years later, was sung for us by elderly folk there, misplaces the accent, causing rhythm of song and rhythm of game to disagree. However, there can be no quarrel with what could, in many instances, be simplification for practical reasons such as aiding the reading and writing of complicated time patterns and syncopations.

Guinea War (as sung in ceremonies)

47

Guinea War (simplified version)

In spite of these weaknesses, the music transcriptions made by Helen Roberts add a valuable dimension to Beckwith's book. Many of her samples can still be heard or drawn from elderly folk. Others have already slipped into oblivion. The collection, therefore, provides some priceless information, in addition to sources from which supplementary and comparative studies can be made. This is considerably simplified by Beckwith's care in stating the names of places and sometimes of informants involved in the primary research.

Valuable Publications, Out of Reach: Enlightened Jamaicans Reaching Out

The work of Beckwith, Jekyll and their collaborators was informative and enlightening. It is a pity that such books had to be published abroad, and heard of, let alone seen, in Jamaica almost by accident. If they had been readily available, they would have opened the eyes of the many local people who were stirring and beginning to question the validity and direction in which Jamaican minds were being pointed.

Gradually, though, there came Jamaican educators such as J.J. Mills, Philip Sherlock and Robert Verity, who were aware of the richness and importance of the Jamaican heritage. They recognized and stressed the significance of the stories with which old folk and paid helpers regaled their young relatives and wards. They realized that the words of the songs heard in the countryside and the fields as people walked the three, four, five or more miles to and from work daily had in them vital information about our history and our unrecorded past and that their ancestors' attitudes and techniques for survival were of importance to Jamaica's development. They helped people to see that, contrary to the impressions (and more), that had been given, there was much beauty in Jamaican music and other arts. The choirboy sound and bel canto were expressive and beautiful in their context, but the sound of voices at a nine-night ceremony spreading over the countryside, of drums of Revival throbbing in the hills, of the soft singing of a mother's lullaby like a trickle of cool, clear water in a cramped city slum were not just expressive in their own ways, but were part of the Jamaican people. These and many nameless leaders of thought began to light the way and dispel the night of ignorance and self-doubt.

The time had come for qualified Jamaicans conscious of the necessity for a context-sensitive approach to the study of their cultural heritage to go further and begin the monumental task of studying and developing a definitive body of work in these areas. Ivy Baxter led the way in dance. Louise Bennett worked avidly to share her extraordinary talent with indigenous speech and to alert Jamaicans to the fact that their vernacular was a language, not "bad English". She has inspired and stimulated two generations of playwrights and poets. Frederic Cassidy added enormously to our understanding of Jamaican creole with *Jamaica Talk*. Claude McKay, Roger Mais, Vic Reid and John Hearne blazed the trail in literature, Edna Manley in art. Music lagged, but the contribution of teachers and social workers such as Lydia Aljoe, Melba Elliott, Zena Stanhope, Muriel Domingo, and scores of others, anonymous but equally talented and caring, must be recognized and valued.

Many were inspired to follow the initiative of Ivy Baxter, exploring dance forms and meeting the challenge of creating a true Jamaican dance expression. These included the tireless Rex Nettleford, Alma Mock Yen, Eddy Thomas and a host of dancers and dance educators, including Sheila Barnett and Barbara Requa. On his own, Neville Black was immersing himself in the folkways of his home parish, Portland, with its Maroon, Revival, Jonkunnu, death ceremony, set dance and village band traditions. Through these and other dedicated dance teachers and choreographers, a Jamaican ethic has evolved and Jamaican bodies have learnt to express themselves and communicate through their own movement styles. At the base has been Jamaica's strong, rich dance heritage found in bruckins, Dinki-mini, Kumina and others less known.

Moving Towards Self-Knowledge and Self-Esteem

With the approach of Independence in 1962 came a growing recognition of the importance of the African roots of Jamaica and the folkways which had grown from them. The Jamaica Festival of Arts which was introduced in 1963 offered many persons their first opportunity to become aware of local arts and culture. The Minister responsible for culture and the arts, Edward Seaga, was not only deeply interested but understood the importance of these largely intangible assets to an emerging nation. He had spent many months living with Jamaican peasant families as a part of his sociological research, and this had given him added insight into the significance of music in the everyday life of Jamaicans. His own social environment had also given him first-hand knowledge of the level of ignorance among "educated" Jamaicans regarding their musical heritage.

The Festival of Arts was designed for a twofold purpose:

1. To unearth and encourage talent in all aspects of the arts, music, dance, photography, culinary arts (for many years interpreted as that which was practised in elegant settings), painting, sculpture, creative writing, drama and handicrafts.
2. To expose orally transmitted cultural traditions.

It was the second aim that brought a wealth of information to the attention of Jamaicans in general, and made them conscious of sights and sounds that had till then been quite unknown to them.

The Festival setting was at first not suitable for the more ritualistic types of traditional music and dance. People accustomed to singing, dancing and participating in other related activities for anything from seven to seventy hours, found themselves limited to only three to ten minutes of presentation. Needless to say, they had not even come to terms with their performance environment (a very important element for them), nor had the songs, the drum rhythms, and the dances begun to flow, before it was time to make way for another group. The performers were hopelessly unfulfilled and the audience could make no sense of what had been presented. In spite of this most unhappy situation, it was obvious that there was a wealth of creativity waiting to be revealed and tapped.

Subsequently, attempts were made to remedy the situation. For instance, the public was invited to visit traditional groups in their own settings for performances, where there were opportunities to converse. Only those who were truly interested went. Although the audience was much smaller, it was also more open-minded and intent on learning. The traditional folk were on their own familiar ground and in control, making decisions at all levels. They sang, chanted, drummed, danced according to their own choosing, and controlled the length of the session and each item. The setting was quite informal and natural, with the audience sitting on the grass or standing around for a better view. They could even move with and join in the music, clapping, tapping, repeating the easily learned refrain: "Cyan fine no money, oh".

Cyan Fine no Money, oh

By the time the next Festival of Arts came around, understanding and respect were increasing. Presentations were allowed to last longer and both sides began to feel more at ease, more satisfied. After some years, the Festival directorate chose more suitable outdoor settings and all but abolished time limits for traditional presentations, which now began to win increasing acceptance. Kumina became especially popular. The rhythm of the drums caused widespread excitement and the songs with the strange words were fascinating. It was, however, Mrs Imogene "Queenie" Kennedy, less than five feet tall, no more than ninety pounds in weight, who most captivated Jamaica. Her voice was heard on radio with its first characteristic long note (Aaay . . . quali, quali) growing through a chant into the song and rising loud and clear over the drums and any number of percussion instruments that might be playing at the time.

Queenie did more than most to gain widespread respect for African-based Jamaican traditions, and for people like herself: people of limited formal education, but possessing electrifying personalities and exerting firm control in their own settings. Their confidence in self and in the Creator's cosmic plan is remarkable, their ability to solve problems and cope with life enviable. Queenie led the way, bridged gaps created by centuries of self-contempt and ignorance and opened doors in what had appeared to be solid brick walls. She was living testimony to John Blacking's universally significant belief in individuals and not cultures as the "sources of imagination and invention which are always necessary to solve the recurring problems of relations and institutional organization that hinder human development" [Blacking 1984: 9]. Much of Queenie's strength and effectiveness came from her use of her individuality, imagination and inventiveness.

II
Non-Cult Traditional
Jamaican Music

4

Music for Work, Play and the Spirit

Before electricity had become available islandwide and before the arrival of transistor radios, even as late as the 1950s, people in rural towns and villages and in urban areas not served by electricity were obliged to entertain themselves. They drew largely on the repertoire of folk songs, traditional dances, ring play and other such music that had been inherited from parents and grandparents. Where industrialization and mechanization had not yet taken root, work songs were still used. But beyond such areas, the songs found their way, with other folk music and dance, into a variety of concerts and special events which were invariably featured on national and community occasions islandwide. Seasonal events such as Emancipation Day celebrations on August 1, Easter Monday fairs and, since 1962, Independence festivities, revolved around music and dance presentations. Christmas and the New Year brought not only concerts in halls, booths and backyards but also Jonkunnu and Buru masked processions on the streets.

The music for all such activities was open to anyone who cared to or could participate as well as to those who wished to be audience. This is the type of music now described as "non-cult" in contrast to that of the religious groups outside the recognized churches, for example, the Revivalists. However, whether cult or non-cult, the roots of Jamaica's traditional music have the same origins: above all, the music brought from Africa and the music created in Jamaica by the exiles, but there are also echoes of military marches, sailors' chanties, formal dances and children's games from the great house of the plantation owner, and Christian hymns. All helped the enslaved to survive the brutal system of slavery.

According to Fela Sowande [1974: 85], "For the traditional African, sound is perhaps the most potent spiritual force available to him for conscious use. The properly trained African priest acquired a profound knowledge of the virtues of sound and how to manipulate them."

The slaves working in the fields were not allowed to talk during working hours, but singing was acceptable since it made the work go better. Singing buoyed up their spirits and served many other purposes in their own interest. Songs became vehicles for communication, passing messages, commenting on situations and even ridiculing the master and the man with the whip. As a precaution, names were avoided. A song about birds sung vigorously in chorus had nothing to do with birds. It actually "threw words" at various people with whom the workers had to cope. As the work gang brought pickaxe or fork down with force, references to John Crow (a scavenger), parrot (chatterbox), woodpecker, blackbird (the farmer's foe, living by robbing his cultivation) related to unpopular individuals and needed no further explanation. An innocent-sounding song could announce a prohibited meeting which had to be a closely guarded secret.

Our African ancestors seem to have known instinctively how to use sound to outmanoeuvre the boss and his carefully engineered system. Music became an important means of expression and communication. Ideas, news and comments that could not be spoken, could be sung. Worksongs were even used for resting in between acts of labour.

Both music and words of the house-hauling song "Sally" illustrate this. I recorded it in 1968 while it was being sung by men in the parish of Westmoreland. Although the practice is dying, it has long been the custom for carpenters in Westmoreland to build wooden houses in their yard space and have them towed away. As each one was ready to be moved, it was lifted onto logs to which ropes were attached and hauled by a team of men to the buyer's chosen location, a method said to have been handed down from the days of slavery. For house-hauling, singing to keep the workers moving in concert was absolutely vital.

Sally

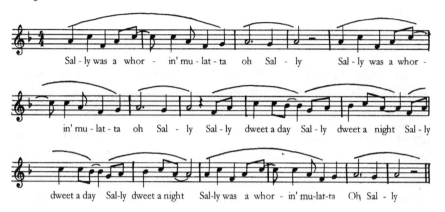

Sally was a whorin' mulatta,	*[Prepare]*
Oh Sally.	*[Haul]*
Sally was a whorin' mulatta,	*[Prepare]*
Oh Sally.	*[Haul]*
Sally dweet (do it) a day,	
Sally dweet (do it) a night.	*[Rest]*
Sally was a whorin' mulatta,	*[Prepare]*
Oh Sally.	*[Haul]*

In most songs used with hauling, phrases for work and phrases for preparation alternate equally, even if at sometimes irregular intervals. An example is found in "Pull Away":

[Prepare] Busha / ha one steamboat a run over yonda (2 bars)
[Haul]   / Pull away yankee / pull away (2 bars)
[Prepare] / Pull away to London / pull away home (2 bars)
[Haul]   / Pull away, Yankee / pull away (2 bars)

It continues:

> [Prepare] / When I was in A/merica
> I / hear the soldiers / groaning   (4 bars)
> [Haul]   / Ah . . . / Ah ah ah / ah
> / Pull away   (4 bars)

In "Sally", out of four phrases, only three are used for the actual work. One is used for resting. This could make quite a difference in eight hours' work. So in addition to using singing to do the boss's work and to please the boss's ear, the labourers used it to pause in their very onerous task. The slave masters welcomed the singing since it suggested that the "hands" were working and happy. But according to my informant in Westmoreland, "Them (the masters) like the singing, but them never know how it use."

Had the masters paid attention to the words of "Sally", they might have been displeased by the song's social commentary. Sally is described as a "whorin' mulatta", referring to the practice of the plantocracy who fathered children by field or other slaves, then sent dark-skinned progeny to the fields and kept light-skinned (mulatta) ones for service in the great house. Field slaves considered these girls as, at the very least, cheap entertainment for great house society and passing guests. So, while the dark-skinned were supposed to feel inferior because of their colour, they were in turn looking down on their lighter-skinned relatives.

Music was often, and still is, used to "cleanse the spirit". Life on earth was considered to be a school during which human beings could work through problems and shortcomings in order to progress spiritually. It was therefore very important not to allow negative and destructive emotions to hold oneself back. It did not matter that the destructive emotions were caused by the sustained subhuman treatment meted out by the masters and their agents, who were sometimes referred to as "young souls". Anger and bitterness generated by the harsh realities of life had to be recognized and thrown out. Songs about souls that had passed through suffering and hardship boosted the morale of the slaves.

Note the mention of David in the following song.

Cymbal a Go Roll

Although the road be rocky and steep
I ask my Saviour to be my guide
And when I turn my eyes up to heaven
I see Mary at her Master's feet.
An' me say bam, Uncle Rufus

Sen' me dung a Browns Town
Fe go hear dem sing.
Dem cyan sing at all
An' a rum dem want
A Mama Tully yard.
King David slew Goliath
With a sling an' a marble stone.
Chrise is coming an' me no wan no condemnation.
An' me pick up me cymbal (and)
Me lick down me cymbal
Cymbal a go roll and cymbal a go roll
An' cymbal a go roll away.

This song has been a part of Jamaican death ceremonies for at least four generations and it is sung nowadays by persons aged between twenty-three and seventy-one as 'caught' from parents, grand- and great-grandparents. Heard at four widely separated ceremonies, the tune varied slightly but the words were virtually the same.

Oral sources suggest that "Cymbal" has been a favourite for at least 150 years, which would put it at about the same time as the abolition of slavery and before the Great Revival of 1860–1861.

Lines 5 to 10 of the song suggest that the people at the "dead yard" will not even sing, because their only interest is rum. The juxtaposition of references to Jesus and references to rum shows clearly how traditional folk in Jamaica as in other old cultures saw no clear line of demarcation between sacred and secular. With regard to the line "King David slew Goliath with a sling and a marble stone", I was told that this showed that Jamaican slaves did not need "white people weapon" in order to conquer. This also underlined the importance of another folk hero, Anansi, the Spider, brought from the Gold Coast (Ghana) by our ancestors. In Jamaica he underwent a certain amount of change in order to be most often seen to be winning. Small, and as vulnerable as the slave plantation workers, seemingly powerless, Anansi had to overcome obstacles and to master situations by brains and trickery rather than by brawn. Unlettered Jamaicans can be very wise, intelligent and articulate. Often when it suited them they chose to appear dim, and to pretend to be humble and submissive. In this way they avoided imposed responsibility or unpleasant situations and unobtrusively learnt survival skills. As a popular proverb says, "Play fool to catch wise."

"Cymbal a Go Roll" was paraphrased in 1968 by a forty-year-old casual worker versed in the wake tradition in rural Jamaica. He saw it as expressing and pointing to basic beliefs and philosophies of ancestors and those of succeeding generations who clung to their parents' teaching. As he told it, life was very hard in the "old days" (presumably during both slavery and plantation society). But the "Boss Man" could only hurt you. He could not "hinder" you. When he was questioned about this, it emerged that the concept of physical evolution was quite foreign and of no interest. On the other hand, of prime importance was the "spiritual journey", a sort of spiritual evolution, whereby one progressed through various life stages towards the "mercy seat" or perfection in the presence of the Great Creative Spirit.

After Jesus had been introduced to the black population, the Christ Spirit was accepted as an unfailing guide, hence the request for help in line 2 of "Cymbal", "I ask my Saviour to be my guide". The vision of Jesus on the cross, in line 4, also was of great significance. The rest of "Cymbal" is a remarkably clear statement on the use of music for cleansing and therapy. In order to pass the test and not "be condemned" the singer plays the cymbal. "Cymbal a go roll, cymbal a go roll away."

In many Jamaican songs, there were references to Biblical characters whom Jamaicans adopted as folk heroes:

a) Daniel – who escaped unhurt from the lions' den [Dan. 6: 4–29].
b) Jonah – who was ejected from the belly of the whale [Jon. 1: 4–17; 2: 1–10].
c) David – who killed a giant Goliath with the simple sling and marble stone [1 Sam. 17: 30–45].
d) Noah – seemingly crazy, building an Ark on dry land but which later, as the surrounding waters rose, turned out to be the means not only of saving his family and their animals but also of perpetuating all living creatures [Gen. 6–8].

e)   Jesus – who conquered death [Luke 24]. Note that for them Jesus
     was the body/temple in which the Christ Spirit lived on one of
     the occasions when God sent his powerful Spirit for good, to
     help and to teach human beings on earth. This Spirit is expected
     to return in a future Messiah.

These characters recur repeatedly in Jamaican lore. Their victories
over seemingly impossible situations generated the hope so vital to the
spirit of the abused and downtrodden black population, and justified
their faith in the Triune God.

Daniel God

Daniel God surely will deliver (x2)
If you only look to him by faith
Daniel God surely will deliver.

Noah

Noah build the Ark and gone (x3)
Another generation come.

My Journeyman Jesus

My journeyman Jesus (x3)
He journey with me.

In order to survive, it was important to our ancestors that their values were respected and operational in their communities. In the outside world in which they worked, they could pretend to accept and live by the standard of those on whom they depended for material sustenance. In their own environments they had to be themselves, free and unfettered. For continuity, the children, therefore, had to be taught the customs, attitudes and conventions – the cultural values – of their elders. This started at birth, and continued through infancy and the various stages of childhood to puberty. Lullabies, stories with songs, ring games, and the song plays were used for this, as indicated by their words. Loyalty, obedience, truthfulness and other such "virtues" were highlighted. Concentration, cooperation, self-discipline and respect for elders were encouraged.

This survey of the main types of non-cult traditional Jamaican music presents songs, games and dances associated with activities and social events from the cradle to the grave. The first part, which completes this chapter, deals with lullabies, play songs and games for children and adults, love songs and work songs. The following chapter presents Mento and music associated more with celebrations and significant events, including death. Clear differentiation of the categories is not always possible, but the text will provide clarification.

In the case of lullabies, for instance, they were considered to be work songs in the great house setting, since they were sung by the women caring for "massa's and missis's" babies. Used in the workers' own settings, however, they were taken for granted as part of family (often extended) life, and a manifestation of love.

Lullabies

Regardless of the setting in which they are sung, these songs are used for babies and the very young. Jamaican lullabies are both for putting children to sleep and for comforting and amusing them. In the case of the former, the rhythm is gentle and accompanied by rocking or swaying motions:

Bya me Baby

By-a bya me ba-by Ba-by want to slee-py sleep ba-by want to slee-py By-a bya me

ba-by Ba-by want to sleep-y

Bya bya me baby, Baby want to sleepy sleep
Baby want to sleepy, Bya bya me baby
Baby want to sleepy (etc.).

As with lullabies worldwide, it is the music and not the text that is intended to affect the child. Texts, however, often give interesting insights into the adult world, as well as into adult views and attitudes.

Miss Becky Blackwood of Clarendon, who sang "Done Baby" for me in 1966, explained that it tells the child to stop (done) crying, because her mother is in touch with God, the unlimited source of their needs.

Done Baby

Done ba - by done cry You mad- da gone a foun-tain Swee-tie wa-ter ne-ver dry You

get i' dung a foun-tain

Done baby done cry } (x2)
You madda gahn a fountain
Sweetie water never dry
You get i' dung a fountain
Milky water never dry
You get i' dung a fountain.

Lullabies sung to comfort and amuse children are enhanced by clapping, knee bouncing, toe tapping, miming and any movement that might amuse and distract the infant from his or her problem. This type of performance, after achieving its aim, is often followed by the use of the same melody with gentle, sleep-inducing movements.

Accompanying rhythms might be

Play Songs and Ring Games

These songs and games have a long history in Jamaica. Many of them have been adopted and adapted from other cultures and have been "Jamaicanized" by means of syncopation and improvisation, by dramatization and the use of movements progressing from mime and formal greetings to outright dancing. Competition plays a minor role and the emphasis is on participation and having fun. There is rarely a winner or a predetermined duration for most games, which end as the players decide.

Children usually perform play songs during breaks in the school day and between domestic chores. Not as widely used nowadays, they are nevertheless still popular in remote rural districts, and in crowded urban areas where a yard, community playground, or the school playground offers that prized facility, space.

Some Jamaican play songs could have been transplanted or adapted from the European repertoire. They might have been learnt by observation in the great house setting or by participation with European neighbours in areas where ex-indentured workers had settled. They could also be Jamaican versions of themes that appear all over the world.

Sally Water

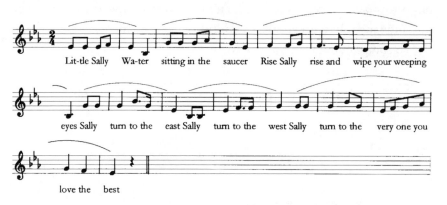

Lit-tle Sally Wa-ter sitting in the saucer Rise Sally rise and wipe your weeping eyes Sally turn to the east Sally turn to the west Sally turn to the very one you love the best

Little Sally Water sitting in the saucer
Rise Sally rise and wipe your weeping eyes
Sally turn to the east
Sally turn to the west
Sally turn to the very one you love the best.

In some places this became:

Poor little Zeddy, put him in the corner
Rise Zeddy rise an' wipe your weeping eyes

Zeddy turn to the east
Zeddy turn to the west
Zeddy turn to the very one you like the best.

"I Come to See Janie" was a popular schoolyard game up to the 1940s. It was considered ladylike enough for girls to play and could also be quoted in grammar classes to assist in the teaching of verbs.

I Come to See Janie

I come to see Ja-nie I   come to see Ja-nie I   come to see Ja-nie, An'   where is she now?

I come to see Janie (x3)
An' where is she now?
She's washing her clothes (x3)
An' cannot be seen
Goodbye (x6)
I'll come back again
I come to see Janie (etc.)
She's ironing her clothes (x3)
An' cannot be seen.
Goodbye (x6) (etc.)
I come to see Janie (etc.)
She's sick (x3)
An' cannot be seen.
Goodbye (etc.)
I come to see Janie (etc.)
She's dead (x3)
An' cannot be seen.
What shall we bury her in? (x3)
Bury her in black
Black is for the mourners (x3)
An' that will not do.

What shall we bury her in? (x3)
Bury her in white
White is for the duppies (x3)
An' that will just do.

When Janie dies and the colour for her burial has to be chosen, excitement builds up until her "duppy" ("white is for the duppies") chases and catches the next Janie. Beckwith [1928] notes that variants of this game are found in many other countries: England, Scotland and the USA for example. The Opies, famous for their documentation of children's games, also quote songs from the UK and the USA that are similar to ones found in Jamaica.

A ring game which, because of its presence in many Caribbean islands, is thought to have been brought here by seafarers is "Jane and Louisa". In Jamaica it is transcribed in triple time. In some other islands, Tobago for instance, it is written in compound duple (J. D. Elder transcription). Apart from that, the melody, words and performance are virtually identical. As in so many other ring games, a casual contact ends with dancing.

Jane and Louisa

Jane and Louisa will soon come home,
Soon come home, soon come home,
Jane and Louisa will soon come home
Into this beautiful garden.

In this game, two girls (Jane and Louisa) first walk into and around the ring in opposite directions. With the next verse:

My love, will you 'low (allow) me
To pick a rose?

they mime picking a rose from each girl in the ring, then choose a partner and waltz with her during the last verse:

My love, will you 'low me
To waltz with you?

The partners become the next "Jane and Louisa", and the game is repeated as many times as the players choose.

"In an' Out the Windah (Window)" is another game found in many countries and in many versions, including "Bluebird, Bluebird in and out the Window" and "Outside Bluebell, through the Window".

In an' Out the Windah

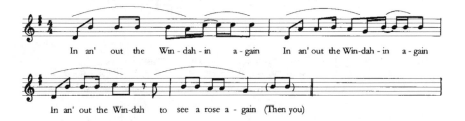

In an' out the Win-dah - in a - gain In an' out the Win-dah - in a - gain

In an' out the Win-dah to see a rose a - gain (Then you)

In an' out the Windah – in again (x2)
In an' out the windah
To see a rose again.

In each of the variations, the person going in and out of the circle of players, with arms making arches or by their sides, chooses a partner, and obeys the instructions given by the words of the song. "Mother Rolan Daughter" is another example of this type of game.

Mother Rolan Daughter

The grass so green, the lemon on a tree
A bunch of roses fallin' down
Turn to the eas' an' turn to the wes'
An' turn to the very one you love the bes'
Take a lily an' a lily white rose
Bring her across the ocean.
Give her a kiss an' a one two three

An bruck (dance) Mother Rolan daughter
Bruck Mother Rolan daughter (x2)
Bruck Mother Rolan (x2)
Bruck Mother Rolan daughter.

According to Beckwith [1928] this game was played in various parts of England as "Madame Roland", "Rosy Apple, Lemon and Pear", "Uncle John", "Mrs Kilburn's Daughter", and "Tread the Green Grass".

Brown Girl in the Ring

A modern version of this game, "There's a Brown Girl in the Ring", reached the top of the pop charts in the early 1980s, thanks to a group of young people, West Indian in origin, living in Europe. As in other "In an' Out the Windah" family of songs, the movements are inspired by the words of the song.

There's a brown girl in the ring,
tra la la la lah
For she like sugar an' I like plum.

One player who walks on the inside of the ring is told in song to:

Skip across the ocean:
Show me you motion,

at which everyone imitates the movement, anything from a simple gesture to a complicated dance step:

> *Stand and face your partner,*
> *Wheel an' tun (turn) you partner.*

Player and partner change places, and the game continues.

Pass the Ball

> *Pass the ball and the ball gone roun'*
> *Mawga (meagre) Nanny show me where the ball gone roun'*
> *Play boy, play boy, play boy play*
> *Mawga Nanny show me how the ball gone roun'.*

and

Biddy Biddy

Biddy biddy hol' fas', los' my gol' ring
One go to London, come back again. $\Big\}$ *(x2)*

"Pass the Ball" and "Biddy Biddy" are different in both time and lyrics, but are played similarly. One person, the "guesser" is inside a circle of players standing shoulder to shoulder. An article is passed behind from hand to hand, until the guesser correctly identifies who has the item at any given moment. The person caught holding the item becomes the next "guesser".

Children in many parts of the world probably play pointing games like "Bingo". In the Jamaican version, everyone sings:

Bingo

A farmer's dog was on the road
An' Bingo was his name
B-I-N-G-O, B-I-N-G-O, B-I-N-G-O
An' Bingo was his name.

At the same time, the player at the centre of the circle points in turn to the other children standing in the circle. The one at whom she is pointing when the song ends changes places with her for the next round.

There are also games played in a line instead of a circle. Among these is

Nanny, Nanny, T'read (Thread) you Needle

73

Long long t'read   Long eye nee-dle   long long t'read   short eye nee-dle   Long long t'read

show me how you t'read you nee-dle   Long long t'read

T'read oh, t'read oh, long long t'read
Show me how you t'read you needle, long long t'read
Long eye needle, long, long t'read
Short eye needle, long, long t'read
Show me how you t'read you needle, long, long t'read.

This game is played in both Britain and the USA. Players join hands in a curved line. The first player passes under his or her own and the second player's joined hands; player two under the second and third and so on until everyone has had a turn. The players then move in reverse order until the line is as it began.

"Rocky Road" is in the "London Bridge is Falling Down" family. Although played similarly, the words become very Jamaican and are often improvised to suit different occasions. Full of teasing and horseplay between boys and girls, when played in a traditional setting it becomes more than a game. It develops into a dramatized dance procession.

Rocky Road

Right through right through the rocky road   } *(x2)*
Sing Charlie Marlie call you

Dem big mout' gal we no chat to dem   } *(x2)*
Sing Charlie Marlie call you

Unlike "London Bridge" there is no "Call for the chopper to chop off your head". Each couple that runs through simply becomes another arch, until it is decided to stop the game.

The Train Game from St Ann, Jamaica's garden parish, seems to be a truly Jamaican play song. St Ann has never had a passenger train service, yet from there has come a song about the train that runs through a neighbouring parish. Fifty or so years ago, people living in that part of the island travelled to Kingston mainly by a mail coach which connected with the railway train at either Linstead or Ewarton. This inspired a game in which players form a line and shuffle forwards and backwards, as the lyrics state.

Linstead Train a Come

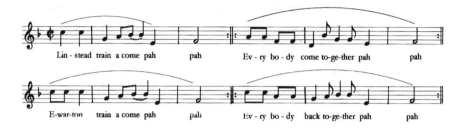

Lin - stead train a come pah   pah   Ev - ry bo - dy come to-ge-ther pah   pah

E-war-ton   train a come pah   pah   Ev - ry bo - dy back to-ge-ther pah   pah

Linstead train a come (is coming) pah, pah (x2)
Everybody come together pah, pah (x2)
Ewarton train a come, pah pah (x2)
Everybody back together, pah pah (x2)

Ring games are still sometimes played at wakes for the dead, mainly by adults, late at night. Children would by then be expected to be indoors. In any case, even though different age groups might play the same games, they would do so separately or on different occasions. Even at "moonshine dahlins" (darlings), where the atmosphere is informal and convivial, the two age groups do not play together. Held out of doors on moonlight nights, these "dahlins" were popular backyard entertainment and recreation before the electronic media became so pervasive. Now they are rarities.

Most games are played by both sexes. Boys and men tend to prefer rougher games, but girls and women are free to play them too. Mixing the sexes is avoided mainly because female players fear being injured and male ones feel obliged to be gentler, thereby somewhat spoiling their game. Young boys have no qualms about joining with girls for less vigorous games, but this attitude usually ends at puberty, when they are embarrassed to do so. Youths then look forward to being allowed to perform with the men, who delight in playing games noisily and with vigour in the cool of an evening, or after a few rounds of drinks tempt them to test their mettle and have some fun.

In the "Looby Loo" family is "Call am Fundawah", a game that ends quite boisterously. Players put hand, foot, head "in deh" (there) with much jigging and clowning, then jump towards the centre of their circle, at the verse that says "put your body in deh" and again finally with a lot of gusto at "everybody in deh, Call am Fundawah". "Am" has been used by East Indians in some parts of the island for "him" or "her". The meaning of "Fundawah" remains a mystery.

Fundawah

Ha' one cou - sin up a Seaforth Town Cheer boys cheer Tek him aunt - y coat

throw it through the win-dah Gal a wey you call am Call am fun-da-wah Gal a way you call am

Call am fun - da wah Put you han in deh Call am fun - da - wah Put you body in deh

Call am fun - da - wah

Ha' one cousin up a Seaforth Town, cheer boys cheer (x2)
Tek 'im Aunty coat throw it through the windah
Gal a wey yu call 'im, call am fundawah (x2)
Put you han' in deh, call am fundawah.

Rowdy Games

Games in which the aim is to break into or out of a circle can become very boisterous.

Bull a Pen [Jekyll 1907: 202]

Me da   leh leh leh Me da   leh leh leh bull a pen   oh   gin-ger-ly de bull a bruck

pen gin-ger-ly A gal-lo-way   bull gin-ger-ly A Mount Sin-ey   bull gin-ger-ly Bull a bruck

pen gin-ger-ly

Me da leh leh leh (x2)
Bull a pen oh gingerly
De bull a bruck pen gingerly
A Galloway bull, gingerly
A Mount Siney bull, gingerly
Bull a bruck pen, gingerly.

In "Bull a Pen", there is a ring of "cowhands" holding tightly to each others' wrists. There is one bull inside the ring and another outside. They paw the ground, and bellow belligerently at each other, while trying to break the circle and have a rough mock fight. The cowhands, who must have strong wrists, try to prevent this, but eventually one or the other bull breaks through. There is then a rather theatrical fight which ends when the cowhands drag the combatants apart.

Two Man a Road

Two man a road, Cromanty boy (Maroon)
Two man a road, fight fe you lady
Two man a road, down town pickney (town boy)
Two man a road, fight fe you lady
Two man a road, Cromanty win oh
Two man a road, Cromanty win.

Sticks are used in this rather rowdy game. On each side of the "road" is a line of girls, one rooting for the Cromanty boy, the other for the town boy. Each boy stands in front of his line armed with a stick. The girls egg their man on with, "Fight for your lady", as each tries to disarm the other and snatch a girl from across the road. Whoever succeeds is the winner. A "doctor" ministers to the loser, before another pair, with new sticks, takes its place. This is one of the comparatively few Jamaican song games that identifies a winner.

Zacky

Zacky you knee cyan ben(d), ben i' dung (x2)
Ben i' dung to groun', ben i' dung
Ben i' like a leaf pon tree, ben i' dung.

The players form a line, each one with hands on the shoulders of the person in front. They sing the line "Ben i' dung", while a "master" with a switch gives instructions in the intervening lines. He uses this on everyone who, in his opinion, fails to carry out his commands properly. The knee bending is exaggerated and accompanied by a lot of twisting of the body. For obvious reasons, this game is now sometimes played just for fun, and without the "master".

Stone Games

Stone games such as "Coverly", which lend themselves to bravura and a show of skill, are favourites. To play "Coverly" well, one must concentrate, and hold the changing pictures in mind in spite of constant heckling and distraction from the other participants.

Coverly (Cobally)

Ri-ver   bank co - ver-ly   Ri-ver to the   bank Cov - er-ly   O yes Co - ver-ly

One di deh Co - ver-ly Take him   put him dung de al-ley

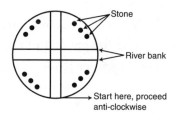

Stone

River bank

Start here, proceed
anti-clockwise

79

This game begins as in the diagram. The first verse is sung by a chosen player:

River bank Coverly
River to the bank Coverly
O yes Coverly
One di deh Coverly
Take him put him dung de alley

After this verse, one stone is removed, and the player must remember the position of the stones and sing accordingly, verse after verse. The fourth verse, three stones having been removed, would be:

River bank Coverly
River to the bank Coverly
None no di deh Coverly
None no di deh Coverly
None no di deh Coverly
River to the bank Coverly (x2)
One di deh Coverly
Take him put him dung the alley.

It is quite a feat to reach the end of the game, all twelve stones having been removed, without making a mistake, yet I have seen children as young as six succeed in doing this.

In "Manuel Road", the most popular stone game, six or more players kneel in a circle, each tapping a fairly large stone on the ground in time to the song. The speed thus established, the game begins in earnest. Players pass the stones to the right. If the movement coincides with the accents of the song (indicating the passing of the stones) all is well. If not, a finger can be crushed as a stone lands on it heavily:

Manuel Road

Go dung a manuel road gal an' boy   fe go bruck rock stone   Bruck them one by one gal an' boy

Bruck them two by two gal   an' boy   Fin-ger mash no cry gal an' boy   Mem-ber a play we da play gal an' boy

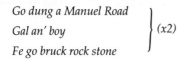

Go dung a Manuel Road
Gal an' boy } *(x2)*
Fe go bruck rock stone

Bruck them one by one, gal an' boy
Bruck them two by two, gal an'boy
Finger mash no cry, gal an' boy
'Member a play we dah play, gal an' boy
(Remember it is only a game)

The message also is, "No one crushed your finger – it was you who had it in the wrong place at the wrong time." As is often the case, there are no set rules. Keeping the rhythm is vital. Breaking it spoils the game and perhaps causes injury to the player. Ask an old Jamaican to teach you a traditional game, and the most likely response will be, "Watch me." Later, one will be invited to try and, if necessary, watch again until the game is mastered. Listening is also very important.

The circle formation is particularly suited to Jamaican attitudes and performance styles. A slow learner can fall out, or an extra person join in without affecting the formation. Players can all see and support each other by clapping, keeping time, or coordinating movements. A player on the inside can be protected, one on the outside excluded, usually with dramatic exaggerated movements.

Games with a History

A Maroon play song: a plantation work song

Most Jamaicans know "Hill an' Gully Rider" as a work song. It, however, started life as a rather athletic game played by men and boys in western Maroon towns. Considering the terrain of the country in which they live, it is quite conceivable for them to have invented a game in which the players' movements simulate the jagged outlines of the hills.

For this game, players hold hands in a curved line. One by one they alternately leap over and pass under the chain of hands without breaking it. In call and response style, the leader is answered by the chorus singing "Hill an' gully".

Hill an' Gully

Hill an' gully rider . . . Hill an' gully (x2)

Then you ben' down, low down . . . hill an' gully

If you tumble dung you bruck you neck . . . Hill an' gully

If you bruck you neck you go to hell . . . Hill an' gully

If you go to hell the devil laugh . . . Hill an' gully
Hill an' gully rider . . . Hill an' gully etc.

I have never heard this game played beyond the limited Maroon area of the Cockpit Country.

Dinki-Mini

Bery Low

Be-ry low be-ry low Be-ry low   Be-ry low be-ry low Be-ry low Cock   a cook a be-ry

low fi mi din-ner   Be-ry low be-ry   low me young gal cock a cook a   be-ry   low fi mi din-ner

Be-ry low be-ry   low mi young gal

Bery low, bery low, bery low (x2)
Cock a cook a bery low fi mi dinner
Bery low, bery low, mi young gal

Dinki-mini people have contributed to the wider community games such as "Bery Low" that use their characteristic dance movement, called "riding". Players form a ring in couples and improvise steps until the last line of the song, when everybody does the "riding" step, one foot flat and the other on the ball, while turning slowly.

Mbele Play

From the most westerly parishes has come mbele. This has travelled only comparatively recently, via videotape, to other parts of the island. In the late 1960s, while in Westmoreland seeking information on Nago people and their practices, I was told of an old man living in nearby hills who sang "funny songs". It was easy to find him. Hearing his songs was another matter, since he was surrounded by a group of chattering, giggling children, ridiculing him. After explanations and appeals, I was finally able to record two songs relatively undisturbed. The old man said that they were "behleh" songs.

In 1974, I asked Professor Kwabena Nketia, noted African scholar and ethnomusicologist, to listen to the recordings. No background information was given. At the end of the two short items, he remarked, "I hadn't realized that you had been to Africa." He was surprised to learn that the elderly singer had been born and bred in Jamaica, so African, he said, were his intonation and vocal timbre.

Ten years later, Daphne Davis, working on behalf of the Memory Bank, heard of a group of people led by Edward Williams who indulged in mbele play. She and several other interested persons were subsequently invited to watch mbele and the Memory Bank was allowed to videotape a session.

> The game is played by both men and women, divided into two teams. They form a circle together; one person from each team goes into the circle, and while the others clap and sing, and after a good deal of feinting, they shoot out one arm and hand towards the other player [Carter 1986].

To outsiders, the game is very complicated but the mbele players know exactly what to do and how winners and losers are decided. Carter has no doubt that the mbele play in Westmoreland "is a descendant of the Kongo Mbele game described in Bentley's *Dictionary and Grammar of the Kongo Language*, published in 1887". Terms used by Mr Williams and his mbele friends are described as "clearly identifiable as Kongo . . . for example, the two positions 'paabula' and 'bulikish' are close to Kongo 'mphaambula' (separation) and 'mmbudikisa' (meeting, joining) and the meanings are appropriate" [Carter 1986].

The songs used are partly in Jamaican Creole, with words not identified by either the mbele players or Carter. Mr Williams explained that they had learnt the songs from their "old parents" but were not told what the words meant.

Finga Jo Jo

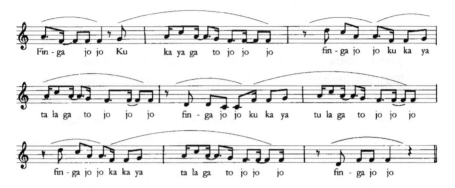

Fin - ga   jo jo   Ku   ka ya ga   to jo jo   jo   fin - ga jo   jo ku ka ya

ta la ga   to   jo   jo jo   fin - ga jo jo ku ka ya   tu la ga   to   jo jo   jo

fin - ga jo jo ka ka ya   ta la ga   to jo jo   jo   fin - ga jo jo

Finga jo jo
Ku ka ya ga to jo jo jo finga jo jo
ku ka ya ta la ga to jo jo jo finga jo jo (x3)

The Jamaica Memory Bank team showed the mbele videotape at the 1986 Conference of the African American Studies Association. Mandondo Pwona, a graduate student at the University of Pittsburgh, told the gathering that he had played the game during his childhood in Zaire, and was fascinated to see its translation to Jamaica.

Pass the navel under a fence to escape:
under a pole for fun

"Mazumba", old Maroon word for navel, is also the name of a game once popular in the Accompong area. It tests the skill and flexibility of participants of all ages who vie with each other "to pass the navel" by bending backwards under a pole held lower and lower by two adults. The game excites a lot of interest and hilarity from onlookers in much the same way as Limbo, its modern version, does in tourist entertainment packages.

Concrete towers still standing in a few Jamaican canefields attest to the fact that watchmen kept an eye on plantation slaves and workers. Mrs Ada Lewis stated that laggards were disciplined, sometimes by the treadmill, and she sang "Jiggi (jig the) treadmill, me boy. Jig i treadmill" (repeated) almost ad nauseam, as a commentary handed down by her slave grandfather. Runaways, she said, were shot at or pursued with the help of dogs. Mazumba reminds us of this technique which was used to escape under rather than over a fence during the days of slavery.

Although this game has not been traditionally used by non-Maroons in Jamaica, the skill with which many black Jamaicans perform the feat of passing the navel under a low pole gives credence to Miss Ada's story. Like the game Musical Chairs, Mazumba has no music of its own. Almost any song can be used to egg on each performer. Speeds vary according to prowess at bending backwards lower and lower to slip under the pole, sometimes no more than twelve inches from the ground. Rhythmic clapping often accompanies this game; for example

or

Emancipation Day, August 1, 1838

In my childhood, "Augus' morn" was an eagerly awaited holiday. Jamaica's Emancipation Day was celebrated with village fairs at which there would be merry-go-rounds, ring play, donkey races, quadrille dances, athletics, sports and lots of delicious food and drink. Old ladies paraded in beautiful starched dresses and colourful headties. Every now and then there would be a glimpse of snow-white petticoats, edged with bands of tucks and tarshan lace. They greeted each other graciously, dropping a curtsey as they said:

Queen Victoria gi' we free
Tidday first of Augus',
Tenky massa.

One of the games that was a regular feature of that special day was:

One Augus' Morn

One Au - gus' morn I went for a walk I met my love with a bunch of
rose I ask for one an' she gave me two By this I know that the love was
mine Dah-lin dah-lin come mek me tell you sweet-est sto-ry lov-ing co-ri-na Joe
Love you so well

One Augus' morn,
I went for a walk,
I met my love
With a bunch of rose.

I ask for one
An' she gave me two
By this I know
That the love was mine.

Each line was echoed on notes that harmonized with the last one sung in the previous phrase. Then came a sort of coda, the words of which we never completely understood:

87

Dahlin, dahlin, come make me tell you
Sweetest story, loving corina Joe
Love you so well.

We enjoyed just singing it, but it was in fact a Bingo-like game. Each round lasted through the song, with the person at whom the player in the centre was pointing when it ended becoming the new pointer.

The final example of mostly adult play songs largely originating in Jamaica or with special reference to our country or history, comes from Moore Town.

A Maroon Play Song

The Jamaican Folk Singers asked Mrs Rennock of the Windward Maroon settlement to spend an afternoon with us to teach songs and stories relating to her, and our, heritage. She chose to teach us what she called a "play". It was more the acting out of a slice of life, than a game.

The theme was similar to that of Lord Randall in that it deals with betrayal, but the outcome is different. In this case, the husband tells his wife that he is off to work at Monklan', and warns her to be true in his absence, and to be particularly wary of Zunzu, the village dude. She assures him that Zunzu will not be allowed to visit her. The dialogue is sung with many gestures. No sooner has the husband gone than Zunzu appears, and there is an affectionate scene. The husband's voice is heard in the distance singing happily. By the time he gets home, Zunzu is nowhere to be seen, and his wife is awaiting him eagerly. He questions her about visitors, and she seems to set his heart at rest. The scene is repeated two or three times, before the husband returns silently and catches Zunzu redhanded. It is on his wife that he turns, and Zunzu makes good his escape. At this point the whole village joins him in condemning her, and sending her packing to her mother.

According to Mrs Rennock, only adults took part in this play but children watched and the girls learnt the virtues of fidelity and clean living. When asked about the boys, she declared that women were more in control of such situations and should learn to "live right" and set the example.

Zunzuman

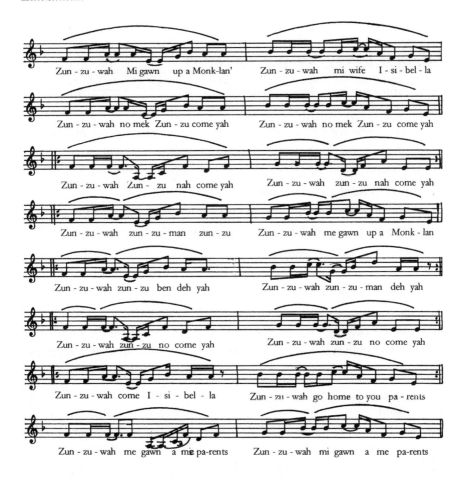

Zunzuwah mi gawn up a Monklan'

Zunzuwah mi wife Isibella

Zunzuwah no mek Zunzu come ya (x2)

Zunzuwah zunzu nah come ya (x2)

Zunzuwah, Zunzuman, zunzu

Zunzuwah me gawn up a Monklan'

Zunzuwah zunzu ben deh ya

Zunzuwah Zunzuman deh yah

Zunzuwah zunzu no come ya (x2)

Zunzuwah come Isibella

Zunzuwah go home to yu parents

Zunzuwah me gawn a me parents (x2)

Migrant Labour Inspires a Game

Jamaicans were in the labour force contracted to build the Panama Canal (1904–1914). The previous attempt (1878–1889) had ended in failure, so the workers returned home empty-handed and embarrassed. Even today with Jamaicans who go to the USA for farm labour the norm is to send money home and return with the means to improve living standards for themselves and their loved ones.

A graphic account of what had happened was given to me by Mr Clifford Strudwick who had been a child in Panama at the time. The fashion of the day was to wear a pocket watch attached to a long gold chain. The watch was tucked into a little fob pocket on the right side of the trousers, while the chain dangled conspicuously from the left. To save face, some of the Jamaican workers bought a cheap gold-coloured chain and wore it as if it had a watch at the end. When Jamaicans at home realized that there was no watch, they teased these "Colon men" by asking them the time:

Colon Man

One two t'ree four Co-lon man a come   One two t'ree four   Co-lon man a come

One two t'ree four Co-lon man a come wit' him brass chain a lick him bel-ly   bam bam bam

One, two, t'ree, four – Colon man a come (x3)
Wit' him brass chain a lick him belly
Bam, bam, bam.

Ask him for the time, an' 'e look upon the sun (x3)
Wit' him brass chain a lick him belly
Bam, bam, bam.

When in later years Jamaicans went to North America as farm workers, the song was updated:

So fast they leave the island, so quickly they come back (x3)
Wit him twang an' chain a lick him belly
Bam, bam, bam.

Love Songs

Slavery militated against the establishment and growth of stable liaisons between workers. The ruling classes feared and actively discouraged any partnerships. Short-lived relationships were all that were required to produce offspring. Loyalty should be shown to the estate, not to a fellow slave or worker.

A man, obviously of mixed blood and nearer to the Jamaican great house system, declared to me in the mid 1970s his unwavering hatred of all white people: my only such encounter to date. One reason given was the brutal and often unprovoked punishment meted out not only to slaves but to anyone known to be close to or showing sympathy for a particular victim. He had apparently learnt this from conversations overheard in childhood regarding great house settings and from observation. From the slave's point of view, constant risk of physical punishment and/or separation could hardly encourage the growth of healthy loving relationships.

In addition, since children for a long time belonged to the estates on which they were born, women were expected to increase their owner's wealth by having as many as possible. A belief that grew up and was nurtured, and is still alive today, was that women were supposed to have a preordained number of children and should, to be healthy, "have out their lot". To be childless, even today, carries a stigma and the dreaded nickname "mule". Able-bodied men also served their masters as stallions do on stock farms. They increased the slave population by liaisons which more often than not were casual, since separation always hung over their heads. This male role lingers on, at great cost to Jamaica and its development.

How could warm, loyal, loving relationships blossom in such a setting? Yet we know that they did. I have not yet found or identified any pre-emancipation love songs. The ages of the two examples to be cited have not been ascertained, but they are at least one hundred years old.

"Three Acre o' Cahfi (Coffee)" was collected and transcribed at the turn of the century by Jekyll. After a stage presentation in the early 1980s, it was identified by elderly ladies who were there as having been sung by their grandmothers. This could place it in the mid nineteenth century. It indicates a sort of betrothal system and the importance of having parental approval at that time.

The girl is sure that she loves the young man whom she considers able to support her from his field of coffee and four acres of undeveloped land. She is therefore puzzled by his reluctance to ask her mother's approval to marry her.

Three Acre o' Cahfi

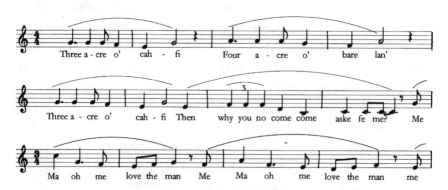

Three acre o' cahfi
Four acre o' bare lan' (uncultivated)
Three acre o' cahfi
Then why you no come come akse fe me? (What is keeping you from asking for my hand in marriage?)

She then sings to her mother:

Me ma oh, me love the man (x3)

and to the man,

Why you no come come akse fe me?

"Fe me Love" ("my love") was made popular during the 1940s by Louise Bennett, Jamaica's foremost professional storyteller and folklorist. In a dialogue with his or her beloved, a lover tells of his or her absolute constancy regardless of circumstances.

Fe me Love

On - ly for me

Fe me love have lion heart (x2)

Strong an' everlasting

Only for me.

If we part an' never meet again (x2)

Fe me love is like a king a reign (reigning)

Strong an' everlasting

Only for me.

Cassidy quotes Williams on a love dance performed in 1826, but mentions no music apart from the goombeh drum. As the dance was "in a ring, to perform a bolero or a sort of love dance", one can, however, presume that there was some type of melodic music. This, judging by the use of the word "minstrel", might have included singing. "The gentlemen occasionally wiped the perspiration off the shining faces of their black beauties, who, in turn, performed the same service to the minstrel" [quoted in Cassidy 1961: 271].

Work Songs

Songs to lighten labour, and more

Our ancestors spent most of their lives working for greedy and self-seeking taskmasters. As a result, there is a vast store of chants and songs used over the years to lighten their labour. Since the music had to agree with the many types of work they accompanied, work songs are not only numerous but also rythmically and stylistically varied.

Under the surface, this music also helped workers to communicate and to protest against the system that enmeshed them, without arousing the masters' suspicion or antagonism. With the help of the songs, they were able to maintain humanness and self-respect in spite of the atrocious conditions and treatment to which they were subjected. The plantocracy approved of this music, since they recognized its potential for improving the work scene, and increasing their wealth. It could therefore be used widely and openly. Well aware of the situation, the workers used work music to get around the system and subtly express their disapproval of it. Sally, the "whorin' mulatta", (p. 57), is a vivid example of this.

Working out of doors

The music used to help outdoor labour was intended to match the rhythm of the work. Most songs for digging, hoeing, hauling and so on were in call and response style. The leader or bomma/singerman did not take part in the manual work. His responsibility was to keep the workers in buoyant mood and moving together. To this end, he had to be quick-witted and able to improvise both words and music.

It was he, the bomma, who would ridicule the system or even the man standing by with the whip, to the delight of the work gang or "bobbin" answering in chorus vocally as well as with work movements. The speed, style and design, whether with bomma and bobbin phrases alternating or with everyone singing as led by the bomma, depended on the type of work being undertaken.

Songs for field work

Bartilby

Rain and breeze a go blow Bar - til - by oh......................................

Oh Bar - til - by oh   Drop the pick a hard mek me   hear Bartilby

Oh....................................   Oh Bartilby oh

Rain and breeze a go blow Bartilby (x2)
Oh . . . oh Bartilby oh,
Drop the pick a hard mek mi hear, Bartilby (x2)
Oh . . . oh Bartilby oh.

Bring Me Half a Hoe

Bring me half a hoe, run come gi' me yah
Bring me half a hoe, come gi' me yah

Call	*Busha want i' fi go dig up pitatah*
Response	*Bring me half a hoe, come gi' me yah.*

The tempo and style of "Alligator da Walk", a Maroon song for agricultural labour, is quick and bright. They were working for themselves on lands granted to them in the Treaty of 1738–1739 which gave them ownership of the "lands on which they had settled".

Alligator dah Walk

Al-li-ga- tor dah walk pon road oh   Leh   leh   leh   leh   leh   leh

Leh leh leh leh leh leh, leh leh leh leh leh leh
Alligator dah walk an' roll oh
Leh leh etc.
Alligator dah walk pon road oh
Leh leh leh leh leh leh leh.

Loading bananas

Banana boats were loaded in different ways. Workers usually carried the bunches on their heads from truck, cart or train past the tallyman for his checking. This particular song was used within living memory for loading USA United Fruit Company ships at Port Antonio on the north-eastern coast of Jamaica. In this case, after each bunch had been tallied, the carrier set it down on a pile and returned for another bunch. The bunches were then passed from hand to hand in time to the lusty singing of "Checkerman" by the line of men. The last person passed each bunch to a packer on board the ship.

Checkerman

Check - er - man   one gone sah Check-er-man   two gone sah Check-er-man   three gone sah Check-er-man

four gone sah   Mark me tal - ly come o - ver   One a dem gone Miss-a Hall me deh yah mm - mm

Checkerman one gone, sah
Checkerman two gone, sah
Checkerman three gone, sah
Checkerman four gone, sah
Mark me tally come over
One a dem gone, Missa Hall, me deh yah (I am here).

The most famous Jamaican banana-loading song, "Day Oh", has long since been popularized by Harry Belafonte. The words remind us that people sometimes laboured through the night, when it was cool. The banana loaders urged the tally man to work quickly and efficiently so that they could return home at dawn, when "day da light", usually for a substantial breakfast of farm produce: hot coffee or chocolate with roasted plantain, breadfruit or yam made more tasty with spicy seasonings, coconut oil and perhaps a bit of roasted codfish. Ripe bananas or citrus fruit might have rounded off the meal.

Sugar boiling

Before sugar and rum were produced in mechanized factories, the cane juice was boiled in large copper containers. A "fireman" stirred the sweet liquid with a long wooden paddle. In order to keep the juice boiling yet not sticking at the bottom, the heat had to be carefully controlled. This was done by constant communication, sung as well as spoken, between fireman and boilerman. They could not see each other at work so, when more or less heat was needed, instructions were given by the boilerman and repeated by the fireman to ensure that the message was going through correctly.

Fireman Oh

Fi-re-man oh fireman   oh   un-der-neath dere   burn   Fi-re-man oh fireman

oh Do me man oh A me   Fireman a bottom oh

> *Fireman oh, fireman oh*
> *Underneath dere burn,*
> *Fireman oh, Fireman oh*
> *Do me man oh*
> *A me fireman a bottom oh.*

Hoisting utility poles

It is interesting to note that this song, used for fishing and whaling in the southern Caribbean (collected by Roger Abraham), was recorded by me in Jamaica. Government linesmen sang lustily to accompany their work as they hoisted lightpoles along a busy main road. They were greatly encouraged by my interest.

Blow Boy Blow

The Cap-tain ask me what for din-er Blow boy blow say san' fly leg and

mos-qui-ta li-ver Blow Bil-ly boy blow you blow to-day you blow to-mor-row

Blow boy blow you blow to-day you blow to-mor-row Blow Bil-ly boy blow

The captain ask me what for dinner
Blow boy blow
Say san' fly leg and mosquita liver
Blow Billy boy blow
You blow today, you blow tomorrow, blow boy blow
You blow today, you blow tomorrow, blow Billy boy blow.

Fishing songs

It has been hard to come by fishing songs through primary research in Jamaica since it is considered unlucky to sing sea songs on land. I did not have the courage to accept fishermen's invitations to go to sea with them in their canoes and fishing boats, chiefly because I had sung a selection of European sea chanties for them and they had dismissed them as being for "pond fishing". Their seas, they claimed, were often too rough for any but religious songs asking for the Creator's protection.

However, when seas were calm, the rowdy and often risqué songs they sang to keep spirits buoyant were such that they would not perform them for "a lady". The following was sung for me by the fisherman husband of the woman who had supplied our household with fresh fish from my childhood. He still saw me as a child and sang accordingly.

Sailor Boy

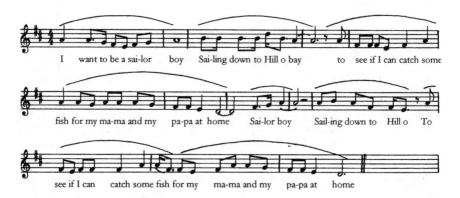

I want to be a sailor boy
Sailing down to Hillo Bay
To see if I can catch some fish
For my mama and my papa at home.
Sailor boy, sailing down to Hillo
To see if I can catch some fish
For my mama and my papa at home.

Working indoors

Some work songs like the floor-cleaning one, "Missa Potta", discussed in chapter 1, were used to comment on topicalities. As a result, they have been valuable sources of oral history. The song tells of a tenant farmer unable to meet her obligation to pay her rent in red peas instead of cash. She makes excuses but in vain. The landlord wants only to be paid, and orders her out of his yard.

Apart from the information supplied by Monica Whyte about rent for agricultural land being paid in kind rather than in cash, I have been assured by children and grandchildren of people (many of them black) who owned over fifty acres of land and rented plots to tenant farmers that such situations would have been commonplace up to the early 1930s. They say that farmers lost much of their crops because of birds, goats and other stray animals, but landlords had to be strict in order to protect themselves from lazy and cunning tenants.

This type of song was used by groups of women in the same way as field songs were used by gangs of men. Cleaning large rooms on hands and knees, using brushes made from dried coconuts, was strenuous labour. Women working in neighbouring houses would, therefore, help one another. Six or eight, from three or four houses, formed a group and worked from house to house. The labour would thereby be shared and there would also be a certain amount of very welcome socialization to further minimize the strain.

Other types of domestic work such as dusting, sweeping, pounding cassava, grating dried coconuts, washing and ironing, were usually accompanied by singing, but did not have songs of their own.

Manual labour was such an all-pervading feature in the life of black Jamaicans that music from other areas of activity was borrowed to accompany it. For example, the Maroon game "Hill an' Gully", collected as such by Martha Beckwith early in the century, is now known and used in field and on stage as a work song.

Work movements and rhythms also inspired play activities, such as stone passing games. I remember women in my childhood, sitting facing piles of stones, breaking them for covering dusty or water-pocked roads. They worked rhythmically, whether singly or in groups, to let the "music carry the work" and make it easier for them. The same rhythm was transferred to games such as "Manuel Road", described earlier in this chapter.

I am convinced, too, that work movements played a significant role in the evolution of mento, Jamaica's indigenous style of music whether for song, instrument or dance.

5

Mento and Other Styles for Dance, Entertainment and Ceremony

Mento is the music of Jamaica. It is Jamaica's indigenous dance, song, and instrumental style. The music is relatively slow, in quadruple time, and its most characteristic feature is the accent in or on the last beat of each bar.

From childhood I have observed gangs of men swinging pickaxes during field labour and I can confirm the link between their movements and the accented fourth beat in mento. In order to effect a strong downward movement on the first beat of each bar in songs used to accompany this most common type of agricultural labour, there is an almost equally strong upward movement on the previous beat.

Muma me Wan Wuk (I Want to Work)

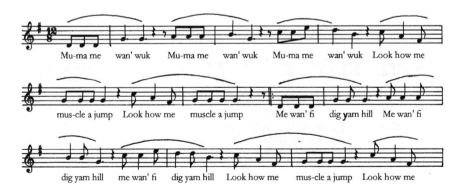

mus-cle a jump

Muma me wan' wuk (x3)
Look how me muscle a jump (x2)
Me wan fi dig yam hill (x3)
Look how mi muscle a jump (x2)

This similarity is evident throughout mento and digging songs. Speeds may vary, but accents never do, maintaining the characteristic fourth beat syncopation. The tunes are in major keys with regular, neatly balanced phrases which lend themselves to harmonization by the primary chords. Other chords and modulations are rarely heard. However, international pop beats and the modern popularity of reggae with its steady beats have been influencing the performance of both mento music and mento dancing. The 1 2 3 4 accent has become less pronounced, though the movements of older persons (those over fifty) maintain the traditional accentuation, even to diluted mento music. Younger people are now trying to recapture the old mento style. It was interesting to note in Costa Rica (1986 and 1987) that late nineteenth and twentieth century Jamaican migrants and their first and second generation offspring playing and performing to mento music placed a very marked accent on or in the fourth beat of the four in a measure bar, retaining performing styles that are weakening in Jamaica.

Mento tune "John Tom"

In performance, a lot of florid ornamentation is improvised, especially when the fife or piccolo is used, though guitar and banjo soloists also sometimes embellish the basic tunes to great effect. Soloists are encouraged to exhibit their skill at improvising in sections of the music called "breaks". The characteristic 1 2 3 4 1 2 3 4 accentuation provides the underlying rhythm, but skilful instrumentals produce an overlay of interesting cross rhythms.

The playing of mento requires both a quick imagination and the ability to improvise, which are not necessary for most other existing types of pop music performance, and so it attracts very few young musicians. The skill needed to create suitable lyrics and the work involved in learning several verses of a song have made it almost impossible to keep young lyricists in this genre of writing.

Until the 1940s, mento was widespread and popular in Jamaica but it gave way to more easily accessible foreign popular music on radio programmes and gramophone records. Trinidadian and Eastern Caribbean calypso also superseded mento in club and hotel entertainment. It became necessary for village and other bands to add calypso to their repertoires at the expense of the local mento music, a situation which continued until the Jamaica Independence Festival began to feature and emphasize mento in its annual competitions and presentations. Nowadays, mento bands are used most frequently for maypole and quadrille dancing, or on special invitation at national, community or privately arranged events.

Mento has special appeal in traditional settings but is not likely ever to compete strongly with either calypso or media-projected international pop styles. In spite of their faithful fans, mento musicians and lyricists are not in demand. The number of bands has, therefore, been steadily decreasing, leaving not more than five that enjoy great popularity and high reputation. These hold the attention and motivate spontaneous movement, even from mixed audiences in North America, Europe and the Caribbean.

A mento band consists of three types of instruments, for melody, harmony and rhythm. Any combination of the following instruments is possible.

1. melody: fife, piccolo, harmonica, saxophone, clarinet, electronic keyboard;
2. harmony: guitar and banjo, which also play melodically, rhumba box or double bass on the bass line;
3. rhythm: drums, maraccas, grater and nail, sticks, a variety of improvised instruments and body sounds.

The piano is also sometimes used to span all three areas. Typical mento bands use five to nine instruments, but some very satisfying mento sounds have been produced by big bands.

In traditional mento dancing, couples "rent a tile". There is little movement of the feet, but a lot of activity – circular and parallel to the ground – in the hips. Body contact is not necessary, but is often a feature of this dancing. Up to the 1940s there were many mento bands which included brilliant pianists, guitarists, flautists, players of other wind instruments and percussionists. The length of a dance-hall mento was quite unpredictable. It depended on interplay between dancers and musicians, and could be from five to twenty minutes long. Dancers as well as musicians often expected that they would need a change of clothing and either came prepared or went home to freshen up and return to continue. Some had to be satisfied with sitting it out until dry enough to resume dancing. Drinks sold well, and there was a lot of lively improvisation as couples joined each other or exchanged partners for new formations. Such dances produced real intermingling and socialization.

The voice is important in mento music and is often used with the instruments. Even when not sung, mento music is always associated with words. In many cases, a tune may have two or more sets of words; examples are "Dip an' Fall Back" and "Win de Sweepstake" which are cited under narrative songs, and "Gimme Back me Shillin" and "Mango Walk", well known in Arthur Benjamin's Jamaica Rhumba.

Mango Walk

Me mu-ma ne-va tell me say fe go man-go walk Sey fe go man-go walk say fe go man-go walk Me

mu ma ne - va tell me say fe go man-go walk fe tief aff de num-ba 'le-ven Come now dar-lin'

tell me fe true O tell me fe true O tell me Me ne - va go a no man - go walk an

tief aff no num - ba 'le - ven

> *Me muma nevva tell me say fe go mango walk,*
> *Say fe go mango walk (x2)*
> *Me muma nevva tell me say fe go mango walk*
> *Fe tief aff de numba 'leven (to steal Number Eleven mangoes)*
> *Come now darlin' tell me fe true*
> *O tell me fe true*
> *O tell me*
> *Me nevva go a no mango walk an tief aff no numba 'leven*

Mango trees can bear hundreds of the fruit each season. In days gone by, the trees often grew in profusion on Crown lands and therefore were seen as common property. No one was bothered if people helped themselves generously. The attitude became one of seeing mangoes as 'unstealable', and this at times caused problems when private property was treated as Crown lands. Even today it suits some to see everyone's mangoes as common property, though the justification has changed. If challenged, "pickers" (they are very hurt at the slightest suggestion of stealing or praedial larceny) are quick to defend themselves with quotations from the Bible: "The earth is the Lord's and all that therein is." They never recall anything about eating "by the sweat of thy brow".

The other set of lyrics using the same tune is about money. Since the song came from colonial times, the coin in question is the British shilling, with the lion rampant on one side. There has been a lovers' tiff and the man is demanding his money back.

> Gi(ve) me back me shilling wit' the lion pon i' (it)
> With the lion pon i'
> With the lion pon i'
> Gi me back me shilling wit' the lion pon i'
> Gal (girl) you mussi (must) take me for a fool.

Verses were improvised to suit different occasions, but everyone could confidently join in the chorus.

It is almost impossible to ascertain whether or not some mento songs are true folk songs or were written by itinerant singers of yesteryear such as Slim and Sam. "Dip an' Fall Back" and "Win the Sweepstake", which also share the same tune, are two examples that are probably the work of street singers but, like all the others of uncertain ancestry, they have been accepted as part of our folk repertoire. "Dip an' Fall Back" also has alternative lyrics (see p. 111).

Dip an' Fall Back

Dip an' fall back Now when the war was o-ver an' ev-ery-thing was scarce An'

man was ex-per-i-men-ting with things to fill them pace We had a lot of food but the

meat was out of stock So to get a blend we re-com-mend The dip an' fall back

Chorus: *Dip an' fall back (x2)*
My advice there is nothing nice
Like the dip an' fall back.

The words of the chorus relate to a popular and inexpensive savoury dish eaten as our Nago and Ettu people eat fu-fu or tum-tum or as dips are used at elegant affairs. The verses are self-explanatory. The war was, of course, the Second World War.

1. *Now when the war was over*
An' everything was scarce
An' man was experimenting
With things to fill them space
We had a lot of food,
But the meat was out of stock
So to get a blend we recommend
The dip an' fall back.

Verse two gives alternative names "dasheen" and "full me up": "rock an' fall back", and so on. Verses three to five give the recipe and manner of eating.

3 *Now you get a shad or herring*
An' put it down fe (to) soak

Get a bone dry cocanat (coconut)
You don't need no pork
You grater dung the cocanat
An' put it on fe bwile (boil)
Till the custard start fe sekkle dung pon
　　　　de cocanat ile.

4. Now you take the shad or herring
An' put it on fe (to) steam
With the pepper, tumattis (tomato), skellion (spring onion)
Until it form a cream
No stew beef or mackerel
Herrin', pork or sprat
Can be so sweet when you start fe eat
　　　　de dip an' fall back.

5. Then you crush the boil banana
An' eat it wit' the dip
Get a mug a bebrige (beverage)
An' so you dip you sip
An' if de war should come yah (here)
An' boom (bomb) begin to drop
I woulda face a tank or a long range gun
　　　　fe me dip an' fall back.

6. Mass John say, "Take me lan(d)
Take me mule an' take me dray
Take me married wife an' me t'ree
　　　　sweetheart away,
Take away me house an' take (a)way me
　　　　burial spot,
But doan skylark, or I bus (burst) you(r) head
Fe me dip an' fall back.

Another set of lyrics using the same tune is about betting at horse races held at Knutsford Park, Kingston. This course was abandoned in 1959, and became New Kingston, a bustling business area.

Chorus: *Win the sweepstake*
Win the sweepstake
Every murmur was,
"Do me Lord, make a (me)
Win the sweepstake."

1. *Me go a Knutsford Park*
On the las' big sweepstake day.
Me never really know that
Some people coulda pray
But when the horse them line up
An' the drum begin to roll,
Every murmur was
"Do me Lord, make a
Win the sweepstake."

One woman took her ticket to an obeah man to ensure success. He kept it, instructing her to "eat a farthing fine salt every morning as you wake, drink no water, eat nuttin' at all: An' you wi' win the sweepstake." The song stops short of announcing the winner, but no one seems to care. It has become a perennial favourite.

Calypsos by their very nature have more direct appeal than mento. Most calypsos designed for general use have clever and amusing words set to catchy tunes. There is often some sort of chorus in which everyone can join, and the rhythm is bouncy in a way that almost compels participation. Mento rhythm impels most Jamaican bodies to respond, but seems to present problems to non-Jamaicans. As far as the lyrics are concerned, even younger Jamaicans find them amusing but not suitable for participation. Mento songs often refer to persons and incidents guardedly, so that only those close to the subject fully understand the references. This obscurity means that visitors and the general public are not as attracted to such songs as to the easily understood calypsos and dub-style songs. In today's world of amplified sound and resounding steel bands, the mento band, playing acoustic instruments in normal listening conditions, needs to be listened to with more attention than most people are willing to give in a pop or light entertainment setting. As a consequence, the mento repertoire has virtually stopped growing. Topicalities are now commented on in reggae or dub-style songs.

In colonial days, subjects and situations that elicited approval or censure, or needed to be rinsed out of people's minds in order to avoid self-destroying emotions such as hatred and bitterness, often found their way into non-cult traditional songs: songs for work, death ceremonies, recreation. Mento songs had the most extended lyrics. They told of or commented on aspects of life and attitudes to it with subtle and ironic wit.

As people have become more confident about expressing themselves openly, and as increased and immediate communication media have made events and every shade of opinion from abroad instantly accessible, the style of topical songs has changed. Modern Jamaica, especially the youth, sees life in quite a different perspective. What older Jamaicans call tact they call hypocrisy: avoiding confrontation by getting round problems is condemned by them as cowardly and, at times, dishonest. Mento songs were not expected to change anything except, perhaps, the morale of those who created and used them. They poked fun, rather than attacked. In the 1950s mento laughed at a widespread strike with these lyrics:

> Strike, strike, strike all aroun' me is strike (x2)
> Jamaica the lan' of wood an' water,
> Madda an' son, fahda an' dahta,
> All you can hear from mornin' 'til night
> Is strike, strike, strike!

Lord Fly then notes that the only things that will not strike are the locally made matches.

Reggae in the 1980s crossed swords with the local establishment on the legality of ganja (marijuana) with a clear statement to "legalize it!"

(Peter Tosh), and with internationally relevant attitudes in Bob Marley's "Redemption Song": "Emancipate yourself from mental slavery . . . have no fear for atomic energy" for no one can "stop the plan", and in his "War" he denounces the "philosophy which holds one race superior and another inferior", and wishes to see it "finally and permanently discredited and abandoned everywhere".

The satire and gentle humour of mento are definitely passé. Many older Jamaicans regret this, with no alternative but to accept or even only tolerate change as another sign of "progress".

Bruckins

Soon after the establishment of the Folk Music Research Unit in 1967, Melba Elliott, a Government Social Welfare Officer, invited me to spend a day at Manchioneal in Portland. I quickly accepted, since groups from that town had consistently won gold medals in the annual Festival of Arts. They had excelled in staged but "authentic" and full-blooded presentations of traditional work, play and mento songs. The newly publicly presented Bruckins Party was also to be found nearby. Several other visits to Manchioneal followed for research, and also to share its rich music and dance traditions with other Jamaicans as well as visitors. These included UNESCO specialists in 1970 and delegates to the International Folk Music Council Conference in 1971.

Bruckins had first been made known to the country at large in the 1960s through the Festival of Arts. The costumes, music and dance steps were fascinating, but it was not until Hazel Ramsay and I were able to make contact with the performers on their home ground that its significance really began to be appreciated.

There was only one Bruckins group on the island. Led by the elderly but active and alert Mary Turner, the group included four to five musicians and twelve or sixteen dancers, of whom at least three were over eighty years of age. One was deaf to speech, but never missed a step. Even after walking two or three miles to the Community Centre where we met, no one ever accepted a seat. They immediately changed into their costumes, blue or red dresses or shirts, according to the set each was in, veils or crowns, and some with both, and claimed the bouquets or swords that they would carry. The dancers paired off and waited, those in blue a little away from the reds.

Bruckins began as a celebration of emancipation from slavery on the first of August 1839. According to informants reporting, as told by grandparents and other elders, after the "disappointment" of 1834, they waited to see if emancipation had really come – no strings attached – before celebrating. More than music and dancing, it was also a competition of skill and endurance beginning at nightfall on July 31 and continuing till dawn on August 1, which all the couples greeted with the following songs and dances.

Day deh pon Dawn

Day deh pon dawn (x4)
O day deh pon dawn.

The music, played by side drums using measured, military-sounding beats accompanying a small group of singers, dictated the sequence of dances.

De Queen a Come in

De Queen a come in (x6)
Oh yes a beautiful sight.

Red Queen a come in (x6)
Oh yes a beautiful sight.

Blue Queen a come in (x6)
Oh yes a beautiful sight.

The main characters were King, Queen and Courtiers. Reds and Blues each had the same number and type of characters, and it was these who vied for public acclaim throughout the night. The winning Set was chosen by the volume and length of applause each received on the first morning of August.

Bruckins involves much parading, or "bragging" as the performers call it.

Walk an' Brag

Walk an' brag, oh Tilly.
Walk an' brag as you like, Tilly.
Nobody walk like you, Tilly.
Walk an' brag as you like, Tilly oh.

The couple or couples summoned by the music proceed round the booth using dignified, stylized steps before dancing in the prescribed area.

Recreation aroun' da Bood

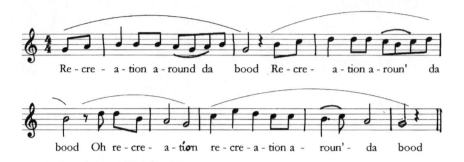

Recreation aroun' da bood (booth) (x2)
Oh recreation, recreation aroun' da bood.

The dancing is characterized by stately dipping and gliding movements, with deceptively simple-looking leg movements in front, at the side and behind, one foot sometimes barely touching the floor, if at all. Another feature is exaggerated posturing with swords. The music varies little, yet skilled dancers can whip audiences into a state of excitement which in turn eggs them on, heightening enthusiasm and interest for the arrival of the next competitors. It is then up to them to prove their worth.

Bruckins impresses everyone with its strict conventions, usually staid music presentation and the variety of movements that the best dancers create out of what seems to be quite a limited traditional vocabulary.

It is noteworthy that two of the most frequently used Bruckins songs mention Queen Victoria by name. In the minds of some of our most senior citizens, it is to "Missis Queen" that we owe our freedom, regardless of what history records. Many letters and appeals against injustice, neighbourly or national, are still directed to the Queen of England. Although modern Jamaicans often disagree strongly with these attitudes, we must respect them since they reflect the concepts of those who had actually experienced the horrors of slavery/plantation life and the contrasting jubilation when they ended, or who were told of them by grand- or great-grandparents.

Jubalee

Jubalee, jubalee,
This is the year of jubalee.
Augus' mornin' come again (x2)
Augus' mornin' come again.
This is the year of jubalee
Queen Victoria give we free (x2)

Noble Queen Victoria

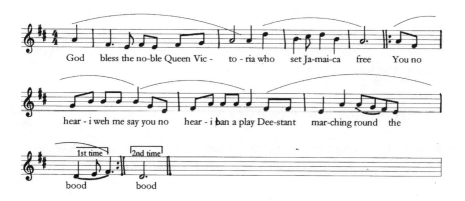

God bless the noble Queen Victoria
Who set Jamaica free
You no heari weh me say (hear what I say)
You no heari ban' a play
Deestant (decent) marching round the bood (booth) } *(x2)*

Bruckins is sometimes used for raising funds to defray expenses. It then includes an interlude of concert-like entertainment with auctions of items being performed and of specially made and decorated hard-dough bread or fruit cake. A popular form of village fun and fund-raising, this type of programme is also used at "Pleasant Sunday Evenings" and "Tea Meetings".

The Tea Meeting format includes wordy orations (preferably polysyllabic) which excite admiration and applause for the sound of the words rather than for their sense. Performers can be paid by members of the audience to stop in the middle of an oration or song. They might also be paid more to return after being put down, or to repeat an item that had been "enjoyed". Quite a lot of money can be raised in this way. Real Tea Meetings may stretch for many hours but are full of good humoured teasing and laughter. In the case of an interpolation into a Bruckins party, the Tea Meeting would not be allowed to steal the show. It would be brought to an end as soon as enough money had been raised. In all cases, the climax is the auctioned unveiling of an elaborately decorated loaf or cake, or someone promoted as a great beauty. She often turns out to be a man or a very plain woman – another source of amusement.

As with Tea Meeting, Bruckins has been gaining a sizeable following. Youth in Portland, its home parish, have learnt it from enthusiastic and knowledgeable members of their communities. Each year it is a centrepiece of our Festival and, as of old, the air is festive, the presentation stately and imposing.

"Story Songs" and Ballads

In his enlightening and informative study of the music of Africa, Kwabena Nketia tells of the important "songs of the elders" which:

> . . . remind people of the past, and of the values of a society, and require some knowledge of oral tradition before one can understand them. They have been described as historical songs in the literature on African music, even though, with a few exceptions, what they generally provide is not detailed narration of events, but brief allusions to significant incidents and genealogies [Nketia 1974: 196-97].

A similar situation exists in Jamaica regarding numerous mento songs as well as in ballads and story songs, which are few. The ballads that have been found to date are based on songs and stories from the great house side and show none of the tendency towards the secrecy that characterizes so many Jamaican mento, work and other traditional songs.

Prior to radio and easily read print media, singers wandered from place to place offering broadsides for sale or performing news and gossip-filled adaptations of popular folk songs for a small fee. A song based on one such adaptation was popularized internationally by Harry Belafonte, himself of Jamaican ancestry, as "Jamaica Farewell". This song had originally referred to a race horse called Barkwood, which had been having a very successful run at Knutsford Park race course in Kingston. His strength and stamina became so legendary that they earned him a song with the line, "Barkwood belly like a' iron bar". Later it was changed to titillate night club and tourist audiences and became "Iron Bar", one of the songs that as children we were not even allowed to play on the piano. "Jamaica Farewell" is gentle and nostalgic, and a far cry from both Barkwood and "Iron Bar".

The only real ballad that I myself collected told of Lord Randall, and came from northern Clarendon. Many Scots settled in this part of Jamaica after serving their indenture. Dr Peter Cooke of the School of Scottish Studies (Edinburgh University) states that features of both the tunes and the words of songs collected in the Scottish islands are found in this Jamaican ballad. The story comes in many forms, including "Zunzuman", the Maroon play song discussed in chapter 4. The husband goes off on business after bidding his devoted wife a loving farewell. No sooner has he left than a lover appears. For one reason or another the husband returns unexpectedly and there is an ugly scene. In Lord Randall's case, after receiving news of his lady's perfidy, he hurries home, across many streams in the craggy Blue Mountains:

He walk a mile, he swim a mile
Till he reach Newcastle his home.

The ensuing scene is passionate and bloody, as the aggrieved husband kills his rival.

In the second example, an indigenous story song, the name of the hero has been changed, since, I was told in 1972, the family of the gentleman in question was sensitive about his notoriety.

The Man from Southfiel'

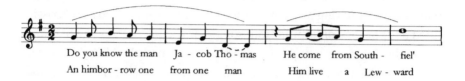

Do you know the man   Ja - cob Tho - mas   He come   from South -   fiel'
An himbor - row one   from one   man   Him live   a   Lew - ward

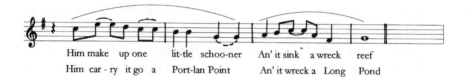

Him make   up one   lit-tle   schoo-ner   An' it sink   a wreck   reef
Him car - ry   it go a   Port-lan Point   An' it wreck a   Long   Pond

Do you know the man Jacob Thomas?
He come from Southfiel'
Him make up one little schooner
An' it sink a Wreck Reef.

An' him borrow one from one man
Him live a' Leward
Him carry it go a Portlan' Point
An' it wreck a' Long Pond.

When it was sung for us by blind Miss Becky Blackwood of Rocky Point in Clarendon, Hazel Ramsay and I had no idea how long it would take us to get to the meaning of this short and simple song. After months of searching for maps that could show us all the places mentioned and then examining them in vain, we returned to Miss Becky. She had no idea where Leward was, but, pointing confidently, she told us in a very matter of fact way that Long Pond had been "over there, but the sea took it in". No one had ever heard of Leward. Eventually, the seafaring wife of a British High Commissioner suggested that it was derived from the nautical term, leeward, meaning on the sheltered side. In the Jamaican context, as in this case, it usually signifies westward. We also found Wreck Reef off the coast of Clarendon on a large geological survey map. The picture was complete.

Putting elements of tales told in Rocky Point together with others told over a year later at Treasure Beach in St Elizabeth, we managed to work out an interesting and informative story.

"Jacob Thomas" lived at the turn of the century. He was a farmer of peas, corn and small stock and every so often he took produce and animals to Kingston where he would sell them and buy supplies unavailable in his part of the island. So he travelled three or four miles from Southfield to the coast, then made the rest of the journey by sea, though that too could be fraught with problems. Jacob made many friends on the way and it is this that led to his acquiring a reputation for wild living. They drank, gambled and lived riotously every time Jacob stopped at Rocky Point, for instance, to stretch his legs, get some sleep and water his animals. Some older residents seemed to think that the two unsuccessful attempts to reach Kingston, as mentioned in the song, were judgment for Jacob's carryings-on. Songs such as these "allude to significant incidents" and "remind us of the past" as in the African "songs of the elders" mentioned by Nketia. Their stories are hidden between the lines.

Jonkunnu

As late as 1945, radio was a rarity in rural Jamaica. We were therefore not then bombarded by the hard-sell Christmas commercials that nowadays herald the approach of the festive season. In many parts of the island, however, preparations for Christmas were well underway by November.

In my village, for instance, donations of money were being received, gifts of groceries, toys, clothes and household items collected, dried fruit was soaking and stocks of ingredients for Christmas puddings and other special fare were growing. Schools and churches would be preparing music, costumes, readings and recitations for end of term and church programmes. Freshening up of walls with paint, white-washing of stone and tree trunks and bushing of yards and public areas would have begun in earnest. By roadways, heaps of stones to be broken would begin to appear as Government's annual Christmas work programme got under way to help people in special need of "Christmas money". Dorcas and other community-based societies would be nearing the "launder and package" stage of garments made for distribution to the needy of the village.

Every night islandwide, the sound of Jonkunnu or Horsehead/Buru drums would confirm that Christmas was approaching. Venturing near the yards where Buru rehearsals were being held, one might hear songs such as:

Chrismus a Come

Chris-mus a come me wan' me la-ma Chris-mus a come me wan' me la-ma

Chris-mus a come me wan' me la-ma Chris-mus a come me wan' me la-ma

Tenk you for the Chris - mus Tenk you for the New Year

Tenk you for the chance to live an' see an- a -tha year

Chrismus a come, me wan' me lama (finery) (x2)

Chrismus a come, me wan' me lama (x2)

T'enk you for de Chrismus

T'enk you for de New Year

T'enk you for de chance to

Live an' see anadda year.

At other places, Jonkunnu musicians would be practising their trills and turns far into the night. Christmas had become an important marker of the passing years during slavery. No birthday revelries for us. Living to see one more Christmas was considered a blessing worthy of thanksgiving and celebration. It was also a time for giving and receiving gifts: an egg, two coconuts, a handful of peppers, a pint of peas from worker to great house: extra rations, a hand-me-down dress or pair of shoes, a bottle of wine in the other direction. At Christmas on some estates, Master and family served workers at table to a fine meal.

Jonkunnu or its variant Horsehead/Buru processions would have taken to the streets on Christmas Eve and again on Christmas Day, Boxing Day and up to or on New Year's Day. They were the long awaited public entertainment by and for the black population, though they might be invited to dance, play and have a drink in private yards en route. In earlier times "householders" and some "set girls" entertained within houses only. These female indoor performers were commented on as early as 1808 by James Stewart in *An Account of Jamaica and its Inhabitants*. He observed:

> On New Year's Day it was customary for the negro girls of the towns . . . to exhibit themselves in all the pride of gaudy splendour, under the denomination of blues and reds . . . These girls were wont to be decked out with much taste, sometimes at the expense of their white and brown mistresses, who took pride in showing them off . . . The most comely young negresses were selected, and such as had a fine and tutored voice, they paraded through the streets two and two, in the most exact order, uniform in their dress, and nearly of the same stature and age. They were accompanied by instrumental music; but they usually sung together . . . [quoted in Cassidy 1961: 260].

The blues and reds of the set girls are a reminder of the costumes worn by the Bruckins dancers of Portland.

Masters were compelled by law to give at least three days' holiday to all workers at Christmas. Hence its importance in the lives of people who for the rest of the year hardly knew one work-filled day from another.

Slaves and plantation workers celebrated their hard-won holiday with feasting, music, dancing and masquerades. Central to these celebrations were processions of men, women and children led by prancing masqueraders and musicians.

There is a wealth of information about these Christmas revelries from historians, sociologists and others, but comparatively little is said about their music. However, Martha Beckwith in her thorough account of the festivities does give some information on the music. Beckwith's *Christmas Mummings in Jamaica* was published by the American Folk-Lore Society, New York in 1928 as Part II of her *Jamaican Folklore*. She considered Isaac Belisario to have been "by far the fullest authority upon Christmas merry-making of this period [early nineteenth century] in Jamaica".

Most of Belisario's writings were lost in the 1907 earthquake, but his coloured plates were salvaged, and are still widely used and accepted. Gardner, one writer quoted by Beckwith in an 1872 essay, stated: "At the Christmas carnival the younger women adorned themselves with all the finery they could procure . . . Gaily adorned, the damsels paraded the streets in parties, known as the Reds and Blues or the Yellows and Blues, each seeking to outshine the other . . ."

Beckwith noted that although the full-length and animal masks and other characteristics of Jamaican Christmas Mummings hark back to West Africa, the houseboat, carried on Actor Boy's head in the Jonkunnu band, is not mentioned in that context. Counterparts of it appear, however, in several festivities in Morocco, Italy, Provence, the Shetland Islands and in the tomb of Hussein and Hassan carried by Shiite Mohammedans during Muharram. In 1921–1923, she observed groups in many different areas and commented on the groups led by the mummer characters Ewan and Swabe:

> Both Ewan and Swabe were accompanied by girls who sang and kept time by means of 'shakeys' made out of little gourds filled with shot and stuck on the end of sticks, and by two men who played on drums. The large drum, called 'Bon', was simply a keg with a piece of goat-skin drawn over the end and beaten with sticks. The other, called 'Goombeh' was shaped like a stool with two or four legs, covered on top with goat-skin

which could be tightened by driving in pegs so as to spread the legs. The player sat with the drum held between his knees and played it with both hands each hand keeping its own beat [Beckwith 1929: 10].

Beckwith also mentions that although one lead singer told her that she always performed the songs in a graveyard on the night before the street procession, according to her "best informed and most outspoken informants, John Canoe, apart from in Maroon country, was simply 'to make fun'."

In my experience, neither Jonkunnu nor Buru, which includes satirical songs, has been of importance in Maroon culture. This is not surprising. Since these celebrations were closely associated with slavery and plantation life, Jonkunnu would hardly have been a symbol with which Maroons would have wished to associate.

Beckwith also supplies information about the plays presented by some Jonkunnu groups. This probably accounts for her using the title "Christmas Mummings", since these plays are drawn directly from the farcical scene of the Doctor in Old English festival mummings such as "Golishan" and "St George and the Turk". I saw such a play in 1968 in a St Elizabeth village, quite near to places mentioned in Beckwith field reports. The speeches were verbose, the manner melodramatic and exaggeratedly Shakespearean, and the incidental music stiltedly based on European melodies. Villagers as well as visitors found it all very entertaining in a ridiculous sort of way. The inevitable sword fight and miraculous healing, so skilfully enacted, drew shrieks of delight from children in the audience.

On the music, Beckwith herself says:

John Canoe songs are not sung at any other time than in connection with the display of the John Canoe cap and dance during the Christmas holidays. As a special licence has to be obtained from the government in order to take a John Canoe company out upon the road, the time of the performance is strictly limited to a period beginning on the night before Christmas and ending sometime during the first week in January. Every year new songs are composed for the occasion and the old ones practised until each company has at its command a large number of songs, new or traditional. There seems to be evidence that some songs refer in a particular way to the ceremony of taking out the dance. Others are strongly impregnated with ideas of idolatry and sorcery; this is perhaps one of the reasons why the better element among the coloured people of Lacovia disliked the John Canoe mummings and seek to put an end to them. By far the larger number of songs are satirical or plaintive references to persons and incidents or everyday life, and hence convey a true impression of the working of the Jamaica negro's mind under the stimulus of emotion [Beckwith 1928: 17–18].

In *Jamaica Talk*, Cassidy asserts that the first account of Christmas dancing by the slaves with "cows' tails (tied) to their rumps" was given by Sloane in 1725, and the first mention of "John Connu" made by Long in 1774. Long described noisy masqueraders in grotesque masks and costumes, dancing and leading a drink-sodden crowd in revelry which sometimes led to illness and even death. Cassidy discusses a number of theories about the name and derivation of what we rural Jamaicans have known as Jon(g)kunu. Some of them are far fetched and he does not agree with Beckwith on the value of Belisario's observations. He concludes that the most likely source of the name is the Ewe language of East Ghana and Togo. He also provides two comprehensive lists of Jonkunnu characters.

The first list includes "Royalty" (from the Sets), Champion, Warwick (a villain reminiscent of mummers), the Devil, Wild Indian and Indian Girl (showing a more recent influence from North America), Sailor and Whore Girl (who "dance vulgar all the time" but in fact represent the black Jamaican's view of the loose-living mulatta girls in the service of the great house and its guests), Messenger Boy (dancing with female as well as male characters), Doctor and Dispenser (of trade companies), Jockey (local) and Pitchy-Patchy, who might possibly be the Jamaican version of "Jack-in-the-Green", the principal mask of the English chimney sweepers, according to Barnett [1979: 29]. Pitchy-Patchy kept masqueraders as well as the surrounding crowd in order by cracking a cattle whip. The second list includes some of the above, with additions such as Drunkard and Matron.

Characters varied considerably from place to place, but by and large represented similar groups or origins. All Jonkunnu characters were male: when necessary they dressed in female garb. There was always an easily recognized leader responsible for the schedule of items, pauses, performances and the procession, as well as the collection and later distribution of monetary gifts along the way.

When Jonkunnu and its variants were part of the environment of both urban and rural Jamaicans, people from all strata of the society, even if disapproving of them, would have been aware of their music, dancing and street activities. Cassidy notes a citizen's complaint in the Jamaican *Daily Gleaner* in 1951 that the paper was encouraging "Jonkunnu, commonly called Horsehead", with its "demoralizing" and "vulgar" dancers just as the police had succeeded in suppressing it. In conclusion Cassidy states:

> John Canoe is now a thorough mixture that takes many forms, some of them obviously debased. But at the centre is still the figure of a masked dancer who makes the procession, prancing wildly and shouting, in a traditional African dance. Bowditch''s famous description of his reception in 1817 by the King of the Ashanti, may be recalled. The English visitor saw Captains and warriors who wore rams' horns on their heads . . . leopards' tails down their backs, and horses' tails at their belts dancing processionally past; flag-bearers 'plunging and springing from side to side with a passion of enthusiasm'. The bands were principally of drums, horns, and flutes . . . jawbones of human victims were hung on the drums [Cassidy 1961: 26].

Jonkunnu music was provided by bamboo, and later plastic, home-made fifes, and side drums. Styles varied depending on the character being featured. Jackna Green or Pitchy Pitchy danced differently from Devil or Bride, for instance, and this was, of course, evident in the speed, accentuation and texture of the music. For unspecified or group dancing, the fife played short repetitive snatches of melody in a quick and agitated manner.

Fife Tune

Interspersed with trills, these melodies were accompanied by a rhythm and frequent rolls of the drum:

Buru: a variant of Jonkunnu, found in Clarendon and St Catherine

Buru/Horsehead used three drums: bass, fundeh and repeater; the drums that, according to Count Ozzie, were adopted by the first Rastafarian musicians. They are still played by them. The composite Buru rhythm of these drums in slow quadruple time was

Singing was an important component of Buru. Local incidents which could inspire songs of ridicule and/or censure would have been noted during the year. Each group would prepare and present its choice of one or more such songs. These, added to others which had been handed down recently or through many generations, would become the current repertoire. Many of the lyrics were "earthy" and considered unfit for "decent ears". Jonkunnu and Buru bands were not allowed on the streets while Church services were in progress at Christmas and New Year.

Since 1980 there have been comparatively few practising Jonkunnu groups of even mediocre standard. They are based in St James, Westmoreland, St Ann, Portland, St Thomas and Kingston. There are a few Buru groups that still operate traditionally, but their activities depend largely on patronage from affluent citizens, business houses or industrial organizations. Dianne Gordon's unpublished study of Buru as it existed in 1980 provides valuable information on this masquerade tradition.

Today, the best groups are sponsored in performances for community and national occasions and for the tourist industry. This gives them opportunities for exposure and to augment their earnings from farming, ad hoc trading and casual labour. At the same time, this also tends to dilute traditions, as pleasing audiences and employers takes precedence over authenticity.

Groups that appear at Christmas and New Year are often poorly masked and costumed, under-rehearsed and straggling. No longer do they attract a crowd of dancing, prancing admirers. They are considered to be a nuisance by most other road users and they are often berated for "begging". Since their demeanour and performance are frequently sub-standard, it is not surprising that their requests for money are resented. The young see them more as objects of ridicule than as having anything to do with them and their heritage.

These masqueraders usually know where to find those who encourage them to continue and to improve. They walk many miles to ask for water, and a chance to rest at the homes or business places of these people. Sadly, we seem to be seeing the last of another facet of our cultural heritage.

Set Dances

Quadrille and others from the ballrooms of Europe to slave quarters in Jamaica

Ivy Baxter, premier choreologist and pioneer researcher of Jamaican dance, states: "Quadrille here is a mixture of European steps and Jamaican quality in music and movement." I would add that most of the music is based on European melodic and harmonic styles and phrase structure.

The Jamaican quality mentioned by Baxter could refer to the typical types of improvisation and embellishment, syncopation and the characteristic accent on up beats.

Quadrille tune

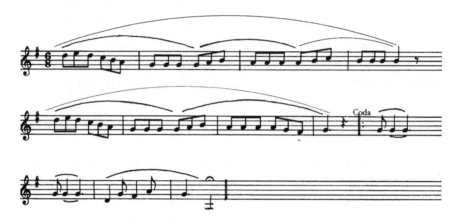

Jamaican quadrille has been described as the creolization of eighteenth and nineteenth century European ballroom dances. These dances reached us by way of the great house. After travelling to the USA, they had become square dances. New Zealand Maoris at the 1986 Edinburgh Festival told me that they too dance quadrille.

There was a very interesting encounter when these Maoris listened to the Jamaican village band. At a workshop, the mainly Scottish audience was asked to comment on any similarities noticed in the quadrille music about to be played since, in Jamaica, one segment was called Schottische. No one commented. Afterwards, the most senior Maori lady assured me that she had noticed marked similarities between the Jamaican Schottische music and that used by them in New Zealand for a dance which they too called Schottische. It suggested that music dispersed by Europeans in these colonies had survived there, while fading away at home, which, we presumed, in the case of the Schottische was Scotland.

Schottische as danced by the Jamaica Festival gold medal group from Buff Bay is in slow triple time which suggests that it must have come to our shores early, taking its speed from the slow polka Schottische and its time from the original Ecossaise. It would be interesting to trace the journey of the polka and mazurka (pronounced "mazulka" in Jamaica) which are also included in our quadrille suites. There is probably less mystery about these. The polka has retained its quick duple time, and probably took the route from either Bohemia or the Balkans [Gilbert and Lockhart 1961: 42] throughout Europe where "it spread like an epidemic" to the great houses across the Atlantic. The mazurka, a traditional Polish dance, "spread to Germany in the mid-eighteenth century, then to Paris, and in the early part of the nineteenth century to Britain and so to America" [Scholes 1941: 547]. He could have added, "and the Caribbean". There Mazurka too has retained its time, tempo and style and, as originally happened in Poland, is sung as well as danced.

Mazurka

Try dear don't tell a lie   Try dear don't   tell a lie   Try dear don't   tell a lie   Or

I will ne-ver ma-rry   you   Try to tell the truth mi   dear   Try to tell the truth mi   dear

Try to tell the truth mi   dear   And   yu will get the ring mi   dear

Try, dear, don't tell a lie (x3)
Or I will never marry you.

Try to tell the truth, mi dear (x3)
And you will get the ring, mi dear.

Jamaican slaves, and other workers, learnt quadrille from their masters either by casual observation or as they played for these ballroom dances. Instruments used included fiddle, merrywang (later, guitar) and shakkas.

In addition to adapting the music and style of great house dancing, the Jamaicans extended the range and increased the number of "sets". Ballroom quadrille retains formal dress and deportment while camp-style quadrille uses couples in various formations and far more spontaneous and improvised music and movements based on the particular dance figure.

The music and movements, of course, interacted, the one influencing and motivating the other. Of the maximum eight figures used, the most original and typically Jamaican is the fifth figure which is danced to mento music.

Instrumentation also became increasingly Jamaican. To the small great house band, rhumba box, bamboo fife and drums were added. Piccolo, trombone, clarinet, saxophone, harmonica, banjo and mandolin have also been used.

Quadrille, and variants such as the Lancers with eight couples, were a lively part of village life up to the middle of the twentieth century. Apart from being featured at community fairs, picnics and holiday celebrations such as Emancipation Day (August 1), Easter Monday and, in colonial days, Empire Day, they were kept alive at regular sessions arranged by elderly enthusiasts. If instruments were short, voices and clapping sufficed.

Costuming is considered important. For ballroom-style dancing, men and boys wear cummerbunds, bow-ties, waistcoats, standing collars, smart trousers and well-shined shoes. Women wear well coordinated ensembles planned round a formal gown and evening shoes. For camp-style, dress is less formal and more peasant-like in effect.

The Jamaica Festival began the handing-on of these dances to young performers. This has continued under its own momentum, giving quadrille and other set dances new life. There are fewer practising groups, but enthusiasm is keen and standards remain high. One major problem is the decreasing number of village bands. Taped and mechanical music just cannot motivate dancers or generate the excitement stimulated by the human interchange between musician and dancer. Jamaican youth is being encouraged to take over from the traditional musicians, but it is a hard struggle with the easy alternatives of discos, synthesizers, video, television and all the other modern fingertip means of entertainment.

Death ceremonies: music to help the spirit on its way

Our African ancestors must have brought many memories of music and rituals relating to life stages. Traditions regarding birth, initiation, marriage and death would have been observed consistently, regardless of the country from which our people were transported. Under slavery, it would have been extremely difficult to preserve most of these traditions. Giving birth was only a brief interruption in the round of toil. Initiation no longer applied: the exiles and those born here would forever be "boy" and "girl" in the eyes of their masters. Marriage was for real human beings, not slaves, who were property in human form. Only death was the same, and here a welcome respite from their short, miserable existence as slaves or plantation hands and a happy prospect of reunion with ancestors.

In spite of their fear of gatherings, the masters seemed to have allowed funerals and death ceremonies to be held without interference. Music played an important role in these ceremonies: music to comfort the bereaved, to cheer and to help the spirit on its way. Many accounts of death ceremonies have been given by writers from before Emancipation up to the present time. Judging by these, the basic form and content of the main rites have not altered significantly. We can, therefore, discuss recent or contemporary observances here.

Music still plays a vital role at all wakes for the dead, from the "set up" on the night of the death, through to the "nine night" on the ninth night and even to the thirtieth and fortieth nights after death.

Professional Wake Chairmen, such as the well-known "Uncle Ref" in Rae Town, are sometimes engaged to oversee the proceedings and lead where necessary. They sometimes travel long distances in order to carry out their duties. In any case, there must always be someone acting as master or mistress of ceremonies, and working on behalf of the bereaved, so that they can be free to attend to personal matters.

The Jamaican wake moves at a leisurely pace at the "prompting of the spirit". Music is interspersed with prayers, readings and various kinds of speeches: eulogy, sermon, exhortation, remonstration.

Toward dusk on the appointed day, people drift to the wake house, also called the dead yard. Many take gifts of food or flowers; others clutch coins, or have notes securely placed in shoe, fob pocket or brassiere, in readiness for an appropriate time of giving. Greetings vary from a simple pressing of palms to unbidden outbursts of weeping or long assurances of sympathy, hope and undying friendship. Soon a hymn is "raised" – "Rock of Ages", "Abide with Me" for example, or a well-known chorus:

Sleep on Beloved

Sleep on beloved, sleep and take thy rest,
Lay down thy head upon thy Saviour's breast
We love thee well, but Jesus loves thee best
Goodnight, goodnight, goodnight

The need for a change is probably sensed by the Chairman, who responds by "tracking" another hymn, "reading" each line just in time for the singers to pick it up.

As Pants the Hart (as "tracked")

chase so pants my heart O Lord for thee And Thy re -

deem - ing grace

A joyful chorus could follow, accompanied by hand-clapping and body movement:

What a wonderful ting, a very wonderful ting
To be free from sin and have joy widdin
And to be a joint heir with Jesus my King
What a wonderful, wonderful ting.

Drums are not used. Boom pipes (lengths of bamboo which are either struck on the ground or blown into to produce one to three bass notes) might be. After lengthy and vociferous praying or reading from the Bible, another hymn or chorus might be raised.

Ladies will have been busy preparing to serve fish, hard-dough bread (specially made and decorated for the occasion), bammy (cassava bread as made by the Arawak Indians) and coffee. Men will have been busy mixing drinks with a base of white proof rum, and checking that stocks are ample, since some take it neat or with only a little water. Precious ice is chipped and put into large containers.

People from many strata enjoy the fellowship, music and other traditions of wakes, including the food and drink. They come from far and near, by car, bus, motorcycle, bicycle, cart and on foot. It is not unusual for persons who have never met any member of the bereaved family to travel 40 or 50 miles (Jamaica is only 144 miles long) to attend a wake. They will be warmly welcomed. Some will be "outsiders" because of their ignorance of wake traditions and of the family's affairs. Even local residents who are not aware of details concerning the deceased and his or her relatives, or of wake customs, will be outsiders. They will not pick up subtle messages often hidden in songs nor will they know how to respond when words say one thing and mean another. Those in the know, from far and near, will for instance feel free to laugh without causing offence. Outsiders are more guarded.

As the crowd grows, and the booth or the reception area of the house becomes crowded, there is increasing need for ice-cold water and other drinks. Visitors also spill into the yard. At this point someone outside might start a riddle or storytelling session. Jokes might be exchanged, and the lighter mood develops into ring play and perhaps dancing. For this a banjo or guitar is welcome, but voices and hand clapping are adequate.

In the reception area secular songs will have started to creep in. There is now little sadness, and the bereaved, too, will be joining in songs which raise a laugh as much by presentation as by content:

When me Father a Go Dead

When me father a go dead
Him never make no will
But him lef' one cow
Fe (for) the whole a we (all of us)
An me bigger bredda (brother)
Rob i' way from we
Glory be to God,
Me ha' fe me own (I have my own)
Me own a me own (My own is my own)

Repeated several times, this type of song becomes a real production. Alto, tenor, bass and descant are improvised and body sounds added for rhythmic interest. People mime and dance by themselves or in couples, without making any body contact. It ends with laughter, and a general retreat to chairs, benches, steps, or anything that offers a seat. There is much fanning and chatter, then more drinks.

A well-attended wake compliments the bereaved. Very few invitations are sent out, but the bush telegraph is always efficient. Even visitors from abroad are sometimes seen at these events in remote rural areas. If they have expressed interest in the real Jamaica there is usually someone within earshot who knows someone who is attending a village ceremony or celebration, and is able to arrange transportation.

The host family has no way of knowing how many people will attend. Happy to welcome as many as arrive, embarrassment has nevertheless resulted on occasions when there have been so many visitors that refreshments prove inadequate. It was just such a situation that inspired the creation of one of Jamaica's popular nine-night songs:

Plant me Caffi

Plant me caffi ratta cut i',
Ratta say 'im (him) no drink bush tea
Ratta cut caffi
Ratta cut cocoa
Ratta say 'im no drink bush tea.

The lyrics of this song take us to the hills where coffee is grown, and where rats delight in gnawing the sweet ripe berries. They also nibble at chocolate beans before they are parched and pounded for boiling the delicious rich, dark brown drink sometimes served at wakes. This is quite acceptable as a substitute for coffee, the traditional drink. It is bush teas, made from many kinds of leaves, that are considered inappropriate at such gatherings.

On one occasion when a wake was held off the beaten track by a humble family, the coffee pots were drained dry. Hot chocolate filled the breach for a time, but eventually that supply too was exhausted. In desperation the lady of the house boiled a pot of bush tea. Some of the visitors accepted this as a suitable substitute, but others realized that this was against wake traditions. Out of respect for the family's feelings, no one objected openly. They, however, felt constrained to convey their objections, and did so with the song. In this way, outsiders would be none the wiser as to what was really happening, but the message would undoubtedly strike home. This song has been looked at in detail because it shows both the tendency for older Jamaicans to work round situations rather than confront them and the use of music to censure, praise and pass messages. The messages are interpreted by those at whom they are aimed, yet pass unnoticed by those outside the circle.

The first technique, the avoidance of confrontation, was found to be useful and effective during slavery and the plantation period. It is still used. Emancipation and political independence came at the stroke of a pen. Habits fostered for centuries do not disappear in a day. The second technique, the use of music to convey coded messages, was developed and used to great advantage in earlier times. The approach of a slave driver or overseer needed to be heralded so that workers could be saved from punishment. I have seen it used to warn of the approach of a strict teacher or, in another setting, of police.

It was after many years that the Shepherd of one of my favourite Revival churches confided that he and his flock had once had musical signals by which they would tell how my presence would affect the course of their activities. After I had passed the test, the signals were used to indicate the attitude to visitors who accompanied me. When they considered that my understanding of their sensitivities had made me "one of them", the secret language was no longer necessary.

A song can also demonstrate the use of performance style to throw outsiders off the scent. As will be seen in the section on Tambo, one way to maintain self-respect was by withholding one's true feelings and opinions from the rulers.

In the Jamaican setting, slow, dignified music sometimes masked ridicule and biting satire, while quick, cheerful strains concealed pain and, in the words of Wordsworth, "thoughts that [lay] too deep for tears". We became experts at taking "kin teet" (smiles) to cover "heart bu'n" (distress) as a Jamaican proverb much quoted by folklorist Louise Bennett says,"Tek kin teet' cover heart bu'n".

Every death ceremony is concerned with the spirit of the departed. One of the most typical sounds of a Jamaican wake relates to this. It is the long sustained notes at the end of each line, sometimes fanning out into chords of four or more parts, which are symbolically seen to help the spirit to cross from this plane to the next. There are several traditional songs used for this purpose, for example, "Bethlehem Schoolroom", but hymns such as "Rock of Ages" are adapted for use:

Rock of A . . . . .ges
Cleft for me . . . . . .
Oh what a beautiful river . . .
Let me hide . . . .
However wide . . . .
Myself . . . .
In Thee . . . .

Movements considered appropriate by the participants, invariably accompany this type of performance.

It is believed that the spirit returns to its recent earthly home on the ninth night after death, then after being entertained, leaves for its home in the spirit world. If displeased or restless for any other reason, the spirit may return and become a nuisance. Other rituals are then arranged to keep the spirit down or confuse it so that it will lose its way. In any event, it is advisable for anyone leaving a nine night after midnight to walk backwards or turn around in the gateway to avoid being followed by the spirit. Memorial ceremonies are sometimes held on the thirtieth or fortieth nights after death. The absolutely final mark of respect and devotion is the tombing one year after death. This is not mandatory, but is common in certain cults such as Kumina. After that, it is presumed that the spirit will definitely be at rest.

Three other types of wake with long histories but now fading are Dinki-mini, Gerreh and Zella. All three are surviving in limited areas of rural Jamaica.

Dinki-mini

Dinki-mini is practised in the parish of St Mary, in the northeast of the island. It has come to the attention of outsiders only comparatively recently, and documentation of it is limited. What little exists is available through the work of Hazel Ramsay (of the Jamaica Memory Bank and the Jamaican Folk Singers), the brief comment in Ivy Baxter's *The Arts of an Island*, and Laura Tanna's discussion of it in a *Jamaica Journal* article [1987]. The main source of primary information has been Kirby Doyle, leader of the Roadside group, one of the two remaining Dinki-mini groups in Jamaica. He has attracted the serious and active interest of young people of his parish, so we can at least hope to see the continuation of their activities even when older members of the group can no longer participate.

In April 1987, Kirby Doyle conducted a workshop for the Jamaican Folk Singers. This was a rich source of information. Doyle's grandfather, a famous dancer, used to arrange Dinkis for local dead yards. Doyle states that Dinki is the dance, and that the ceremony at which this dance is performed is also called Dinki-mini. There are special Dinki songs, but it is mainly digging songs that are used. Whatever the song, it is performed in a characteristic call and response style with heavy rhythmic emphasis on the first and third of each four-beat bar. Doyle's group is accompanied by a band of two to four maraccas, one grater, one guitar and one home-made drum set with drum and cymbals operated by a pedal. The other traditional Dinki group, the Rose Bank Traditional Dance Group, uses the "benta", a bamboo ideochord. The dry gourd with a hole at the top is rubbed along the strings at one end to produce a heavy, low and twanging note on the first and third beats of each bar. Two thin bamboo sticks play an ostinato rhythm at the other end of the long bamboo instrument.

The speed is leisurely, in keeping with the slow, sinuous body movements of the dance and the unique leg movements.

The dance begins with men and women standing alternately in a circle. They pat the ground to draw attention and "make contact with the earth" (Doyle) then walk, single file, following the leader. The leader goes to the centre for a solo dance, then, standing in front of one of the ladies, invites her to join him in a dance at the centre. When he rejoins the circle, she in turn invites a man to partner her, and so on until everyone has had a turn. They all dance:

Sambo Yellah Skin Gal

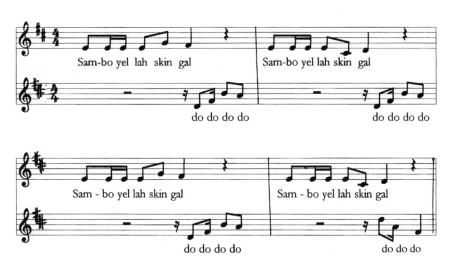

Sam-bo yel lah skin gal · Sam-bo yel lah skin gal

do do do do · do do do do

Sam - bo yel lah skin gal · Sam - bo yel lah skin gal

do do do do · do do do

Samba yellah skin gal (x4)
do do do do

In the basic step, shoulders circle backwards and forwards and the head is held erect, eyes looking straight ahead, hips rotate and arms are bent at the elbows. The most interesting and deceptively simple-looking movements, however, are in the legs and feet. Knees are bent and turned inwards, the left foot – the one in front – is usually flat, the other on the ball. The right foot brushes in front of and behind the left one on first and third beats while the left shuffles forward. This is varied with occasional turns and sudden stops, with the torso inclined to one or the other side and, at times, pelvic contact between the couples.

Through the work of devoted teachers in St Mary and courses at the Jamaica School of Dance, the knowledge of Dinki-mini is being passed on to children. Still, too often the form of practices handed down for generations is left without an understanding of the substance; so many see only gyrating hips, and "sexy" bodily contact. Some it shocks, others it titillates. Let us hope that increased knowledge will bring greater understanding and respect for ancestral traditions that respond to death and loss with a symbolic celebration of creation and new life.

Dinki-mini, like other wakes, often includes ring play and general merrymaking. Since death is only a gateway and, in our case, most probably leading to better conditions, though we miss our loved ones, it is a joyful occasion.

Gerreh followers would not always agree with the last statement. They think that human beings gloss over faults and failings once people die, and that the departed have more to answer for than is usually admitted. It has therefore been known for a Gerreh group to gather a little distance from the "dead yard" and sing of things as they see them. One example is "A drunkard reach his home at last", injecting cold reality into the occasion.

Gerreh is practised in the most westerly parishes of Jamaica, Westmoreland and Hanover. From the night after death until the burial, people may gather to "jump gerreh". Ring games and dance songs, accompanied by bamboo boom pipes, hand-clapping and other body sounds, are performed with very energetic movements. A popular addition to the usual activities is the bamboo dance. Youngsters dance with great agility and precision on two lengths of bamboo held parallel to the ground and kept in constant motion.

Zella, according to Kirby Doyle, is the Portland parish equivalent to St Mary's Dinki-mini.

Though Dinki-mini and Zella have strong links with Jamaica's African past, they have lost their cult-related features. The following chapter shows that there are, however, many types of traditional Jamaican music that have retained features which identify them as cults.

Dinki-mini dancers

Benta: an instrument used for Dinki-mini

III
Cults and Cult Music
In Jamaica

6

Maroon, Tambo, Goombeh, Ettu, Nago

T he practices of cult groups in Jamaica demonstrate the African-inherited tendency to integrate song, dance and instrumental accompaniment in the musical event. Broadly speaking, they adhere to shamanistic and spiritist concepts inherited from African ancestors, in some cases with a mixture of Christian beliefs.

Although details and lifestyles vary, the world view of each cult demonstrates a philosophy of life which the members have retained from their African forebears. It is based on the belief that the primary aim of life is to maintain and, when necessary, re-establish harmony and balance between all levels of creation. Communication between departed ancestors, spirits, gods, the supreme God and the living for guidance and direction, and being in tune with one's spirituality are crucial to achieving and maintaining this balance. In this quest music, dance and, in the case of Kumina and other strong African retentions, language play vital roles.

Two characteristics distinguish cult from non-cult. The former prescribes (1) formal, declared membership, and (2) some activities in which only members can participate. This participation may be limited by use of an ancestral language, secret procedures or learned practices with which only members of the cult are familiar. (The word "cult" is not normally in the vocabulary of members of such groups but has been accepted by them.)

There are several cults in Jamaica and they vary widely in many respects. They differ in degrees of secrecy and in criteria for membership. For example, Maroons are members strictly by ancestry (to date, only one person, the writer, is known to be a fully invested Maroon); Revivalists, by the acceptance of beliefs, forms of worship and a lifestyle that reflects these; Rastafarians, by accepting beliefs, practices and observances that set them apart from the general populace in obvious ways. To some cults, possession and trances are desirable and sometimes integral on specific occasions, for example, Revival, Kumina, Maroon, Goombey. To others, Rastafarian, Ettu, Tambo and Nago, they are not.

Cult members, other than the Rastafarians, see matter as the manifestation of spirit and so consider that problems existing in the world of matter originate because of conflict with the traditional principles laid down by the ancestors with whom the living are still closely connected. These problems must therefore be solved at a spiritual level. A solution does not simply require church-going and ritual involving the ancestors, but also a spiritual transformation with the help of the ancestral spirits.

Cult members believe that spirits, and especially ancestral spirits, have extensive knowledge of all that goes on at the different levels of life and consciousness. If suitably respected and approached, they communicate with, protect, guide, direct and generally play an important role in the daily life of the community and its members. If neglected or offended, they react accordingly by withdrawing support or punishing the culprits. They are able to provide the necessary information concerning the cause of and methods of solving the effects of disharmony on earth. This belief focuses on a view of life wherein the lines of demarcation between what the average person may view as the real, tangible world and that of the unreal world of spirits and gods are in a sense non-existent. The "dead" are a real part of the living world and are all around us. Hence the belief that the body, mind and character of the living can be taken over or possessed by a god or a spirit. At death, one part of the soul, which they consider to be dual, returns directly to the spirit world, while the other continues its attachment to mortal matters and events. It is to this part of the soul that the living must constantly direct their attention.

Whether the problem be legal, social, medical, physical or psychic, since the cult group's cause and effect theory sees most disharmony or disease caused by spiritual short circuits, it is the cult leader with higher special knowledge and expertise who must initiate the spiritual solution to the earthly problem.

The cult leader mediates between the human and the spirit worlds. This flows from the ability to communicate with the gods and spirits, to find ways to transcend the barriers between worlds and to interpret the advice and instructions of the unseen messengers or guides. It must be remembered that in order to find solutions, one deals not with the effect, but with the cause. It is often necessary to go beyond limited minds to determine this, which is in the cultist's view at least as valid as going to doctors, counsellors, lawyers or psychiatrists.

Music in its integrated form of song, dance, and instrumental accompaniment is a primary channel through which the cultist communicates with the gods, spirits, beings, and forces of nature that influence his or her world. The rhythmic aspect of music, in particular, is used to help people to attain an altered state of consciousness which enables the unseen spirits to communicate the necessary information that the group needs in order to deal with suffering and distress, and promote justice, health, happiness, and wholeness. Hence the need to give to these spirit helpers proper respect, thanks for help received, and constant appeasement.

Rouget [1985: 325] points out that "music is the instrument of communication between subject and group" and the group is just as indispensable to the blossoming of trance as the two others (possessed and possessor), since possession cannot function without being theatre. He also notes that music motivates the dance whereby trance states are achieved. This is true of Kumina where it is primarily the rhythmic aspects of the music that urge the devotees to dance until someone becomes entranced. It is easy to observe the onset of possession trance as the drums crescendo and build up excitement. At this time, the support of the group and rapport with it are crucial. Adepts sometimes seem incapable of resisting the general excitement and the call of the drums. The queen and musicians, however, must withstand these influences so that they can continue to direct the activities and interpret messages that are passed from the spirit world through the possessed one(s).

In fact, where the music of the cults is concerned, the picture is quite complex since there may be closer links between some cult and non-cult music than between that of different cults. Some cults even borrow from non-cult sources. This is not surprising, since many secular activities are indulged in by faithful members of cults. Few cultists would hesitate to participate in mento dancing and, if so, it would probably be for personal reasons. Some cultists are specialists in quadrille and square dancing. Several consider pop music and dancing quite in order and join in as long as there are no body movements which they or their leaders consider vulgar, and the setting and environment meet with their standards regarding decor, dress and general demeanour of participants. There have been instances in which secular dance and Revival music have crossed into each other's territories. The Revival chorus "If I had the wings of a dove" was the first Ska song.

If I Had the Wings of a Dove

If I had the wings of a dove,
If I had the wings of a dove,
I would fly
Fly away
Fly away and be at rest.

A lament created by Revivalists for use at ceremonies relating to death owes its origin to the mento song "Mango Walk" in chapter 5.

My Company

My company is going far and I am left alone. (x2)
My company, my company,
My company is going far.

There is little difference between the Rastafarian music and the dance steps that are used for recreation by the general populace and those used by Rastafarians in some ceremonies. In the latter instance, the range of music is wider, and includes chants unsuitable for dancing as well as choruses with words of religious significance, for example:

"Little Samuel, oh."
"Speak, Lord, thy servant heareth."

This chorus is one borrowed from the Revival repertoire. "O let the power fall on me, my Lord" is another. Each cult's use of its own performance style and accompanying rhythms gives the chorus a new sound: In the case of the Rastafarians, unacceptable words are changed. "My Lord" becomes "Far-I" (Rastafari) and "Heaven" becomes "Zion". The basic melody remains the same.

Some Maroon and Kumina songs centre on the same subject. The Maroon warrior, Nanny, for instance, is one. Maroon and Kumina people respect each other and welcome shared subjects, though there is no attempt to adopt any musical similarities. Both these cults guard their music, and approve only limited use by outsiders, such as for artistic theatrical performances. Imitations are sometimes used lightly in Festival presentations but these are disowned and ignored by both serious Kumina devotees and Maroons as being beneath their notice.

Music of other cults, "the smaller ones", Tambo, Goombeh, Nago and Ettu, varies greatly from that of the major ones already named. Equally marked are the differences in the music of each of these smaller cults. Even where there are language and kinship links, as there are between Nago and Ettu, their melodic, rhythmic and instrumental styles are quite distinct. Although both use the tin drum, the sounds are easily distinguishable because Ettu uses a goatskin drum also, while Nago does not.

Some of Jamaica's most articulate leaders of Revival (Kapo), Kumina (Mrs Kennedy and David Cummings), Rastafarian (Count Ozzie and Brother Everald Brown), and Ettu (Miss Phyllis Williams), for example, have maintained that the arts, especially music, dance and language, are used by people who have retained the ancestral traditions of the "ole arrivants" to establish and maintain a state of harmony within themselves, and between them and (1) gods, spirits and other entities in the unseen but very real world; (2) human beings; (3) animals; (4) plants; (5) the elements – all of which are seen by such persons as having life from the Creative Source flowing through them.

As with other cultures in which traditions are passed on orally and in which cults exist, secular as well as sacred rites are practised in Jamaican cults. However, since the themes, songs, movements, and instrumental accompaniments of secular and sacred rituals sometimes overlap, it may be difficult to classify and categorize the practices of cult groups into clear divisions.

The Maroons

To gain a better understanding and appreciation of the music of the Maroons, it is first necessary to understand the history and culture from which their music is derived. Beverley Hall-Alleyne's 1982 article, "Asante Kotoko: The Maroons of Jamaica" is useful in this respect.

Hall-Alleyne presents an overview of the Jamaican Maroons, dating their origin from 1655 when the British invaded the island. During the takeover, some of the Spanish settlers' slaves escaped and established three independent communities in St Catherine and Clarendon. Several later uprisings caused more slaves to escape into the mountains and join the Maroon communities already established. Initially, the Spanish Maroons were hostile toward the British Maroons, but by the early eighteenth century, the two groups had begun to integrate. Windward Maroons were in the East, while the Leeward Maroons were in the West. Today, there are four main Maroon communities: Scott's Hall in St Mary, Charles Town and Moore Town in Portland, and Accompong in St Elizabeth.

For decades the Maroons waged guerilla warfare against the English soldiers in the rugged territory of the Blue Mountains and the Cockpit Country. Although the English did capture Nanny Town in 1734 they could not crush the Maroons. Finally, in 1739, a treaty was drawn up between the Windward Maroons, led by Cudjoe, and the government. It was signed at Accompong. The Leeward Maroons in the Blue Mountains agreed to a similar treaty. However, the treaties incorporated clauses that put the Maroons at a disadvantage and, to some extent, in the service of the English.

Clause VI:

That the said Captain Cudjoe and his successors do use their best endeavours to take, kill, suppress or destroy either by themselves, jointly with any other number of men, commanded on that service by His Excellency or Commander-in-Chief for the time being, all rebels, wheresoever they be throughout this island unless they submit to the same terms of accommodation granted to Captain Cudjoe, and his successors.

Clause IX:

That if any negroes shall hereafter run away from their masters and owner and shall fall in Captain Cudjoe's hands, they shall immediately be sent back to the chief Magistrate of the next parish where they are taken; and those that bring them are to be satisfied for their troubles as the Legislature shall appoint.

Clause XIV:

That two white men, to be nominated by His Excellency, or the Commander-in-Chief for the time being shall constantly live and reside with Captain Cudjoe and his successors, in order to maintain friendly correspondence with the inhabitants of the island.

These clauses have caused gaps in understanding and lack of warmth between the Maroons and certain Jamaicans, even today, over two hundred years after the signing of the treaties. It is still felt, in some quarters, that the Maroons were responsible for the British capture of Three-Fingered Jack, the arrest and hanging of Paul Bogle, who is now a national hero, and the massacre of scores of his followers in Morant Bay Square and other parts of St Thomas in 1865.

Edward Seaga related in the *Memory Bank Newsletter* of March 1987, from field research done in the mid 1960s: "A centenarian at Belle Castle in St Thomas, told of the day during the Morant Bay uprising in 1865 when soldiers marched into the community, tied a villager named Thomas Cash to the pimento tree in the churchyard, and shot him dead for being a Paul Bogle man."

Yet as a result of the terms of those treaties, the Maroons today hold a unique position in Jamaican society. The land given to the Maroons at that time is not taxed by the Jamaican government and no Maroon is allowed to sell even the smallest portion of it. Each "clan" owns a section which is inherited by succeeding generations. By Clause 12, the Maroons were given "full power to inflict any punishment they think proper for crimes among themselves, death only excepted". This also still holds good. Jamaican police cannot, for instance, arrest a Maroon within his territory for smoking ganja (marijuana) which is punishable by law elsewhere in the island.

Each Maroon town has its own political leader or Colonel who is chosen internally. The Accompong Colonel is elected every three to five years, but in Moore Town their leader retains his post for life. The smaller Maroon towns also have Colonels who are chosen by elections about which outsiders are not informed.

Community affairs in Accompong and Moore Town are directed by the Colonel and a council of eight to ten members appointed by him. Ritual matters are in the hands of persons with particular powers, including healing, the ability to contact ancestral spirits and interpret their messages, knowledge of the ancestral language, drum rhythms and Maroon history and traditions. The Colonel's approval or permission is sought in all matters. He in turn may seek advice from his councillors or any individual of his choice. He and the council settle disputes, make all decisions relating to the day to day life of their charges. Since 1966, Colonels have been farmers and teachers. It is important for them to have a very thorough knowledge of Maroon history and heritage. There are no reliable up-to-date figures relating to the population of Maroon towns or of Maroons scattered in various parts of the island and overseas, but it is estimated that they number less than four thousand.

An interesting journey taken by some western Maroons resulted from their being tricked by a governor in 1795 at the end of the Second Maroon War (see page 163).

Hall-Alleyne also examined the varying ethnic backgrounds of the Maroons of Jamaica. They consisted of:

a) Coromantees (mainly Akan slaves from the Ghanaian Gold Coast and Ga, Adangme, and Ewe slaves from neighbouring areas);
b) Non-Coromantees (from the Slave Coast, i.e. Volta to Benin);
c) Creoles (descendants of Africans born either on the plantations or among the Maroons);
d) Indians (Arawaks and Mesquito Indians brought in by the Spanish and British from Central America).

These groups fused and created a distinct Maroon culture based on African retentions, resistance to enslavement and a strong sense of independence.

Other aspects of this Maroon culture include:

* the location of the communities in areas inaccessible to their enemies and providing the Maroons with natural defences;

- the Maroon economy which evolved from wild hog hunting and fishing to agriculture;
- the structure of Maroon political organization with its government machinery consisting of the Colonel (head of the political hierarchy), his Cabinet or a Secretary, a Major and a Captain, and a Council.

Hall-Alleyne argues that a Jamaican Maroon culture still exists, despite the increasing encroachment of the mainstream cultures, particularly in Maroon music and dance and, to a lesser extent, in the erosion of the linguistic remnants of African dialect, Asante and Twi. The strongest survival, however, is the Kromanti Play or the Kromanti Dance. Hall-Alleyne describes this as the main ritual for summoning Maroon ancestral spirits to intercede with the Supreme Being "Nyangkipong", or "Onyangkopong", on behalf of the living who seek solutions for personal and social problems. The Kromanti ceremony is usually closed to outsiders, except under special circumstances.

Another Maroon ritual that has survived and is still practised among the Scott's Hall Maroons is the "cutlass" initiation ceremony through which outsiders wishing to work in the Maroon community gain access to the community to the degree necessary for their work:

The ritual is performed in the context of a "dance", where there is most usually singing, dancing and drumming, and the novitiate is brought into the dancing circle and gestures performed over his or her head and body with the afana (cutlass) [Hall-Alleyne 1982: 20–21].

Religious dances, called "business" dances, include songs and music named after the particular ethnic groups that brought them. There are, for example, "Papa" (Popo), "Mandiga" (Mandingo) and "Ibo" songs. These "ethnic" songs and dances have distinctive styles of their own and are also used to invoke ancestral spirits and to induce spirit possession.

The ceremonies can be categorized broadly as ceremonies to heal or to respond to distress. As in many African ceremonies, the spirit enters the dancer-woman or dancer-man to instruct him or her about the solution to the problem. After possession, the possessed dancer becomes a "Horse" and his or her possessing spirit is respectfully referred to as "Granfa" and "Granfara" (Grandfather) or as Pakit or Pakish. Under possession, the nature of the malady and the correct antidote will be revealed to the dancer [Hall-Alleyne 1982: 19–20]. The use of "weeds" or herbal medicines is much more important to Maroon ceremonies than to Kumina. The pharmacopoeia has existed for centuries in the wild and natural hilly territories inhabited by the Maroons, often consisting of pockets of flora and fauna in the mountains of Jamaica. The dancers know about the properties of herbs for physical and mental problems and how they should be prepared and used, whether as a drink, ointment or bath.

Maroons are proud of their history and heritage, but see no need to advertise this. They exude confidence, and can discomfit the most self-important visitor by their smiling silence, and their innate secretiveness. Languages of words, abeng and drum, as well as music and dance are crucial in the maintenance of their exclusiveness and their independence.

In carrying out fieldwork on traditional music and dance, I found that the Maroons were the most secretive of all the cult groups in Jamaica; therefore, the quality of information gathered depended largely on the

Maroon area of Cockpit Country

relationship between the particular Maroon community and the individual researcher. The different communities are tight-knit and isolated from one another, each with its own Colonel. It was not until the late 1960s that the leaders of the various communities met together, due to the efforts of Barbara Kopytoff, a researcher. The words and rituals used are kept secret even from some young Maroons, who are regarded as having little respect for the old ways.

It was only after I had been invested as a Maroon (a distinct honour, for anyone not born so), that certain traditions and words were used in front of me. Obviously, the strong sense of secrecy among the Maroons is due to more than two centuries of struggle to survive as free and independent nations within a nation itself imposed upon by foreign cultures. It is an honour, for example, for an outsider to be invited to see Peace Cave – where the treaties between the British and Cudjoe were signed. This is done with great dignity by the Accompong people.

The Maroons are noted for their use of the drum and abeng (a cow's horn with the tip sawn off and blown through a square hole at the concave side) which have been traditional forms of communication among the communities, warning them and sending messages across difficult terrain.

The abeng is common to all Maroon areas and is still used in Moore Town and Accompong to relay messages. By the abeng, villagers are summoned by the Colonel, deaths and accidents announced, and important items of news reported. According to Maroon oral history, abeng signalling was crucial to their guerilla warfare against the British. Today, in all Maroon villages, the instrument is an important symbol used on ceremonial and festive occasions. The signals reproduce the pitch and rhythmic patterns of a fairly small vocabulary of Twi words from their mother language, in most cases called Kromantin (Maroon spelling) after the Ghanaian port from which many slave ancestors were shipped. Older Maroons can decode the signals with ease but they are not teaching the codes or the language to their descendants whom they dismiss as being "too modern" and therefore "don't care about the old ways." The signaller, one for each village, enjoys special status. He undergoes long and exacting training and is not allowed to blow the abeng at community functions until the current signal man retires, usually due to old age or illness. The day of retirement is a sad one, and I saw it cause many tears to fall in Accompong. On the other hand, it marks an important beginning for the new appointee.

Rhythmic patterns are effected by tonguing, and variations in pitch are made by altering the position of the thumb on the hole at the small end of the horn. During Maroon wars against the British, series of abeng blowers were used in military manoeuvres.

Maroon drum language is kept absolutely secret from non-Maroons. As an initiate, it is my privilege to be told of it, but divulging such information would be a serious offence against all living Maroons, and the ancestors whom that language served.

A quotation from the Colonel's report on my investiture will help to clarify my position:

> On Sunday 23rd June 1973, Miss Olive Lewin . . . was invested as a member of the clan, a Maroon. There had been occasions on which non-Maroons having lived in Moore Town for years and being decent and interested in the welfare of the community, were allowed to enjoy all the privileges, holding of offices within the framework of the Committee excepted, but such persons were never thought of as real Maroons. Miss Lewin's case was completely different. Her investiture was a serious and touching affair. After many speeches and songs, the symbolic ambush was performed, and the words proclaiming her a Maroon in all respects were uttered. The implication, should be clear: there is no Maroon privilege that she cannot enjoy [Harris 1977: 216].

Maroon Drums, Songs and Dancing

The most important Maroon drums are the *prenting* and the *goombeh*. They are both revered because of the roles they played in liberating their people from British harassment. It must be admitted that the Maroons harried, tormented and inflicted much loss of life and property on the colonists. The drums were vital in relaying messages and inducing trances during which special persons went into a state of Myal and warned of impending attacks. This, coupled with the use of the abeng, is considered by Maroons to have given them the tactical advantages that led to the British offer of peace treaties.

Both drums are used on religious and secular occasions. When the prenting is used to accompany and assist in a healing ceremony, for instance, it complements the singing of powerful songs in Kramanti language. Two drums, one male, one female, then play according to the ancestral speech styles, as it were, conversing while the other participants sing and dance. The drums produce no pulse. This is provided from time to time by sticks called aboso. They shift their style and pulse in a way that confuses those not familiar with it. Practising Maroons dance to the resulting musical interweaving without any difficulty. At times the prenting is accompanied in a very systematic and traditional style by the kwat, a length of bamboo beaten with two sticks, and the adawo, a machete struck with a bit of metal.

The goombeh is the prime symbol and revered instrument of Accompong Maroons. A square goatskin frame drum, it has a second wooden frame under the skin which is used to tune the drum. This is done by hitting pegs at the sides which raise the inner frame, causing it to press harder against the skin, thereby tightening it and raising the pitch. When the correct pitch is achieved, one which Professor Nketia assures me is the same as a Ghanaian drum, the goombeh is "seasoned and consecrated" with white rum. Goombeh rhythms are quick and sharp, in keeping with the darting, angular dances that they accompany. These are played over heavy-pulsed patterns provided by two cylindrical drums, approximately fourteen and sixteen inches in diameter. Unpadded sticks are used on these drums, but only fingers touch the heads of the prenting and the goombeh. The original goombeh used during the eighteenth century Maroon wars was used at ceremonies two hundred years later. It unfortunately disintegrated in the 1970s.

In Charles Town the drums used are the *grandy*, similar to the Moore Town prenting, and the Accompong goombeh. These drums are also used in Scott's Hall though sometimes called *monkey* and *saliman*, respectively. In both places the goombeh/saliman is considered male, and the grandy/monkey, female. Prenting (Moore Town Maroons) and Goombeh (as used by both Goombeh people and Accompong Maroons) drum rhythms are similar in pattern, though there is a difference in timbre between the prenting and goombeh drums.

The drum rhythms on festive occasions are quick and decisive. Dancers' feet reproduce the patterns with a skill that outsiders cannot replicate. Rituals and ceremonies use several different drums, singing and movement styles. As the old folk die, they take these with them, and most of the young ones haven't enough interest to spend the necessary time and effort to learn the ways and expressions of their forefathers. Modern audio-visual facilities are helping Memory Bank and others to document these activities for information before it is too late.

All the songs used by Maroons, whether ritually, ceremonially, or for recreation, are traditional. They have been handed down orally and are highly valued by those who use them. No Maroon ritual music is used outside their settlements, and the songs are not even taught to their own children unless and until the elders are convinced that the new generation understands the history and respects the heritage. This may spell the death of a rich tradition, but they prefer that to risking any degradation or misuse of their music.

Maroons have hundreds of songs for inviting the spirits of their ancestors into personal, family and clan affairs. The clans are rarely spoken of by name, though there is clear and unquestioning knowledge of the lineage of each present-day Maroon family. This is important, since there are customs which hinge on this. For instance, when a Maroon returns from war he must remain outside his family group and be cleansed before becoming once more acceptable. This is to ensure that any "blood on his hands" does not defile his family.

Songs and music for secular occasions have lighter, recreational styles and are called *salo*. Hall-Alleyne identifies among the salo songs the Ja-bone (Ja-bone is derived from the use of an animal's jaw-bone as a musical instrument), Saleone, Tambu and Ambush. Ja-bone songs are usually sad songs lamenting the death or injury of a loved one, but there are also happy Ja-bone songs sung to welcome strangers. Saleone songs were originally laments for the Maroons from Trelawny Town who, after a bloody confrontation with the British in 1795, were banished to Halifax, Nova Scotia, and subsequently allowed to go to Sierra Leone.

Maroon abeng

Goombeh Maroon drum

Maroon prenting drummers

Maroon prenting drum

According to Senior [1983: 105], they surrendered in order to save their women and children from dogs imported from Cuba to track down a group of three hundred fighting Maroons after fifteen hundred British soldiers failed to subdue them. As soon as they capitulated, the governor had them seized and placed on board a ship. Accompong Maroons say that these warriors were invited to a feast on board a ship at Montego Bay and only a few, whose descendants still live in Accompong, refused to go. In any case, once they were on board, the ship sailed for Halifax, Nova Scotia. The weather and other conditions made life there very difficult for them. Some adjusted, but others chose to be resettled in Sierra Leone. It was Jamaican Maroons who built the imposing Citadel that guards Halifax harbour.

In Nova Scotia in 1980 I met some of their descendants who have made Canada their home.

Music in the Maroon world cleanses. It also heals. Each type of medicinal weed (Maroons do not call them herbs) has its own type of song and drum rhythms which, used in combination, bring sure, quick results. The music for the ancestral spirits is for instructions and advice which are given through the dancer-man or woman. Sickness and troubles may be cured by simple music and use of ancestral language, but at times a full Kramanti play is needed. In the play's early stages, saleone songs are used, accompanying movements in a ring formation. Tambu songs and drum styles might also be used before serious spirit activity begins. At that point it is Kramanti or Country songs that are used. There is strict peformance order, leading to Myal possession dancing. If the lighter, topical jawbone songs are used at a Kramanti play, they might cause spirit possession but they are not intended for this. They are primarily for work and socializing. One such is "Alligator dah Walk" (chapter 4).

A song worth mentioning relates to a story in the large Maroon repertoire. It tells of an attempt by the British to recapture Maroons after the signing of the Peace Treaty in 1739. They were to be lured through the gate at Rockfort, east of Kingston, which would then be locked, making it impossible for them to return home. They were to be manacled as a further precaution. To add to their humiliation, a Maroon was engaged to forge the handcuffs. This man soon realized what the plan was and, feigning stupidity, began to sing "Mukobriam". No one paid any attention to him, and his constant singing soon became background noise. Came the day on which his nation was to be tricked into submission. His task completed, he lolled near the gate, still singing. He heard the steps of his people approach the gate. They heard his song, and in a ceremonial procession marched towards the gate and away from it three times. The third time they did not return. A message had been hidden in the blacksmith's song.

In 1968 Mamie Rennock, a Maroon councillor and dancer-woman, sang many songs for me. The words of one struck me as strange: "Black nayga (negroes) hate we oh, Weh me da go do?" (What shall we do?) Mamie explained that Maroons had not forgiven themselves for helping the British to capture runaway slaves and, after Emancipation, rebels. Yet they were bound to do so by the terms of the treaty. The song reflected their embarrassment.

The Jamaican Folk Singers took Kumina queen, Imogene Kennedy, on a visit to Accompong in 1979. She was treated with great deference and, in turn, showed deep respect for the Maroon Colonel and elders. Mrs Kennedy later explained that they were familiar with each other's rituals and even shared some songs to entertain visiting ancestral spirits of the other "nation". Links had been made when the Kumina people arrived from Central Africa as post-slavery indentured labourers during troubled times in St Thomas. The new arrivals supported the Jamaican struggles, while the Maroons helped the British, but this did not cause any deep rift between the two groups. Beneath the surface they were together, the Maroons having proved this by centuries of struggle against the British.

One of the Maroons' chief and most successful war tactics had been the ambush. They enveloped themselves in leaves and vines and melted into the surrounding bushes. The British repeatedly walked into clearings where the surroundings would suddenly come alive and close in on them. Even today, the Maroons celebrate ambush, sometimes by successfully camouflaging themselves in the presence of unsuspecting visitors, and sometimes with a dance described below by Katherine Dunham herself in 1946:

> The war dances are danced by both men and women. The introduction seemed to be a disjointed walking around in a loose circle, much like the warming up of an athlete. Then Henry Rowe and I are facing each other doing a step which could easily be compared to an Irish reel. Hands on hips, we hop from one foot to the other, feet turned out at right angles to the body or well 'turned out', in ballet vernacular. This hopping brought us closer together, and I had to watch the others closely to keep up with Henry. We turned our backs and walked away, then turned suddenly again and hopped together. The songs are in lusty Koromantee, and from somewhere a woman procured a rattle and is shaking it in accompaniment to Ba' Weeyums. Some of the men wave sticks in the air, and the women tear off their handkerchiefs and wave them on high as they dance. Henry and I grabbed each other, first one way, then the other. A few of these turns and we separate in a melee of leaping, shouting warriors; a moment later we are 'bush fightin', crouching down and advancing in line to attack an imaginary enemy with many feints, swerves, and much pantomime. At one stage of the dance Mis' Mary and I are face to face, she no longer a duppy but a Maroon woman of the old days working the men up to a pitch where they will descend into the cockpit and exterminate one of his Majesty's red-coated platoons. She grabbed me by the shoulders and shook me violently, then we were again hopping around each other with knees high in the air, handkerchiefs and skirts flying [Dunham 1946: 135–36].

Special Maroon events

I. The funeral of a Colonel

Colonel and Mrs Cawley's home always had a warm welcome for my daughter, myself and anyone else who travelled with me. When he died after a very short hospitalization, we contacted his widow and family, and on the day of his funeral I travelled to Accompong. Everywhere was quiet, but there was no gloom. Interment was to be in the cemetery, after a service in the church where he and his family had worshipped every Sunday.

I was invited to sit with the Cawleys. The service followed the usual church conventions, but the coffin was placed in the aisle by the family pew, facing east, instead of in the customary north/south position at the eastern end of the aisle. Colonel Cawley was still with his kinfolk. On the coffin were an abeng, his official coat, an old musket and a bow and arrow. There was a little sobbing and much drying of eyes. As we left the church, we walked beside, not behind, the coffin. The abeng blower led the way, followed by men carrying the musket and bow and arrow. Towards the end of the funeral, an elderly lady went into a mild state of Myal. The parson was not pleased. As the coffin was lowered and Mrs Cawley stepped forward to toss a handful of earth into the grave, the peaceful air was rent by a chorus of loud wailing.

Thus far, the farewell to their Colonel had been, apart from the brief spell of Myal, Christian. The Maroons now wished to conclude the proceedings in their traditional way. This was not to be. They were sternly reprimanded by the visiting church leaders, and asked to "stop the noise" so that the service could proceeed. To my great disappointment they complied. It was clear how traditions can be pushed underground not only by colonial powers but also by one's own people.

2. Cudjoe's Day

Cudjoe's Day at Accompong falls on January 6. It has become increasingly commercial and overrun by visitors seeking the exotic. Because of this, most of the elderly Maroons have withdrawn from the celebrations. It is still an important day in the Maroon calendar, attracting members of the nation based not only in other parts of Jamaica but also in England and North America. The Colonel, his council and many younger residents of Accompong treat the day with great respect, and try valiantly to control insensitive fun-seekers, researchers and journalists who come from as far away as Canada and California. Some Maroons declare the day to be Cudjoe's birthday, others the anniversary of the signing of the Peace Treaty by Cudjoe for his people and Colonel Guthrie for the British.

Rituals begin the evening before and are resumed early in the morning of January 6. By the time most visitors have begun to arrive, the goombeh drum and abeng have been made ready, and certain important obligations to the ancestors completed.

The town takes on a festive air as stalls are dressed and merchandise, toys, drinks and foods displayed for sale by members of the community as well as visitors. Gamblers and smokers of ganja (marijuana) are also in evidence while the Jamaican police look on. They are invited each year as a precaution in case of any breach of the peace, but have no further powers unless requested by the Colonel to take action.

The narrow winding approach road becomes crowded and difficult to negotiate by midday. The four miles become a continuous traffic jam by late evening.

Many winding tracks lead up and down the hill for half a mile or so, to a large mango tree. This is the site of the traditional celebrations. The drum sits silently there while many pots of pork and ground provisions are cooked nearby, without salt, so that the ancestral spirits can also partake. When in the late morning the Colonel arrives, the abeng is blown and the public celebrations begin in earnest. The goombeh is played, secular songs and dances are led by local Maroons who are joined by visitors who perform basic steps and sing along, even if not with the correct words. The Colonel participates in this from time to time, greets people and keeps a watchful eye on the proceedings. At his bidding, food is shared out for the ancestors, and Maroons line up for a procession led by him, an assistant with a bottle of white rum, the drummer and the abeng blower. This heralds the most serious part of the celebrations. Maroons only should participate, but in recent years several non-Maroons have joined in. It is an offence which older Maroons cannot countenance, hence their withdrawal from much of the day's activities. Younger Maroons do not mind the intrusion.

The procession winds its way to Old Town, the location of the original settlement, pausing at the site of Cudjoe's grave, an unmarked spot in a small clearing. There the bottle of rum buried the previous year is dug up and the new one is buried. Food is left for the ancestors, and after singing, dancing and drumming, the procession moves on to Peace Cave where the Treaty was signed.

The countryside is full of rocky and precipitous hills, small grassy valleys, tree-filled expanses and little garden plots. The cave can be seen from across a field surrounded by shrubs and bushes. It looks like a large rock poised ready to be dislodged, yet it has been there for over two hundred years, a solid reminder of a very special day in Maroon history.

The drums had foretold a British incursion, and scouts had gleaned the information that the troops would pause and refresh themselves in that very clearing on the appointed day. The Maroons planned and prepared. There was only one usable track to that spot and it ran very close to the cave. It was so narrow and rocky that the men could follow it only in single file, so the Maroons balanced a large flat rock along the path in such a way that each soldier would be compelled to step on it, causing it to rock and make a sound. Each time they heard the stone move, the men hiding in the cave knew that a soldier was passing. They listened and they counted. They also watched through a peephole that still exists. When the stone was silent and no more shadows passed, they knew that the whole company had gone by. After allowing time for the intruders to settle down to rest and refresh themselves in the clearing, one of the men in the cave blew the abeng, signalling that it was time to act, and indicating the size of the company of British invaders.

Before the troops had time to realize where the sound was coming from or what it might mean, the bushes came alive and enclosed them. The British were cornered and captured before they had time to arm themselves. It was a decisive victory for the Maroons, and the last encounter before the treaty was proposed.

At the signing, Cudjoe insisted on sealing the treaty with the blood of both signatories. Thumbs were cut and the blood made to drip into a glass of rum, from which both drank.

The Maroons revere Peace Cave. On January 6, after performing in its shadow, the procession heads back to the mango tree, some two miles away. On arriving, there is one more dance, then as "Clear Road oh" is sung, all who wish to may follow the main procession in the direction of the school, the yard of which was once the old military parade ground. The drum is set down at intervals and introduces short song and dance performances. After a final steep climb, the parade ground is reached. One more dance, then the drum is left there, silent, until the Colonel collects it at sundown. He keeps it until it is again needed. Sometimes this is one year later, at the next Cudjoe Day celebrations.

3. *Nanny Day*

Nanny Day is a feast day celebrated in Moore Town on a day, usually in October, decided by the Colonel and Council of the Windward Maroons. In former times, all who made their way to the celebrations on that day were treated as special guests by the Maroons.

Nanny had been the most feared Maroon leader. A brilliant military tactician, she was also attributed with supernatural powers. The British treaty was not to her liking, with its clauses giving the colonizers powers to appoint administrators, approve or otherwise of Colonels, and commissioning the Maroons to capture and hand over runaways and rebels, but eventually she accepted the terms. Grandy Nanny is revered in Moore Town, respected by all Maroons and honoured as a National Heroine by all Jamaica.

As members of the Folk Music Research team drove into Moore Town, the abeng sounded. The message, we were told separately and by different persons, was "Come to the school: our visitors have arrived." We went to the Colonel's house to pay our respects and present him with the traditional symbol of our esteem, a quart of white rum. This rum is used for tuning and consecrating drums, as well as for medicinal purposes mainly to wipe or wash heads, hands and other parts of the body in healing ceremonies.

As we reached the Colonel's front door, Mamie Rennock, who was sitting in a chair on the opposite side of the room, stood and with a strong gesture told me, "Wait!" I obeyed. "Dance come meet me," she said as she began to sing in a language we did not know and, with head held high and arms bent at the elbows, approached me with small, mincing dance steps. I tried to imitate her style of dancing, moving towards her from the opposite direction. When we met, she first glided round me, then taking me by both hands guided me to a chair. She said nothing: nor did I. Other members of the visiting party were then greeted and offered seats.

Soon a message came from Colonel Harris, inviting us to the school. We joined the hundreds of villagers and listened attentively first to gracious expressions of welcome then to his plans for the day.

Grandy Nanny was to be honoured in a short ceremony at Bump Grave, her burial spot, followed by music, dancing and feasting. Some of the provisions, rice, yams and corned pork, had been collected over many months; others, like the buzu (mussels) for soup, and caucoon were freshly gathered. Women had been cooking from "sun up", but they were to continue well past noon to cope with feeding the hundreds of visitors who were arriving. No money changed hands. The Maroons would not permit this. Though by no means an affluent community, they farmed and fed themselves. Sales of surplus ground provisions and bananas, bought "shop food", rice, tinned milk and other supplies and clothing.

The Colonel led us to Bump Grave. There were speeches followed by drumming, abeng blowing and dancing. Many Maroons, including the Colonel, had lengths of caucoon vines wrapped symbolically round them. This had been one of the plants used in their pre-treaty ambushes. One centenarian amazed the gathering by her expert dancing. She was being watched by four generations of Maroons whom she had delivered at birth as part of her work as midwife and district nurse.

Some days later, an official party arriving by helicopter to honour Nanny were treated to a warm welcome by the Colonel and Council, but completely ignored by the rest of the community. There could be no ceremony without the residents' participation, so after pleasantries, the visitors had no choice but to reboard the helicopter and depart. One of the councillors explained to me that an unforgivable mistake had been made. The Colonel had been informed of the visit. Instead the officials should have waited to be invited by him. Their action had been disrespectful, so while good manners dictated that a proper welcome be extended, there could be no ceremony.

Tambo

In 1967 Ivy Baxter told me just enough about Tambo to arouse my curiosity. Her own research into Jamaican dance and, to some extent, music heritage, began in 1956. She spent many nights and days combing rural as well as urban areas, trudging through cane fields, criss-crossing mountain streams, searching, listening and observing in deep concentration through half-closed eyes. From the early sixties we had teamed up in the use of her research findings for community and national events. Ivy would choreograph and teach from my transcription and arrangements of music sung by her or taken from her field tapes. After 1966, we frequently exchanged notes. Ivy's comments on my field work were always cogent and she was quick to detect links and identify opportunities for follow-up and comparative study.

I learned from Ivy that Tambo was a cult found only in Trelawny. Its songs and dances were accompanied by a large single-headed drum played by a man who straddled it, using his heel to change the pitch, and a percussionist who stood behind the drummer using two wooden sticks to beat an intermittent pattern on its sides.

I made contact with Mr Guillermo Laing, the Social Welfare Officer in the Wakefield area of Trelawny where the Tambo people were located. He arranged for me to visit the people and stay overnight.

With my daughter, Johannna, and Denzil Southwood-Smith of the Folk Singers, I drove to Falmouth in Trelawny and then inland some ten miles. Enquiries about the exact location of the Tambo men drew blank stares and shrugged shoulders, even when we were within a mile of our destination. This told a tale which was later verified. Tambo was practised separately and apart from the life of the town, and was considered "backward". No one wanted to admit knowledge of it to strangers.

A session had been arranged at the community centre. By ten o'clock about twenty men and women, members of three separate groups, were singing and dancing to the drumming and "catta 'tick" playing of two elderly musicians. The style of drumming was quite new to me. At the start there was often no discernible beat being produced except by the catta 'ticks. The drummer seemed to be communicating with the dancers in melodic phrases of different lengths, which built up towards a climax, remained at that level and high pitch while the paired dancers shook their bodies in a tight, trembling manner, then at the climax slapped their hips together to synchronize with a loud thwack on the drum. At this time there was usually no singing. The excitement was in the drums and human bodies, while the catta 'ticks then beat an unbroken rhythm.

From time to time, the people argued as to what should or should not be done; whether there should be one or more couples, what the correct sequence of songs was, the words, the tilt of the body, the turn of phrase. The members from any one of the three groups were unwilling to concede a point to either of the others. In answer to other questions, however, they agreed that a goat was sometimes killed to please "them other one" (the spirits) and that many of the songs were laments. This baffled me, since in most items, the speed and crisp sound of the catta 'ticks gave no such impression. To my further questions they explained that they were lamenting three types of separation:

1. from friends and family through slavery and the plantation system: "They sen' mother one way and child another. Maybe they never meet again.";
2. from loved ones through death;
3. from "the homeland, Africa"

Many of the songs were short and repetitive. Some used unfamiliar words, which appeared to be easily understood by the group members.

All Dem Ole One

All dem   Ole one dead an' gawn   All dem   ole one dead an' gawn   All dem

ole one dead an' gawn An' we never to meet a - gain Mourn Day - ka mourn O

mourn Day - ka mourn O mourn Day - ka mourn An' we ne - ver to meet a - gain

All them ole one dead an' gawn
An' we never to meet again
Mourn Dayka mourn,
O mourn Dayka mourn (x2)
An' we never to meet again.

The modal quality of this one was particularly interesting.

The cadence was also reminiscent of a Maroon song from Accompong not far away as the crow flies, further into the treacherous Cockpit Country.

At the time I was not aware of a significant link between Tambo and Maroon people. Nor did I realize why, every time I visited Wakefield, Kongo Town and Friendship, all in Trelawny, the drum was hanging in an outroom and not fully assembled. These pointed to a possible French connection, since this practice is common in Haiti, for instance, but is found nowhere else in Jamaica.

Clinton Black's writings [1958] helped me to put the pieces together. According to him, association with the French Caribbean began in the late eighteenth century at a time when there was a lot of unrest among the Trelawny Maroons, with sustained guerilla warfare and frequent attacks on estates, culminating in the Second Maroon War of 1795. The French Revolution (1789) affected life in the French colonies of the West Indies, including Jamaica's neighbour, Haiti. There had been revolts and violence and bloodshed. Many inhabitants of the French islands fled to Jamaica with their families and faithful slaves. It is possible that these slaves passed on the custom of partially dismantling and hanging up drums used in secret and forbidden ceremonies, since discovery would have resulted in severe punishment. Master drummer Benjamin Reid died before this could be discussed with him.

Tell you Neighbour

1. *Tell you neighbour min' dem goat*
2. *Brown's Town ina fire oh*

3. *Saddle de ram goat mek me ride*
4. *Brown's Town ina fire oh*

and

5. *Me say bury me head but no bury me foot*
6. *Anda (under) cool shady.*

This song, according to an old Tambo informant known only as Bada, confirms information gleaned in Guyana about the burying of feet to prevent slaves put to guard treasure from deserting their post. The song, with its bright catta tick rhythm, sounded rather happy to us outsiders, but we were told very firmly that it was a lament. An example of music used to put the bosses off the scent, as the pain of seeing a colleague wilting from dehydration and exposure was expressed in the song.

Slaves in the early nineteenth century had long suspected that the masters were hiding facts concerning the ending of the slave trade and slavery itself from their workers. Many canefields were set on fire in the resulting seething unrest (line 2). Because great houses were always set on hills, their occupants could see the first signs of fire, and escape. Slaves and plantation hands who lived and worked on the lower levels were more vulnerable with no buggy and horse or even a mule for a quick getaway. With ironic humour, typical of old Jamaica, the song makes light of tragedy (line 3). Line 1 suggests concern, not just for self, but also for the neighbour. The Reids emphasized the absence of bitterness by reminding me of the wake song which says:

> I'm a white man, and I drive mi motor car
> An' the brown man do the same
> I the black man use me so-so foot (only walk)
> But I get there jus' the same.
> I'm a white man use me knife and fork
> An' the brown man do the same
> I the black man use me so-so han'
> But I nyaming (eating) jus' the same.

They escaped however they could. What mattered was not the means, but the escape.

The fifth and sixth lines of "Tell you Neighbour" referred to a practice that had been prevalent during the Spanish occupation. The feet of slaves put to guard treasures were buried in the earth so that they could not leave their post. There, sweltering under the scorching heat of the sun or drenched by tropical rain, the slave sometimes died at his post. Lying in a grave, feet pointing east towards "Mother Africa" gave him a chance to return home.

I commented on the speed and light-hearted sound of "Tell you Neighbour". My informants stressed the need to keep the "real feelings" from Busha or plantation overseer and others on the side of ownership.

Singing light-heartedly of tragedy was one way of doing so. Their explanation made me realize the importance of understanding the background and context of traditional music when arranging and presenting it in performance settings. Listening solely to the musical qualities could easily lead to distorted interpretations.

Although Tambo is practised only in Trelawny, individuals from the cult live in twos and threes in other parts of the island, in the St Andrew hills for example. Once when members from other areas converged on Wakefield, Trelawny, for an evening of Tambo music and dancing, there were fierce arguments about how one set sang or danced. Oral transmission had caused changes which some participants were unwilling to accept. "Right" drumming impelled them to sing and dance, and restored "good humour", until the next argument erupted. They all agreed that the drums and certain songs could affect the "bearing" (fertility) of plants, animals and even human beings by "calling" spirits to address the situation and that Tambo rituals were needed to ensure safe passage and then rest for spirits of departed loved ones.

Some interesting and informative articles have been written on Tambo. Hazel Carter attests to the Kongo connection:

> . . . a few of the Tambo people still know recognisably western Bantu words . . . towa, 'fire' and langu, 'water' among others: . . . bolo, 'bread'. (Compare Kongo nllangu, 'water' which Bentley [1885: 388] gives as from "Coastal dialects"; ko tiya and tubya, 'fire'; ko mmboolo, mbolo 'bread', both from Portuguese bolo, 'cake' [Carter 1986].

Joyce Campbell, dance teacher and Festival administrator, in notes on Tambo (1976) says: "Observers have noted a similarity in dance movements to the Bele in Martinique, Guadeloupe and Trinidad; and also to the Virgin Islands Bamboula, which until the last century could be found in Louisiana, Martinique and Guadeloupe." Here, too, there are French overtones. However, the Bele dance mentioned above bears no relationship to the Jamaican Mbele or Bele.

With the death of most of the elderly second generation Tambo people, including master drummer Benjie Reid, Tambo has changed markedly. Mr Reid's son, Hopeton, an outstanding dancer who seemed to pick up instantly every message from his father's drumming, is probably the last such dancer. Mr Reid had been helping his grandson to develop his talent as a drummer, but the lad had not achieved a satisfactory level when his grandfather and mentor died. He now plays expertly but in the new style that has evolved, with more rhythmic pulsations and hardly any of the free-phrased and sometimes melodic drumming that characterized Tambo up to the very early 1970s. The new dancing is improvised but predictable, unlike the old style when the dancer had to establish close rapport with the drummer in order to respond to his spontaneous phrasing.

Tambo is no longer used to contact ancestral spirits. Since it is now primarily for socializing and entertaining visitors, the role and performance of drumming have changed considerably as have the styles of singing and dancing. The old Tambo folk do not approve, and think that Mr Reid and the others who have gone before watch with displeasure.

Goombeh

Goombeh is fast fading from Jamaican life. It is one of Jamaica's least-known cults, and very little if any scholarly research has been done on it. At its core has been one extended family living in a cluster of small houses tucked away in the woods behind the more affluent houses that line the main road running through Lacovia in St Elizabeth. Once a small village, Lacovia quickly grew into a bustling town after 1968 when bauxite mining began nearby. With increasing prosperity and growth came new attitudes and activities which were inimical to practices such as Goombeh. Younger folk distanced themselves from it, as did the new middle class. Ear-shattering levels of amplified pop music clashed with the sound of drums, and the earthy dancing of Goombeh people accompanied by the high pitched, nasal singing became increasingly "embarrassing" to the record-collecting fans of radio, film and television stars.

As a result, Goombeh attracted no new members even from the core family. By the 1980s, many of those for whom it had been an integral part of life had either died or become too frail to organize or participate in Goombeh activities. They had to depend increasingly on clinics and health officers who made house calls when illness struck. In earlier days such problems, as well as family and other disagreements, would immediately have prompted a ritual. Goombeh people still maintain their belief in the interest and power of ancestral spirits and Almighty God (probably because of the influence of nearby Christian churches) to solve problems and cure ills of all kinds. Practice of these beliefs has shrunk and the people have retreated to the confines of their living areas for the occasional gatherings to sing, drum and move as best they can in honour of their ancestral spirits. By 1987, possession by spirits occurred only occasionally, since few participants had the energy to dance as required for this to happen.

Goombeh takes its name from the square frame drum which accompanies the dancing and singing used to invoke assistance from helpful spirits or to counteract the work of mischievous ones. The drum is the same as the one by the same name which is used by Maroons of Accompong, north of Lacovia. Neither group recognizes links with the other, though the drumming is similar in intensity if not in actual rhythms.

The cult concerns itself mainly with physical and psychological healing, for which spirit possession is considered essential. The one possessed relays the advice and/or instructions received to the group. In order to achieve the possession or myal state, members of the cult sing in a loud, high pitched, nasal manner, while some of them perform a fast and vigorous dance referred to by them as the myal dance. Movements are angular and at times violent, with dancers darting about, covering a lot of space, performing acrobatic feats and throwing themselves to the ground. They claim that these movements are directed by ancestral spirits and there is no need to fear that they will injure themselves.

The drumming is quick and energetic with rhythms similar to those used by Accompong Maroons on their goombeh drum. Many of the songs are performed in short, disjointed phrases.

Poor Wilhel

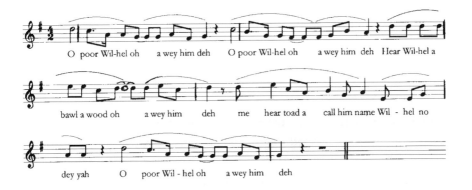

O poor Wil-hel oh   a wey him deh   O poor Wil-hel oh   a wey him deh   Hear Wil-hel a

bawl a wood oh   a wey him   deh   me   hear toad a   call him name Wil - hel no

dey yah   O   poor Wil - hel oh   a wey him   deh

O poor Wilhel oh, a weh him deh? (where is she?) (x2)

Hear Wilhel a bahl a wood oh,

A weh him deh

Me hear toad a call him name (asking for her)

Wilhel no deh yah (is not here)

O poor Wilhel oh, a weh him deh?

(Note: In the Creole, "him" is used for both he/him and she/her.)

A Goombeh woman explained that spirits of their "foreparents" contacted and advised them when they "went into myal", mainly through the dancing. Once advice is given it must be followed, or severe punishment by illness or other problems may result. Wilhel had to wander in the woods for three days because she had disobeyed the instructions of a spirit. In order to remedy that situation the offended spirit was placated by music and dancing. Wilhel returned to the settlement, carried out the previous instructions (not identified) and all was well.

Ettu

One of the small cult groups, Ettu was brought to the attention of Jamaicans outside Hanover, its home parish, in the 1960s. Mrs Zena Stanhope who later became Mayor of Lucea, the capital of Hanover, had won their confidence by her long-standing interest in their activities and attention to their needs. She was therefore able to persuade them to enter the Jamaica Festival of Arts, non-competitively, in the early 1960s. In 1966 Mrs Stanhope was quick to invite me as Folk Music Research Officer to visit her home and meet several Ettu people. They drummed, sang, danced and introduced me to the ritual use of bizzy (the Jamaican name for cola nut which grows in that area) for purification, and tum tum or fufu, breadfruit or yam pounded into a smooth mass, pinched off and, using fingers only, dipped into a dish of stew and swallowed without chewing by the cultists and their guests. This is a sign of friendship, especially as everyone eats from one dish of tum tum and dips into a single bowl of stew.

The use of words such as bizzy/cola nuts, fu fu/tum tum, in both songs and conversation and which were not understood by non-Ettu people suggested that another link with Jamaica's African past had been found. This was later confirmed by visiting Africans, including the late Dr John Akar of Sierra Leone, who had studied African dance forms and their music, and Professor Fela Sowande of Nigeria, who was able to communicate with Ettu people using Yoruba words. In 1976 Nigerian musicians at the American Festival of Folklife in Washington DC identified links with Ettu performers in language, intonation, melody and cooking methods. Unfortunately, apart from the documentation of field tapes, only a few pages have been written on Ettu and, up to 1987, there had been no scholarly identification of the unfamiliar words used as has been done with Kumina. There was, however, some informal identification of words as Yoruba by Dr Marie Panenbaum during an Ettu ritual. The people themselves explain that their old folk did not translate their language: "Them never teach we."

From my own experience with Ettu people, I have established that Ettu has been practised in Hanover by people claiming to be direct descendants of Nigerians brought to Jamaica as slaves between the sixteenth and nineteenth centuries. Members of the cult are conscious of carrying on activities and cooking styles and using words learnt through contact with and eavesdropping on their "foreparents". As with other cult groups, its primary focus is on invoking ancestral and other spirits for help in earthly matters. There may be, however, other purely social and recreational purposes for Ettu rites. According to the late Miss Phyllis Williams, then eighty years old, dancer, musician, herbalist and most articulate informant in the last remaining group, they depend on their ancestors to advise them in matters such as healing and betrothals. Ancestral help is also required to ensure rest for spirits of the departed. Because of this, the ancestors must be entertained and appeased from time to time and respected at all times. For specific purposes, a dinner is "built". The main foods are tum-tum or fu-fu, to be eaten in the traditional manner, soup or stew of okra, spices and annatto seeds, and offal. Some food is earmarked for the spirits, and therefore cooked without salt. This is never eaten by adults, but can be given to children.

Both Ettu rituals and Ettu "plays", whether used for human or ancestor entertainment, include feasting, music and dancing. The repertoire of songs is reported to have been inherited, each by a particular person from a specific ancestor with no additions by contemporary cultists. The vocal timbre is nasal, but gentler than that of most other Jamaican cults. The songs are sung by the whole group accompanied by two drums. Many of the songs use three to five notes within a small tonal range and consist of short phrases repeated with little variation for the duration of a dance. This can be from two to four minutes. "Eni Burroke" is typical.

Eni Burroke

E - ni e-ni bur-ro-ke E - ni e - ni bur-ro-ke e - ni

Eni eni burroke
Eni eni burroke (several times)

One Ettu drum is of tin, the other a double-headed goat-skin drum, both played with fingers. The skin drum now in use belonged to the grandfather of one of the present master drummers. It is over one hundred years old. The tin drum, an empty kerosene oil container, with its almost continuous quick triplet figures, produces a tone which at times tends to overpower singers as well as the skin drum, which is played firmly but intermittently.

Dancers perform solo, except when one is "shawled" in congratulation by another dancer. Each dancer is called when his or her song is played and sung by the accompanying musicians. There are obvious and close interactions between dancer and drums, with no attempt at pleasing or relating to anyone outside the group. There is absolutely no thought to general audience appeal. Throughout the dance, feet are flat and in contact with the earth. Men dance with more energy and agility than women, who use subtle or angular hip movements, body erect or slightly tilted forward, with knees bent. Only a small space is covered. When a dancer performs well, he or she is shawled, as a mark of appreciation and encouragement by the leader or queen who steps forward with a long scarf and throws it round the dancer's neck. The shawler then presses the dancer's torso backwards from the waist, and 'stretches' his or her arms in turn, by raising each one diagonally from

Ettu drummer and dancers (the drum is made of tin)

the shoulder. The dancing area in front of and facing the drums is rarely occupied by more than two persons, dancer and shawler. Occasionally a singer will be carried away by the drumming and join the dancer, but will soon return to the group standing and singing at the side. Because of the importance of contact with the earth, stage performances of Ettu are not taken seriously by the group. In addition, for the same reason, all meaningful plays are held out of doors and in touch with the ground.

Ettu plays, if secular, often begin with a greeting song which might mention guests by name. Short dramas are sometimes enacted with songs and spoken dialogue interspersed. These are usually topical and humorous. Plays are used for "birth night" parties, pre-wedding celebrations and death ceremonies. They may also be used to solicit advice from ancestral spirits, as for instance in choice of marriage partners. In addition to feasting, music and dancing, such a play might include a blood sacrifice. Ettu people claim that possession is not necessary, since the ancestors speak to them through dreams or signs which can be interpreted by special members of the group.

Ettu members are very sensitive to signs and signals within their group. These may have subtle nuances that go unnoticed by outsiders, yet have quite definite meaning to insiders. For instance, each dance is brought to a close by a signal from dancer to drummers. It seems simple and straighforward, yet requires specific coordination between feet and right arm which proves difficult for non-Ettu persons to master without very careful observation of several dancers.

In 1987, the one remaining Ettu group had less than twenty members, and an average age of over eighty. A promising younger group which was being groomed and trained by an adult member disintegrated when the adult emigrated. We are therefore, sadly, seeing the last of real Ettu in Jamaica. In spite of age, however, the drummers and some dancer/singers are strong, alert and agile. For instance, Miss Phyllis Williams, frail in appearance at over eighty, still showed surprising mental alertness, creativity and charisma. At the Commonwealth Institute's Caribbean Ancestral Voices exhibitions in 1986, she amazed everyone, not only by her stamina, but by the strength of her personality. When she danced, sometimes with her back squarely to the audience, attention was riveted on her. This, in spite of the very unspectacular and uncompromising style of dancing. At the end of each evening after the applause died down for the entire group of Jamaican peformers then presented on stage, she would step forward. Raising her hand and looking downwards, she would say, "Wait". Those in the audience who had stood, would sit. She then sang gently, and improvised words relating to that evening's proceedings, usually to a well-known European tune. She held the audience in the palm of her hands until she chose to bow several times, both arms raised from the elbow, and retreat from the stage. Backstage, she was always the centre of a circle of admirers whom she kept amused by her subtle wit, and amazed by her confident fielding of questions. Miss Phyllis and other Ettu members had made an equally powerful impact at the American Festival of Folklife in Washington DC during the summer of 1976.

Nago

The retention of Yoruba attitudes to land, the upbringing of children and certain life styles is characteristic of the Nago cult. It was practised regularly in Westmoreland up to 1979 when floods caused the people to scatter. Houses, workplaces and farms were inundated for weeks, and many Nagos lost all their belongings. They took refuge with family and friends outside the area that had been home to them and their ancestors for several generations. Nagos, like the Ettu people, claim direct descendance from Nigerians brought to Jamaica as slaves who, they state, had always lived in Westmoreland and worked on the sugar plantations and dairy farms in that parish. Leaving their homes was a sad necessity which caused the disintegration of the Nagos as a group. Individually, members continued to identify strongly with their traditions, but since most of them were almost or over eighty, it has been virtually impossible for them to cope with meeting and carrying on their activities. Even when the Jamaica Memory Bank arranged to get them together, though they welcomed this, not more than five were able to respond.

Very little scholarly research into the Nago cult has been undertaken, and it is now probably too late. In 1970 Professor Chief Fela Sowande was sponsored by UNESCO as a guest of Jamaica's Folk Music Research project. He identified Yoruba cooking and eating styles, as well as words used by elderly persons in Abeokuta, a Nago settlement. Professor Sowande looked and listened for African survivals in music and its physical and spiritual environment. He identified these and other important links. His highly specialized and advanced music training together with practical and painstaking research in traditional African cultures made his comments and observations invaluable. He put sounds and customs into a West African context, and helped us to understand them from new historical and cultural perspectives. When he spoke with the Nagos, they understood each other in a way that made other Jamaicans feel like foreigners. After the visit he wrote:

> I am an Egba of the Yoruba, my hometown being Abeokuta in Western Nigeria. By no stretch of the imagination could I have foreseen that I would travel thousands of miles to Jamaica to visit another Abeokuta at Waterworks in Westmoreland, to meet with a ninety-six-year-old lady with a head-tie and a face that brought my late Egba mother vividly before my eyes, and possessing a stock of Yoruba words in surroundings which looked in places like a transplantation of areas of the Abeokuta in Nigeria of my youth [Lewin n.d.: 2].

Subsequently, a bedridden matriarch, Mrs Agatha Johnson, was visited by the writer Wole Soyinka, who was amazed at her understanding and use of language and customs recognizably of Yoruba origin.

Some years before Professor Sowande met the Ettu people, I had made my own journey of discovery to Westmoreland. At a workshop for in-service teachers, I was told of a place named "Abekitta" in Westmoreland where Nago people lived. They used strange words and sang even stranger songs. Subsequent enquiries furnished no further information on the location of "Abekitta", as my urban contacts called the place. Even residents of Westmoreland had only vague memories of Nago songs and their singers. Nothing had been heard of them for several years. The trail was cold, yet there seemed to be something exciting in the very exclusiveness of my quest. So early one morning, determined to find these people, I set out from Kingston for the far end of the island.

Westmoreland was remarkable and rewarding for the folklorist and ethnomusicologist. The prejudice found against folk arts and the self-consciousness about being Jamaican that one found in certain other areas did not exist there. One could depend on being helped by citizens from all walks of life and on a widespread eagerness to become involved in the preservation and study of Jamaica's cultural heritage.

To visit Westmoreland unexpectedly for an indefinite stay presented no problems, with the doors of the Carnegie home always wide open as their contribution to the Jamaica Folk Music Research Project. As soon as I arrived, I shared my problem with my hosts. We seemed to be making no progress as we asked everyone for directions: cook, gardener, school child, police trainee, Custos, doctor, passer-by, but eventually, the advice was, "Drive along the Waterworks Road and ask for Abekitta and for the Nago people." On the road to Waterworks, three schoolboys who had been walking in that direction accepted my offer of a lift, and we were soon exchanging stories about our grandparents. Up the road, I saw a very old man sitting on the "banken" staring into space. We pulled up beside him and had a short and rather disjointed conversation. Two strapping, confident men joined us. They recognized me as an ignorant town dweller in love with their parish, offered their help and joined us in the car.

Our first stop was at a typically neat little home on the main road where they introduced me to a tall, stately woman. She proudly told us that she was a Nago, a direct descendant of West Coast slaves. Her speciality was cooking. She had just won a prize in the national Festival for a Nago dish and was happy to describe the various dishes that she was an expert at preparing. One particular description threw my mind back to student days, and the meals that West African friends often prepared. They used to call it fu fu; she called it tum tum.

As she spoke, using many unusual words and describing lifestyles that harked back to West Africa, it became clear that we were at the start of a thrilling journey into our past, a journey that might take many years, overcoming countless obstacles, but one for which no effort would be too great. Our Nago lady told us where to find "Beokuta" and other Nagos. The schoolboys bade us goodbye and the rest of us continued our journey as directed. Half an hour later we were being welcomed by a voice coming from a tiny cottage. I went nearer and when I had become accustomed to the darkness of the room, saw an old man sitting motionless on a stool. After what felt like an age, he invited me into the house, blessed me and thanked me for visiting him. I, in turn, thanked him and told him what a joy it was to be in such a beautiful place and to have had the pleasure of meeting him. We then conversed in a rather formal way.

During the course of our conversation he told me of his grandparents who had been full-blooded Africans. They could not communicate with each other in the same language, but each grandparent spoke in his or her own tongue with other members of the community. Eventually their everyday speech became a mixture of African and Jamaican words. He himself was a Nago and ate Nago food, but he could not remember any of their songs. He offered to take me to meet other Nagos who might sing for us.

When we arrived at their place, there were gracious introductions all around before I could melt into the background and listen to their reminiscences. They used words that were completely foreign to me, and speech rhythms which made it difficult to understand even their Jamaican Creole. When eventually they were satisfied that I could say "Abeokuta" using the proper pitch and accentuation for each syllable, they told me how the land had been theirs since the abolition of slavery and that their ancestors had preserved several customs and habits which had been brought to Jamaica hundreds of years before by their West African ancestors. Unfortunately, as children they had been barred from adult gatherings and even forbidden to go to specific spots. However, they had eavesdropped and "caught" some of the songs. These have been sung by succeeding generations, at death ceremonies, birth night parties and on other social occasions which ancestral spirits attend.

Spirits sometimes request a "play" at which they are entertained by a feast of tum tum, stew, curried goat flesh, white rum and loosely organized dancing. At other times a ritual is arranged to solicit advice on matters affecting members of the group or to assist departed spirits to find rest. Nagos state that these are special and treated more seriously.

Nagos have no leader as in the Revival Shepherd or Kumina Queen tradition. People join in as they wish, dancing to the accompaniment of songs and a tin drum. They relate to each other in twos or threes and sometimes dance solo, using shuffling earth-hugging steps. Dr John Akar considered their movements to be essentially African in style.

Professor Fela Sowande was later to prove without a doubt that both words and songs by the Nagos were of Yoruba origin. A Nigerian on assignment to Jamaica's Ministry of Agriculture identified the song as an old Yoruba hymn. Only a rough idea of the Nago music can be given by our standard musical scoring and phonetic spelling.

Amasunduwah

Amasunduwah (x2)
Amasunduwah Tata lu
Tata lu (x2)
Amasunduwah
Amasunduwah Tatta lu.

7

Revivalism and
Rastafarianism

Revival

Revival is Jamaica's main African-Christian cult, embracing Pukkumina and Zion. It is still possible today at a street corner or village square to come upon a gathering of soberly dressed people often with heads wrapped with white or brightly coloured lengths of cloth, lustily singing religious songs to the accompaniment of drums, tambourines and hand-clapping.

This kind of meeting is like the tip of an iceberg above the main body of Revivalism. It is designed to attract members who, it is hoped, will accept the doctrines of the cult and eventually become totally immersed in wide-ranging activities, some closed to non-members. Such gatherings still occur but far less frequently than in the past. Indoor services have become more popular and prevalent, and the groups now call themselves Revivalists. This is because they came to realize that Pukkumina, usually called Pukko by them, had become "Pocomania" on the lips of most people outside their groups, and which is taken to mean "a little madness". However, Cassidy says in *Jamaica Talk* that this supposed Spanish link "is by no means likely".

In the same work, Cassidy states:

Virtually all the Christian churches and sects are represented in Jamaica .
. . Christianity is certainly the predominant religion. Yet, as a by-product
of the historical situation, many elements of Christianity, both doctrinal
and ritual, have overflowed the bounds of any of the Christian churches
and become mingled quite inextricably with the remains of African cultist
practices brought over by the slaves and still having a considerable hold
on the folk more than a century after emancipation (1939). It is quite
impossible to draw sharp lines of distinction among the multiplicity of
mixtures already produced and still continuing [Cassidy 1961: 232].

This "multiplicity of mixtures" still exists and probably partly
explains the varied and sometimes contradictory information available
from literary sources. Some confusion has also been bred by
misunderstandings due to the frequent spelling of pukkumina as
"pocomania". Referring to pukkumina, Seaga says:

It is customarily spelled 'pocomania', which is often justified as the proper
form by relating the practices of the cult to the alleged Spanish translation
'a little madness'. However, this appears to be a case of antipathy about
the cult being made to conform with the phonetics of that term, for there
is no evidence of Spanish linkage or derivation. It is perhaps more closely
linked semantically with Kumina, surviving as a purely African religious
cult which absorbed Myalism and became prominent in the second half
of the last century after introduction, it is said, by post-emancipation
African immigrants to the St Thomas area in the 1850s. More strength is
given to this interpretation by the fact that the Great Revival [1860–1861],
as the forerunner in inspiration of the revival cult, took place at around
the same time [Seaga 1969 : 4].

Myalism (Hausa "maya": sorcerer) mentioned by Seaga was an
African-derived cult practised in Jamaica during the 1840s in which spirit
possession was essential. This often took the form of violent movements

and dancing. When this type of possession occurs at Maroon, Kumina or Revival events, it is called "going into myal".

The roots of the Great Revival were both African and Christian. The impetus, no doubt, was given by missionary Christianity, especially the Baptists, which for various reasons had always been more inclusive as far as membership was concerned. The Baptists joined with Moravians, who had in the past been rather exclusive, and other nonconformist churches to form the backbone of the movement. But the means of achieving salvation implicit in the Great 1861 Revival were far more African than European. The Great Revival died and was succeeded by other movements; as in turn the Great Revival had been aided by Myalism and some forms of the Native Baptist Movement. (The origin of the Native Baptists can be traced to free Negro preachers who came from the USA as early as the 1780s [Seaga 1969: 3, 4].)

In its blend of Christian and West African concepts, Revival has included in its spiritual experiences, singing, dancing, instrumental and body percussion accompaniment, healing, divination and spirit possession as integral to rituals.

Revivalists clearly differentiate between religious groups operating in Jamaica as follows:

I. "Spiritual" groups

    a)   Those that believe that only Christian powers, Divine and Satanic, can possess and influence the living.

           These include Church of God, Jamaican Freeway Baptist (Bedward), Shilo Apostolic, City Mission, Pentecostal Holiness, all of which classify themselves as "churches", and Revival, including both Zion and Pukkumina which are seen as cults.

    b)   Those that believe in possession by gods and spirits as handed down by their African ancestors, for example, Goombeh and Kumina.

2. "Temporal" groups

        These oppose the belief in spirit possession and include Anglican, Moravian, Presbyterian, Methodist and Seventh Day Adventist.

In addition to regular Sunday services, feasts and fast-days of the Christian calendar, Revival activities are scheduled as the need arises for a variety of purposes, including:

1. prayer and street meetings, to win converts
2. baptism
3. baths and fasting for purification
4. feasts for thanksgiving tables or duties
5. mourning or memorial rites
6. contacting the spirit world for help in earthly matters in any other way as directed by the Shepherd/Mother/Leader.

The chart below represents characteristics of Pukkumina and Zion, mainly based on Seaga's research, confirmed and elaborated on by my own observations and participation.

	Pukkumina	Zion
Ritual	Begins on Sunday, short sermons or exhortations, explanations re function, singing interspersed with prayer, Bible reading.	Any night, short sermons or exhortations, prayer, singing, Bible reading. Accompanied by drums.
Table/Altar	Elaborately spread with fruit, loaves of bread, cakes, wine, water flowers, candles lit. Food and drink set aside for spirits, the rest distributed among those present.	Elaborately spread as for Pukkumina. Food and drink. Some distributed among those present before midnight. After the distribution, the meeting ends.
Activities	a) Ritual "Labouring" after Table broken until dawn. Speaking in tongues. Monday, the "bands" travel in the spirit world until pre-dawn. On Tuesday, sacrifice, more travelling until Wednesday morning, when there is a feast. Use of lime, salt and washing blue prohibited. b) General Healing. Attention to social and psycho-physiological problems.	Drilling by the Shepherd or Mother follows the speeches etc. Speaking in tongues. A sacrifice may be offered either before the meetings, when the Table is broken or on the next day. A feast concludes the meeting at about midnight of the 2nd day. Use of salt and washing blue prohibited. Healing. Attention to social and psycho-physiological problems.

	Street meetings, prayer meetings and "tables" for special concerns.	Street meetings, prayer meetings and "tables" for special concerns.
Spirits	The Triune God of Christianity at the zenith, to whom prayers directed. Ground spirits and Fallen Angels who are not considered evil, but move nearer, more concerned with earthly matters, and available for requests for assistance and advice. Spirit possession therefore sought.	Heavenly Spirits, the Triune God of Christianity, Apostles and prophets. All lesser spirits considered evil and to be avoided. Spirit possession not important since moral principles and not super-natural intervention are of prime concern.

Music and movement are integral to all Revival ceremonies and rituals. The songs which set the scene for spiritual trance and possession are usually performed with melodic, harmonic and rhythmic improvisations. This can be quite remarkable when large groups of Revivalists demonstrate their creativity in spontaneous group improvisations, the most satisfying of which are then absorbed into the permanent repertory. The songs and choruses used are mostly adaptations of Western-style hymn tunes and therefore the melodic and harmonic content show a strong Western influence. Most Pukko tunes are in duple and quadruple time. Zion tunes are sometimes in triple or compound time. However, the example given demonstrates the strongly African-Jamaican treatment given to these Western metric schemes, with much syncopation against contrasting rhythmic patterns provided by the instrumental and body percussion accompaniment. Accompaniment for Revival is provided mainly by membranophones and idiophones as well as by rhythmic body sounds such as clapping, stamping, moaning and loud overbreathing called "groaning" or "trumping". This overbreathing is used to induce trance states. Movements include nodding, rocking, sidestepping, processions and dancing. Some Revivalists move with feet resounding rhythmically while repeating the trance-inducing choruses until contact is made with the spirit world.

As in some of the other cult groups, the wearing of certain colours or the use of some colours on the flags in Revivalist enclosures is significant. Although colours may carry a message of peace or upliftment, the most important significance is that of attracting spirits to the ritual.

Ceremonies, rituals and services differ according to each band or group consisting of Shepherd/Mother/Leader, post holders who have specific tasks, for example, reading Bible lessons, preparing vessels and ritual paraphernalia, and members who attend on a regular basis. Members of Revival bands are held together by devotion to their beliefs and to their leaders, not by family or ancestral links as in the Maroon and Kumina cults.

Revivalists often attend services at established churches, particularly the Roman Catholic where the ritualistic and down-to-earth approach to Christianity is more attractive to them than that of the Protestant churches. Although the roots of Revival were planted firmly in the Baptist family, the differing attitudes to rituals, spirits and spirit possession have caused the two to drift apart. No matter what other churches they might attend, Revivalists go regularly to their own places of worship.

Revival is a way of life for its members, but they do not show this as openly as, for instance, Rastafarians do. The Shepherd or Mother is expected to provide guidance, advice and assistance in all matters religious as well as secular. Harsh rebukes and even corporal punishment are given to members without hesitation and accepted without question whether in private or in the presence of a congregation. Leaders who seem to be reluctant to discipline their "flock" quickly lose authority and the respect of their followers. These may be from forty to two hundred beyond the central core of leader and post holders.

Pukkumina chorus

This is sung several times to syllables such as la, na, da. Each repetition is varied rhythmically as well as melodically. Simple two- to four-part harmony is improvised with voices sometimes singing an octave apart and/or in parallel fifths.

Zion chorus

Sung in the same style as the Pukkumina chorus, triple time identifies it as a Zion song since Pukkumina tunes are always in duple or quadruple time.

Christian hymn tune as sung by Revivalists

(Tune "Christchurch" sung to various syllables during trumping and labouring.)

Singing words inhibits improvisation which is considered essential in both Pukkumina and Zion. Hymns are sung according to the book only on formal occasions such as services.

Revivalism continues to be central to the lives of considerable numbers of Jamaicans directly and to even more, less directly. These latter do not consciously accept the tenets or practices, but respond naturally and fervently to the music and ceremonies.

With the growth of American-prompted Pentecostal and Evangelical groups in Jamaica, disapproval of Revivalism has been increasing. Speaking in tongues is acceptable, but spirit possession and blood sacrifices are seen as evil, and at times described as "devil worship". Seaga [1969: 13] says: "No doubt both Zion and Pukkumina offer their followers spiritual, social and, at times, economic aid which is to them available in an accepted and satisfying form."

These cults have been moving towards more structured forms of worship, from under the stars to within tents and church-like buildings. It is no longer appropriate to meet under trees or in an open space on a regular basis. A lot of money may be spent on buildings varying from simple sheds to elaborate structures. "Collection" is taken at every meeting, and special offerings requested when extra funds are needed. Social and economic change will continue to cause modification, but I believe that as long as Revival continues to satisfy certain needs in the

Kapo, Revival Shepherd, leading a chorus

society, it will remain alive. Any alterations will be cosmetic rather than profound.

Rastafarianism

The most modern manifestation of African thought in Jamaica is Rastafarianism although it developed in isolation from traditional communal roots. From 1927 Marcus Garvey had set the stage by stimulating unity and cohesive action in black people, and urging them to look at Africa as their Motherland and the source of their culture.

When in 1930 Ras Tafari was crowned Emperor Haile Selassie of Abyssinia/Ethiopia, some who had been stirred by Garvey's message became more convinced that Jamaica's salvation was inseparably bound up with the African "homeland". Haile Selassie was given messianic status, equal to Jesus, by virtue of his also being of King David's line. Ethiopia became the promised land.

With the Garvey movement affecting black people throughout the western hemisphere, it was not surprising that a Jamaican seaman, Leonard P. Howell, returned home inspired to begin a politico-religious movement that re-interpreted the Bible in terms of the needs of Black people. The time was ripe, and in the 1930s, Leonard Howell, Thomas Hibbert and Joseph Nathaniel Hinds began the Rastafarian movement in the hills of St Thomas. The group later moved into the impoverished slums of West Kingston where they were able to galvanize believers. They were united by great dissatisfaction with the British colonial administration's response to the growing ranks of the descendants of former slaves. These were being neglected at a time of economic depression when living conditions and employment opportunities were inadequate.

Rastafarians adopted as their symbol the colours of the Ethiopian flag – red, green and gold. These were seen in clothing, accessories and home decorations, on drums, on walls, in numerous paintings of the Emperor, often depicted as the Lion of Judah, and wherever an opportunity for their use presented itself.

"Selassie I" became an often repeated greeting. "Peace and Love" was soon to be added. The preachings did not seem to tally with that message, and the passionate speeches emphasizing the wealth and beauty of the African homeland, and urging "repatriation" were sometimes interpreted as sedition by officialdom. In December 1933 Howell was arrested for "seditious and blasphemous" language. He had, for instance, claimed that "the spirit of our Lord has returned in this mythical figure", Rastafari. He was sentenced to two years in prison.

In 1937, the Ethiopian World Federation was established in New York in sympathetic response to the invasion of Ethiopia by the Italians in 1935 and the war that followed. Much interest had been stimulated by Western media eager for propaganda aimed against the Fascists and their sympathizers. Jamaica joined the Federation in 1938. In 1940 Howell, who had resumed his Rastafarian activities after being released from prison, established a camp near Spanish Town in St Catherine. He was joined there by hundreds of cultists. In the following year, police raided the camp and again arrested him. This led to another prison term, and a series of confrontations between police and Rastas. The cultists were seen to be inciting civil unrest and considered dangerous to a colonial territory, especially as World War II was then raging. In spite of persecution, and being kept on the fringes of society, the Rastafarians maintained their beliefs, and remained actively involved in several self-help schemes.

In 1955 Haile Selassie gave a total of five hundred acres of land in Southern Ethiopia for any in the African diaspora who wished to farm and settle there. No record exists of the number of Jamaican Rastafarians who availed themselves of this opportunity, but it is reported that individuals and small groups have done so from time to time. In the same year, Rastafarians received another boost when the island was visited by officials from the Ethiopian World Federation of New York.

In 1959 Claudius Henry, primarily a religious leader, and his followers distributed cards which believers thought entitled them to passages to Africa. When no ships arrived, there was disappointment and some consternation. Henry established a camp in the St Andrew Hills for himself and a team including his son and an avowed American Black Power advocate. When the camp was raided by security forces in 1960, arms and a newly moulded grave – allegedly of an executed member – were found. Henry and others were arrested and charged with treason. Some, including the leader, were imprisoned. Henry's son was hanged. The whole episode inspired much alarm among mainstream Jamaicans, and drove an even wider wedge between them and the Rastafarians. Their relations with the police worsened.

A significant milestone in the history of Rastafarianism was the official visit of Haile Selassie to Jamaica in 1966. He was given a tumultuous welcome by his followers and a very warm one by all Jamaica. However, his small frame, light brown complexion and aquiline features were not what many Rastafarians had expected. The visit caused serious misgivings among some, who felt that the visitor could not be the leader or Messiah of their race, and among others, because he disclaimed messianic status and leadership of the cult.

Rather than defect, disenchanted cultists adapted to what they saw as a new situation. One result was that Jamaica, till then a place of exile to which they owed limited or no allegiance at all, became Jah (God)-make-yah (here) and a specially beautiful second home.

Three years later, a Rastafarian convention lasting for twenty-one days was held in a very rundown area of Kingston. It was attended by crowds estimated at three thousand. There were several clashes with the police, and further deterioration of relations between Rastas and the authorities. This led to the dispersal of cultists into other parts of the island.

The Ethiopian Orthodox Church was established in Kingston in 1969. Many Rastafarians have remained outside it, but recognize and respect it.

By the 1970s, the sociocultural influences of Rastafarianism began to be felt among the middle and upper classes of Jamaica. The symbols, the drums, herbs, reasoning, singing, chanting, costuming in all its splendour, dance movements, locks and, most of all, the colours of red, green and gold, along with pictures of the Emperor Haile Selassie decorating their rooms and communal facilities; the leisurely lifestyle with many hours each day spent making music and just quietly socializing, attracted a new generation of nationalistic youth. Many of them had become contemptuous of what they interpreted as superficiality and hypocrisy in the lifestyles of their families, and the irrelevancies of the pervading attitudes to culture and education. They were Jamaica's "flower children", responding also to a strong influence from the arts which were having their own kind of florescence and to which Rastafarians contributed significantly. They were producing art, sculpture, handicrafts, poetry, music and a philosophy which reached well beyond Jamaica's shores. Even Jamaican speech styles and vocabulary have been affected by Rastafarians in many ways.

Rastafarians have as many leaders as there are groups. They include Coptics, Ethiopian Orthodox, Twelve Tribes, Bubbos and many that gather around a dominant figure who may be religious guide or one who teaches and performs music or visual arts, a gifted orator with a message such as repatriation to Africa or one who manages a cooperative commercial concern, such as broom-making or pottery. Many members are individualistic and, though committed to the Rastafarian doctrine, in the final analysis owe allegiance only to Jah (God) and Rastafari (Lion of Judah). Most Rastafarians are very visible, often wearing the colours red, green and gold, having long matted or braided locks and beards, and always ready to philosophize and "reason" with believers and sceptics alike. There are many wealthy and materially successful Rastafarians but it was their earthly renunciation of this world's goods and their simple lifestyle that first attracted middle and upper class followers. Rastafarians do not pressure people, not even their own families, to join the cult, but they are adamant and outspoken in their belief that their devotion to Jah, Rastafari, natural foods and other attitudes to life are the only road to clean, godly living.

Most Rastafarians worship frequently, as the spirit moves them, since they are totally involved in their cult as a way of life. Spiritual guidance is considered essential to peaceful and successful living. Those who belong to the Coptic and Ethiopian Orthodox Churches attend services on Saturdays, their Sabbath.

One of the most talented and revered Rastafarians was Count Ossie (Oswald Williams), pioneer in Rasta drumming and music and a living example of their motto "Peace and Love".

My first visit to Count Ossie and his community on the slopes of the Wareika Hills was in 1963. I had been on a panel of judges before whom he, his drummers and dancers appeared during Festival competitions. I had been transfixed by the sounds produced by the drum ensemble, and especially by Count Ossie's artistry on the repeater drum. Later we spoke, and he invited me to visit their camp, which I did. All the symbols were there and the disciplined, peaceful atmosphere was enhanced by the main objective of Count Ossie, the creation of music that would spread Rasta philosophy.

My admiration for the Count grew with every meeting. It was he who had distilled new sounds from Buru and its three drums, the bass, fundeh and repeater; he had also, in my estimation, added to the spirit and intensity, if not the substance, of Kumina drumming to create and inspire new sounds which eventually influenced the development of reggae music.

Reggae evolved in the 1970s from Ska by way of Rock Steady. Ska was the result of ghetto youths' determination to shed American and European influences in Jamaican pop music, thus affirming the island's political independence gained in 1962. The youth, mainly from Western Kingston, tapped the music and movement of Revival which pervaded their environment. Gradually, actual Revival songs gave way to original material. North American rock music seeped in and transformed Ska into Rock Steady. The heavy Rasta beat, as much as their philosophy and style of social commentary in the lyrics, led Jamaican pop music from Rock Steady to reggae.

Count Ossie could not have been more humble. Apart from being a great musician, he was a fatherly, generous-hearted, gentle human being. Strong and assured in his playing, he never intruded or flaunted his leadership. When he felt that commercialism was threatening the religious base of his work, secular and otherwise, he withdrew with unassuming dignity and allowed others to carry on as they saw fit. He was at ease in an amazing variety of settings; being father to the youth in his community, and ever-helpful friend to the older folk; participating in media and recording sessions, or "giving thanks and praises to Jah, Rastafari, Selassie

I, Lion of Judah" in religious ceremonies; at jam sessions in the hills or improvising with jazz musicians such as Jamaican horn-player Cedric Brooks, or classical players like the British clarinetist Neil Cadogan; sharing his drumming and philosophies with students and staff at Mico Teachers' College or answering the chants of his bandsmen in performance.

Count Ossie was a true Rastafarian, but no one could even picture him being forcefully anti-anything, as many of his fellow cultists have been. He agreed wholeheartedly with the critical view of Western ethics and religions, regarding the latter as consciously deceiving and downgrading the black race. Even the Bible was seen as an agent of the white man's chicanery. How could it not be, when a widely used version was translated by King James, the head of a colonial empire?

Babylon represents, first and foremost, the church and state structures of the West, all that they stand for and the lifestyle which they imposed on the African diaspora. Babylon must be destroyed. An aggressive Rasta is likely to shout "Babylon" as menacingly at a black woman wearing lipstick as at a white visitor whose mode of dress is seen as inappropriate.

For Rastas, Jah is a god of life. Man is created to live forever, but death comes through human wickedness. "The wages of sin is death" is often on their lips. They even modify the negro spiritual which says

And before I'll be a slave
I'll go down into my grave
And go home to my Lord and be free

to

And before I'll be a slave
I'll skip over my grave
And go home to my Lord and be free.

Rastas revere nature and natural life. It is evident in their uncut hair and beards, in their vegetarian diet of natural ("ital") foods, and in the widespread use of "the weed". They justify the last, which has become illegal, by alluding to Genesis 1:29:

> God said, I have given you every herb bearing seed, which is upon the face of the earth, and every tree, in which is the fruit of a tree yielding seed; to you it shall be for meat.

I nevertheless recall hearing Claudius Henry telling a large gathering at a Rastafarian convention in the 1960s that smoking the weed was not, as often stated, an indispensable means of achieving wisdom and enlightenment. He also told the predominantly clean-shaven members that they could be as authentically Rastafarian as any "locksman". The locks and beard attracted disapproval and persecution from large segments of the society, and were therefore useful as tests of steadfastness. Once this had been assured, there was no need to continue to wear locks. It had been quite a surprise for me to see hundreds of gloved women, and white-coated men with no sign of beards, uncut hair or Rasta colours meeting to intone fervent prayers and chants to Jah. They had passed through the testing stage.

The most interesting feature of Rastafarian cult music is the drumming. Three types of wooden drum are used:

1) *Bass drum:* made of barrel staves, twenty to thirty inches in diameter, and approximately twenty inches long. The goatskin heads at each end are held in place and tuned by means of metal braces and pegs. With the drum balanced on one thigh, played endwise and on its side, a deep sonorous tone is produced by striking the centre of the drumhead with a single, heavily padded stick. The basic rhythm is 4/4:

but it can build up to climaxes requiring a lot of strength and passion in order to play sequences such as:

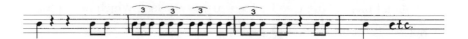

Talented drummers are skilled at varying the patterns on this powerful instrument.

2) Fundeh: eight or more inches in diameter, this drum is held between the player's calves and barely touches the ground. Fingers are held together as both hands strike the centre of the single goatskin head. The body is made of staves, strips of wood or, occasionally, of a hollowed tree trunk. Its basic rhythm is:

Sometimes, depending on the drummer's interpretation of the chant or song being accompanied, the rhythm changes to:

3) Repeater: a shorter version of the Fundeh. Held in the same way, it remains off the surface of the ground or floor. The single head is usually also of goatskin but the membrane of a pelican's stomach, when available, is considered to be even more suitable. Unlike the Bass and Fundeh, the Repeater is played nearer the rim: fingertips are separated to produce an endless variety of rhythms. Repeaters provide complex patterns to complement and sometimes defy the rhythms of the other two drums. Hands sometimes work at great speed, being seen only as blurs.

Other percussion instruments used in Rasta bands include tambourine, grater, shakkas/maracas, and striker bell. Wind instruments such as saxophones are occasionally added. Percussion players also sing and, with the exception of the drummers, become quite mobile, at times executing intricate dance steps.

The words of Rastafarian songs are always meaningful in terms of doctrine, whether original or based on Western hymns, negro spirituals or other songs. Tunes are sometimes borrowed, but the Rasta repertoire is full of melodies created by devotees, and improvised chants which take root.

> *Peace is based on love and justice*
> *Europeans shall find no peace*
> *They despised Haile Selassie's warning*
> *Now they're crying out for peace*

This chant is sung to Martin Shaw's tune "Marching", familiar to worshippers in Anglican churches. The tune of a popular Revival chorus was "captured" by the Rastas and the words adapted to suit them:

O Let the Power

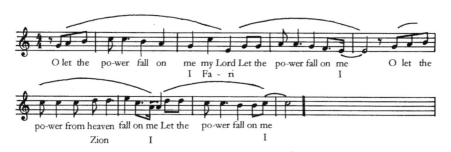

> *O let the power fall on me, my Lord*
> *Let the power fall on me*
> *O let the power from heaven fall on me*
> *Let the power fall on me*

became

> *O let the power fall on I Far I*
> *Let the power fall on I*
> *O let the power from Zion fall on I*
> *Let the power fall on I*

205

Two songs which are popular with Rastafarians as well as other Jamaicans are:

Holy Mount Zion

Holy Mount Zion
Holy Mount Zion
Holy, holy, holy
Holy, holy, holy
Holy Mount Zion

and

Peace an' Love
Peace an' love
Peace an' love I give to you
Peace an' love

The latter is now used as a greeting in some Jamaican church services; an interesting development. The well-known Rasta song of the 1980s "Pass the Cuchie on the Right Hand Side" has direct links to the Buru song "Pass the Pipe" [Lewin field tape, 1967].

Babylon comes in for a lot of strong criticism and comment:

Roll King Alfa, roll King David,
Roll with Babylon away

Gone to give the wicked payment
Great Babylon reward.

and

Babylon you holding' me
  an' you won't let go.
Babylon you holdin' me
  that's all I know.
I need a hammer, a hammer
to hammer them down.
I need a rammer, a rammer
to rammer them down.
With a hammer and rammer
I will hammer them down
With a hammer and a rammer
I will rammer them down

Babylon you holdin' me
  an' you won't let go
Babylon you holdin' me
  that's all I know.

Rastafarians use music and movement as therapy to keep spirits buoyant and cleanse their minds. Brother Everald Brown, now recognized as one of the world's finest intuitive artists, and the late Count Ossie, in particular, consciously sought inspiration to create new forms of music with the power to heal, a belief in line with those of Revival, the Maroon and Kumina people. To date there is no firm scientific evidence to prove that they were successful.

However, I was present when a colleague, plagued for years by acute attacks of laryngitis, was cured after less than thirty minutes of Rasta ministration in Long Mountain. We had both been invited to a rather secret ceremony with all the ritual. She hated to miss it and went, in spite of her disability. The Rastas were very concerned at her state and immediately brought out a bottle of medicine for her. She sipped it slowly, letting it trickle down her throat. The drumming, chanting and praying began, and gradually moved to a powerful climax, as the hot, crowded hut filled with smoke. To my question about the use of an illegal weed, Genesis was quoted, and I was in turn asked, "Why Babylon settle pon Rasta, an' them don't trouble Roman Catholic when them burn them incense?"

My colleague was amazed at the speed with which her throat cleared. Normally it would have taken at least another day of rest and medication for her voice to be so totally restored. For the next three years, after which I lost touch with her, the problem did not recur and she considered her cure to be complete.

Some months later, another colleague suffered an attack of laryngitis. I sought my Rasta friends and asked for some of the medicine that had worked so well. They would have been glad to mix some for me, but explained that it would not work in isolation. The drums and chanting had, they assured me, played an important role in the previous healing.

The music of Rastafarians spreads their message of peace, love and black dignity; it also fights Babylon, and is a most effective bearer of "praise and thanks to Jah". Praising Jah and bringing death to all oppression in any part of the world is the prime function of the important Nyabingi or Groundation ritual. My Rasta friends and informants do not agree on details, but certain principles are widely accepted. The ritual may last for days and is attended by large crowds that may converge from all over the island.

Christmas in the Ethiopian Orthodox tradition is one occasion for Groundation. It is open to all, and engenders feelings of elation and togetherness in those who attend. I can vouch for this, though my experience is limited.

Between 1960 and 1975, in addition to field research, I was deeply involved with members of the Rastafarian movement mainly because of their children in a special school for them in a then very depressed area between a busy city road and the sea. In those days the cult was more homogeneous. It suffered much persecution and harassment in the earlier years, and I myself was sternly warned by members of the security forces to keep away from the Rastas. True, criminals grew beards and locks and hid from the law in Rasta camps, but my infant daughter and myself were safer among our locksed friends than in many uptown locations. Perhaps problems strengthened them and their resolve.

Reggae reached its zenith in the work of Bob Marley and his Wailers, the excellent female group, the I Threes, and artists such as Peter Tosh, Jimmy Cliff and the Third World Band. These led the scores of reggae musicians in taking this modern Jamaican form of popular music to media and live audiences all over the world.

Bob Marley was reggae artist supreme. For his special services to Jamaican music at home and in every continent and island group, he was awarded the Order of Merit, Jamaica's highest honour. When he died, he was given an impressive official funeral. According to Rasta philosophy which focuses on life and negates the power of death, Bob lives. He does indeed, through the ideas propagated and respected worldwide through his songs, and by his legacy of music. He would be quick to acknowledge his debt to the early Rastafarian cultists.

The Social Organization of Cults

It must be difficult for those not familiar with life in Jamaica to accept the fact that in an island of less than 4,500 square miles the beliefs and practices of groups and individuals have been kept secret for centuries. Even now, apart from comparatively few Jamaicans with special interest in their cultural heritage, cults such as Ettu, Tambo, Nago and Goombeh are virtually unknown beyond a relatively small radius. The members themselves see no reason to publicize their affairs. After the long period of slavery and colonialism when they had to be cautious in using drums, which were sometimes banned, and in practising healing, for instance, which usually was seen as anything from backward to evil and dangerous, they are adept at keeping internal matters to themselves. Healing practices were, and often still are, classified as obeah, which remains punishable by law.

Members of these small cults also suffer a certain amount of ridicule from even their own young folk. Consequently, as with the Maroons, significant information, music, dancing and cooking styles are not shared with the younger generation. On the other hand, national and international recognition, as at Focus 1986 in London and the 1986 Edinburgh Festival have been building the confidence of members of these smaller cults. Since no one is ever compelled by birth or anything else to be a practising cultist, without the active and serious interest of younger Jamaicans these cults will continue to slip away as older members become infirm or die. The elders voice displeasure at the efforts of young Jamaicans who copy their music and dancing without understanding and respecting their significance. They find the vocal sounds too "English", the movements "loose", awkward and lacking subtlety, and the drumming reproducing only the main rhythms without sufficient understanding of the real vocabulary.

Membership of Ettu, Tambo, Nago and Goombeh has centred round the most knowledgeable and respected musician/dancer or healer. Ettu still has a queen, but she remains in the background, partly because of physical debility. The group works democratically but at rituals or plays the drummers' role is crucial. In each cult, the healer is particularly important since he, or more frequently she, is the keeper of secret knowledge and can interpret messages from the spirits. When a leader dies, his or her place sometimes is not filled, since there might not be a suitable successor. In such cases, responsibilities are shared by the members considered most capable in different areas as decided formally or informally by the group.

Rituals are planned to meet a need: illness, friction within the group, drought, for instance, or to respond to the request of an ancestral spirit for recognition or placation. These small cults have not worked to a set schedule within living memory, unlike Revival and the Christian calendar, Maroon and their Nanny and Cudjoe days, Kumina and New Year's Eve, and Rastafarians with days specially designated by them, in addition to festivals of the Coptic and Ethiopian Orthodox churches.

Children brought up in homes in which parents are cultists, whether Revival, Rastafarian, Maroon or of smaller groups, cannot escape the influence of the beliefs and practices, but are under no obligation to participate. There is tolerance, as long as the young people's way of life meets the elders' basic standards. There is no compromising if it does not.

Jamaican cultists, on the whole, have great faith in the ability of their supreme and lesser gods to provide sustenance of all types and they surprise non-cultists with their nonchalance about material prosperity. Many of them are semi- and unskilled labourers, farmers, domestic workers or unemployed. Some more affluent members of the society also join cults, sometimes secretly. In all Jamaican cults, members show great concern for each other's needs, and much practical help is given to those who require assistance. The institutions and leaders are assured of regular subscriptions or offerings at services and meetings. Members who are short of cash contribute in kind or in labour, like a day's work in the meeting place, the leader's house or garden.

The pardner (partner) system in which a certain number of persons agree to "throw" a specified amount weekly, each one taking it in turn to collect the total sum each week, is widely used. For example, when twelve persons contribute $10 a week for twelve weeks, a different member of the pardner collects each week $120. This is useful for cultists when special funds are requested. More affluent Jamaicans, even shareholders and people with large bank accounts, also use this method of saving but for larger amounts and usually for a pre-assigned purpose.

The Jamaican climate is, on the whole, kind, so cult members' clothing requirements are minimal. Ground provisions, nourishing fruit such as guavas, bananas, mangoes and cherries, staples like breadfruit, are usually easily available outside of Kingston. Most Kingstonians have family, friends or fellow cultists in rural areas who can assist with providing food at low prices or at no cost.

Since members of cults usually look to each others' needs, even if there is no source of revenue, there is usually very little suffering. Regardless of their particular belief system, all Jamaican cults hold that "as a man soweth so shall he reap" and feel constrained to live accordingly.

IV
Kumina and
Queenie Kennedy

8

The Kumina Cult

K umina is a cult rooted in beliefs and practices brought to Jamaica perhaps by slaves and certainly by immigrants from Central Africa. Songs, some with African language texts, complex drum rhythms and distinctive dance movements, are used in closely knit form, mainly to honour, appease and evoke the help of ancestral and other spirits in solving problems and addressing human needs.

Origins

Since the eighteenth century, several studies of varying depth have been made of Jamaican cults, including Kumina. Views on the origin of this cult differ considerably, especially in the early accounts.

In discussing "Cumina", Patterson [1973] stated that it "existed in Jamaica from at least as early as 1730", when Leslie published his New History of Jamaica. Leslie's comments on the "cumina" cult, in the context of Dahomean ancestral beliefs and practices, caused Patterson to accept that there were Dahomean links. He commented:

> The fact that for the next two hundred and eight years [Hurston's account was published in 1939] nothing is heard of the cult means either that throughout the period of slavery and for the century afterwards these rites were held in great secrecy by the slaves and their descendants, or

that the chroniclers did not pay sufficient attention to them and perhaps meant to include them in their rather vague references to the post-funeral ceremonies of the Negroes. (There is also the possibility that the ritual died out and was later restored.) Secondly, if we assume that Leslie was not completely confounded by his slave informants, the passage from his work quoted above could certainly be taken as one of the most striking pieces of evidence we have on the process of acculturation and adjustment among the slaves.

He notes that the good God mentioned by Leslie, "Who lives in the clouds, is very kind, and favours men . . . that taught their fathers to till the ground, and to hunt for their subsistence" is none other than Mawu the female head of the Dahomey sky pantheon [Herskovits 1941: 2: chap. 16, passim.]. On the other hand, "The evil God" who "sends storms, earthquakes, and all kinds of mischief" and who is feared very much, is immediately recognized as Xevioso, the head of the Thunder pantheon, "the little brother" of the head of the Earth pantheon, who punishes with his "axe" or thunderbolts, "who renders supreme justice" and is associated with lightning, thunder and storms.

Patterson calls attention to the parallel between the Dahomean "good" and "evil" gods, and the Christian God and the Devil. He then asks, "is it not possible that this is an early adjustment on the part of the Dahomean slaves in Jamaica to the vaguely conceived Christianity of the whites?" [Patterson 1973: 201–2]

Zora Hurston's account [1939] mentioned above described a Kumina ceremony but said nothing of origins. Kerr [1963] and Hogg [1960] both suggested strong links between the Kumina and Maroon cults, and that these could have existed before the abolition of slavery. Since the Maroons are of predominantly Ashanti/West African origin, it is implied that Kumina might share this ancestry. Supporting the notion of Ashanti roots is the opinion expressed by Barrett that Kumina came out of the "Myal cult" which developed in Jamaica during the eighteenth century, and that it has resulted from ancestor worship practices of the Ashanti [Barrett 1976].

Intensive interdisciplinary research from linguistic, historical, music/ movement and sociological points of view has now provided new information from which another and more accurate picture emerges.

The highly respected Jamaican historian, H.P. Jacobs, saw Kumina as "based on the beliefs of free Africans who entered the country after slavery". In 1969 he was at great pains to explain why music of this cult seemed so similar to items recorded in Central Africa by the Traceys. He told me that after the abolition of slavery in 1834, plantation owners sought replacements for their lost free labourers. Besides, the African work force had dwindled since 1808 when slave trading was outlawed, and ships no longer plied the middle passage. Recruiting labour from the British Isles seemed the answer. This was done, often with the help of false declarations and fraudulent promises. Not surprisingly, many of these workers became dissatisfied, in addition to finding it difficult to cope with the climate and living conditions. Those that finished their term of indenture were certainly not willing to sign up for another. Once again, the great house society looked to Africa for solutions.

Illegal slave traders had been trying to continue their trafficking in human flesh after 1808 when the trade was banned, but British scouts had been vigilant and turned the ships back. Some went to Sierra Leone, others to St Helena where their human cargo remained. Between 1841 and 1865 indentured labourers were brought to Jamaica from these two centres. Those from Sierra Leone were mainly of Yoruba descent, those from St Helena were Central African, mostly from Angola and Congo. Most of these people settled in St Thomas, at the eastern end of Jamaica.

H.P. Jacobs presumed that the music recorded by the Traceys in Central Africa on the one hand, and by me of Kumina in St Thomas on the other, were similar because they were music of the same people, one set in their homeland, the other transplanted across the Atlantic.

Schuler [1980] substantiates the historical data given by Jacobs. She further provides conclusive evidence of the cultural and linguistic links between Kumina devotees and the Kikongo and Kimbundu-speaking people of Central Africa. The linguistic link was studied in greater depth and verified by Carter [1986], Hall-Alleyne [1984] and Bilby and Bunseki

[1983]. A writer commenting on Kumina some thirty-odd years ago asserted:

> . . . the dancers are supposed to be true 'Bongo Men' or Africans . . . the Kumina songs are sung in 'Bongo' which the singers say is in African language. They really believe it is African and seem to have a small translatable vocabulary which they can use when they want to be mysterious [Kerr 1963: 144–45].

Since then, scholarly work has shown that there is no pretence about the elements of Central African, predominantly Congolese, culture that course deeply through Kumina traditions in Jamaica. Statements such as the following are not lightly made:

> As the work of scholars such as Schuler, Brathwaite, and Lewis has made increasingly apparent, Kumina can neither be reduced to a quaint survival nor dismissed as a fantasy of African reenacted. It is a vibrant and fully living African-based religion. Those who belong to the 'Bongo Nation' and practice Kumina really do consider themselves Africans, regardless of what others might wish to believe about them. Their African identity and consciousness are not designed: they are rooted in the still-remembered historical experience of nineteenth-century African immigrants who adapted their cultural pasts to the new surroundings in which they found themselves, and passed the product on to their children and their children's children. The end-result is that there exists today in eastern Jamaica, and particularly St Thomas, a social and economic network of 'Africans' – people who belong to a bona fide 'subculture' based on an African-derived religion, ideology, and language [Bilby and Bunseki 1983: 3].

Let one more quotation suffice for the present:

> Kumina is, to put it most accurately, the living fragment of an African (mainly Kongo) religion in the Caribbean/Jamaica. It is a fragment because the slave/plantation system did not allow more than fragments: the visible public aspects of the incoming (so-called 'deracinated') Africans were, in

the instinctive interests of control, suppressed: the social language, the social hierarchies, the specialists, the public customary observances, and therefore the officials of symbol, regalia and publicly expressed ritual, link and memory, were destroyed. Therefore African culture in the slave world: KUMINA: to survive: and it had to survive as long as the people who lived/expressed it survived: had to submerge itself, had to accept losses, to adapt: miraculously, creatively did this: persisted and survived. This is not as surprising as it first sounds; and would not be so at all if we stopped thinking of Kumina (religion) in terms of European medieval definitions of it; church, pope, ecclesia; and conceived of kumina (and religion generally) once more as an aspect or focus of culture: so that worship is seen as a particular kind of social observance, based on faith/assumptions, but not in any permanent way separated from other, more 'secular' customs. Indeed we must begin to think of a situation where the word/ concepts sacred and secular are practically meaningless; or rather where they connote a certain kind of intensification of a shared organic experience. Politics, then, psychology, economics, prophecy, medicine, law, poetry, music, dance, art may all be seen as aspects of 'religion' and religion as aspects of all these [Brathwaite 1978: 46].

The Social Organization of Kumina

Some interesting similarities and differences between Maroon and Kumina culture are worthy of comment here. As with the Maroons, one must be born into Kumina. No matter how closely a person is allowed to work with members, even in rituals, or to participate in the planning of activities, unless the blood of Kongolese ancestors flows in the veins it is impossible to be of the Kumina world, the Bongo nation. At ceremonies, instructions and advice may be directed at the whole gathering or confined to the Bongo nation, in which case there may be just enough African words used to exclude non-Kumina people. Translations may be given later, but in private as if sharing secrets.

The main similarities are in the uses of music for healing and festivities, drums and dancing and invocation of ancestral spirits for assistance with earthly problems. Although Maroons have cloaked their ways with secrecy, Kumina tends to be more accessible. Maroons never take their rituals outside their own towns, whereas Kumina leaders will take their services to places where the need exists. The Maroons are a much older society, since Kumina came into existence with the arrival of Central African indentured labourers in the nineteenth century while the Maroons are descendants of Africans who came to Jamaica as early as the 1500s.

An interesting dichotomy is that the Kumina people of St Thomas supported Paul Bogle and his followers in the uprising of Morant Bay in 1865. The Maroons, however, lived up to their treaties with the British by pursuing the defeated rebels. Members of both groups can be, and often are, also practising Christians, finding no conflict between their practices and those of Christianity. Although Kumina people at first hankered for their return to Africa, they eventually integrated into their new society. Maroons have always kept themselves apart, even separate from one another in their own Maroon communities.

Kumina devotees know their family histories, as do the Maroons. Since the primary aim of Kumina is to contact ancestral spirits and gods, it stands to reason that the past to present continuum must be maintained, as when a visiting Kumina person establishes his/her authenticity by quoting family clearly and directly. This can usually be quickly checked and verified. Lines of communication to the spirit world must also use the language of the ancestors.

Knowledge of the language, understanding of the cosmology, acceptance into the "family", are not enough to qualify anyone not born into the Kumina nation as a member. Not even approval of ancestral spirits can do that. This was illustrated to me by an incident in 1983.

I had decided to spend a Sunday writing, but I found it hard to concentrate. The interference with my train of thoughts became too strong and I put the work away with a view to spending half an hour or so listening to music before resuming. This was not to be. An urge to visit Mrs Kennedy, Kumina queen, living some twenty miles away, became stronger and stronger. I would not normally have visited her without having mentioned it to her husband a few days in advance so that he could find out if it would be convenient for her and to bring me word.

Eventually, however, I could not resist the urge, so I made my way unheralded to her home in Waterloo. When I knocked, there was the usual looking through the peep hole. The gate was thrown wide open but Queenie did not greet me in the usual way. She spun quickly round and said, "So you get the message." "Which message, Queenie?" "All morning I was calling you because Beenie [one of her master drummers] take sick; sick bad. When a didn't see you come, a tell him to dress, so that we could help him walk to the corner to take a taxi to Spanish Town, a bus from there to Kingston and then another bus to St Thomas, to him son." His son could then make arrangements to take him to hospital the next day.

My arrival made the whole plan unnecessary, since I would immediately take Beenie from door to door. It was also possible for me to contact the doctor in charge of the hospital and explain who Beenie was, how precious he was, and ask that he take a personal interest. The doctor suggested that Beenie should go to the hospital in the morning and ask for him. When Beenie's son was given the message, he immediately complied. The doctor's diagnosis was that Beenie had a serious stomach ulcer and he was admitted to hospital for treatment. He was discharged some two weeks later, a little weak but in very good spirits.

To the Kumina "nation" in Waterloo, my response to Queenie's message was very significant. It meant that their ancestors had recognized me as a genuine friend and were relaying messages between us. An invisible link was in place. Prior to that, any need for assistance had been sent by human messengers and, of course, the time span had to be anything from half a day to two days. In the case of Beenie, his people thought he would have died without such prompt attention. Their resorting to spiritual communication had been a necessity brought on by the acuteness of the problem and the importance of Beenie as a master drummer to the whole Kumina nation.

Although this incident considerably enhanced my rating with the Kumina people, it still could not make me fit for membership. People of Kongolese ancestry can choose to participate as believers at Kumina functions. Remaining aloof is viewed with deep disapproval, but many of the younger generation, and some who see it as socially advantageous, keep their distance. Others become involved to varying degrees. Leaders are sometimes chosen on spiritual advice to elders, as in the case of Cyrus Wallace. He told Laura Tanna [1982], "Mother Bartlett teach me Kumina ... is really why I become a leader." According to Tanna, "He was initiated into Kumina at the age of fourteen and became a Kumina leader in the 1930s after he moved to Kingston and met Imogene 'Queenie' Kennedy."

Cyrus Wallace and Queenie Kennedy together led Kumina activities in Kingston for many years, then went their separate ways. One fundamental difference in their attitudes, which apparently became irreconcilable, concerned secrecy. Queenie Kennedy, though seeing the need for private rituals, was more willing to make information and ceremonies accessible to outsiders. Wallace expressed his views to Tanna in this way:

> I'm a Kumina leader. I don't play drum at street-side! I don't play drum because when I'm talking my language Kumina language, you fool wi' me, is dangerous. In Revival, you call to God, say 'God have mercy'. But in Kumina you fool wid me you naa have mercy. God move in a different, mysterious way [Tanna 1982].

Once a leader's position has been established, there is no argument. Those who disagree with any aspect of the leadership leave, or are asked to do so. Such action is not taken lightly but to observers on the outside it seems to cause no dissention or protest.

Leaders try to find successors to whom they can pass on the language and deep lore of Kumina. The choice is never entirely in their hands, so if a suitable neophyte is not found, there is no great anxiety. It is assumed that when the leader dies and joins the ancestral spirits, the decision will be made with or without his or her assistance.

The leader is the most important member of a Kumina group or bands (bands is singular in this context). A Queen usually heads the bands, but a man may also lead. Some groups have a Kumina mother and some have a master of ceremonies as well. It is usual for the roles of queen and mother to be held by the same person and a master of ceremonies to officiate at specific ceremonies and rituals. This master of ceremonies may wear a gown or skirt, denoting his subordination, like that of a wife, to King Nzambi. If the leader is male, he too might wear feminine dress, as in the case of David Cummings who led a bands in Barking Lodge, St Thomas. He appoints a master of ceremonies or, more frequently, a Kumina mother to be his assistant.

The leader alone decides on how the responsibilities will be shared. Secular duties are more likely to be delegated, but even the role of lead dancer or lead singer may be passed to someone else, particularly during the early stages of a ceremony.

The sacred duties of the leader include: preparing the site and ensuring the selection of appropriate songs for different stages of the ceremony; leading the singing; leading the dance; ministering to possessed devotees, for example, removing possessing spirits from them; conducting the ceremony so that it achieves the purpose for which it is held; healing; warning; preparing and killing the sacrificial animal; and leading the procession that moves by candlelight to feed the spirits. The reputation of the leader depends to a large extent on how skilfully he or she controls human situations, influences spirit activity and mediates between the two worlds. It should be pointed out that cultists may be mounted by either good or evil spirits.

The secular duties of the leader include making all the arrangements for the food and drinks that are served at the ceremony; ensuring that visitors are made to feel welcome and comfortable; disciplining of devotees; setting the ceremonial table; and in general presiding over every aspect of the ceremony so as to ensure its smooth and successful outcome.

The cyas drummer is probably next in importance to the leader since it is his prowess at the drums and its complex rhythms that invoke the spirits. Also, it is the excitement that he generates that urges on the singers and stimulates the spirits to possess devotees. The lead drummer must work closely with the leader and respond to every signal, every hint. The drummer may himself become possessed by a spirit.

Kumina Beliefs and Ceremonies

To Kumina believers, the invisible world of spirit is real. The world that we see is but a reflection of that world and everything that happens in it is the manifestation (effect) of the invisible and real world of spirit (cause).

In their own words, "Everything suppose to run smooth, but is man get in the way." To achieve this smoothness, divine harmony must be maintained or, when necessary, re-established at and between all levels of life. Kumina devotees state clearly that there are no barriers between the unseen world, human beings and the world of nature, excepting those put up by human ignorance and error. The life-force flows freely from the supreme God, "King Zambi", through every person, animal, plant and element. When there is no interference, health and harmony result; when there is, dis-ease follows, causing problems that can affect personal and/or community affairs as well as the world of nature in a variety of ways.

It is firmly believed that after death, ancestors continue to be interested in human affairs. These they affect for good or for ill, depending on the relationship existing between those in the world of the living and those in the world of the dead. The prime aims of Kumina members are to keep in constant touch with ancestral and other spirits and gods: to appease and honour them continually, and when there is special need, entertain them in ceremonies and rituals arranged to request guidance and advice. It is at these ceremonies that devotees come together under the guidance of a leader and combine in the use of music, movement and the spoken word to attract spirits for help and guidance.

Kumina ceremonies serve various purposes. These include healing, thanksgiving for restoration of harmony or blessings bestowed, rituals relating to death, including memorials for the dead and for tombing, and celebrations such as weddings and anniversaries. They may be held in an open yard, a temporary structure made of bamboo poles covered with coconut leaves, or a permanent structure that has supporting posts placed symbolically at the four cardinal points of the earth.

Tombing ceremonies, however, take place near the grave of the departed. The purpose of a tombing ceremony, which is held one year after death, is to ensure that the spirit is laid to rest and that its ghost will not haunt the earth. This might happen if it is not satisfied with rites performed at the burial.

Death is looked upon as a reunion with ancestors, release from the trials and tribulations of this world, and a gateway to the next. The tombing is therefore a joyous occasion involving drumming at both ends of the grave, singing, dancing and a blood sacrifice. The earth is also trampled prior to the actual tombing.

Before a Kumina ceremony of celebration or to correct disharmony, a table is laid in the ceremonial enclosure with a variety of items to appease the spirits. These include water, sugared water, wine, rice, flowers, fruits, aerated drinks, bread and candles. A small table with foods known to be favourites of the spirits is sometimes placed under or near the main one. It must be noted that all four elements – earth, air, fire and water – must be present in some form on, under, or near the table.

Colours are significant. Blue, white and green for example are used separately or in varying combinations to symbolize peace and reconciliation. They are used to invite spirits relevant to achieving these conditions in personal and communal situations. Red and black are also used, but reasons for this are not shared with outsiders. The colour theme of a ceremony is used for clothing, candles, flowers and in the materials that cover the table and wrap the supporting poles of ceremonial structures.

Preparations for a ceremony begin long in advance. Special hard dough loaves made in significant shapes like a cross, a dove for peace, a star in honour of the skies, must be ordered from one of the few bakers who still make them, supplies of food and drink bought; clothing and linen are carefully laundered; the ceremonial area cleared and swept repeatedly; materials for making the table put in place. These are usually a length of deal board on wooden supports that can be quickly dismantled after the table has been "broken", that is, the edibles shared, and the candles, by then burning low, placed on the ground near the drums. This happens after midnight, fairly soon after the blood sacrifice has been made.

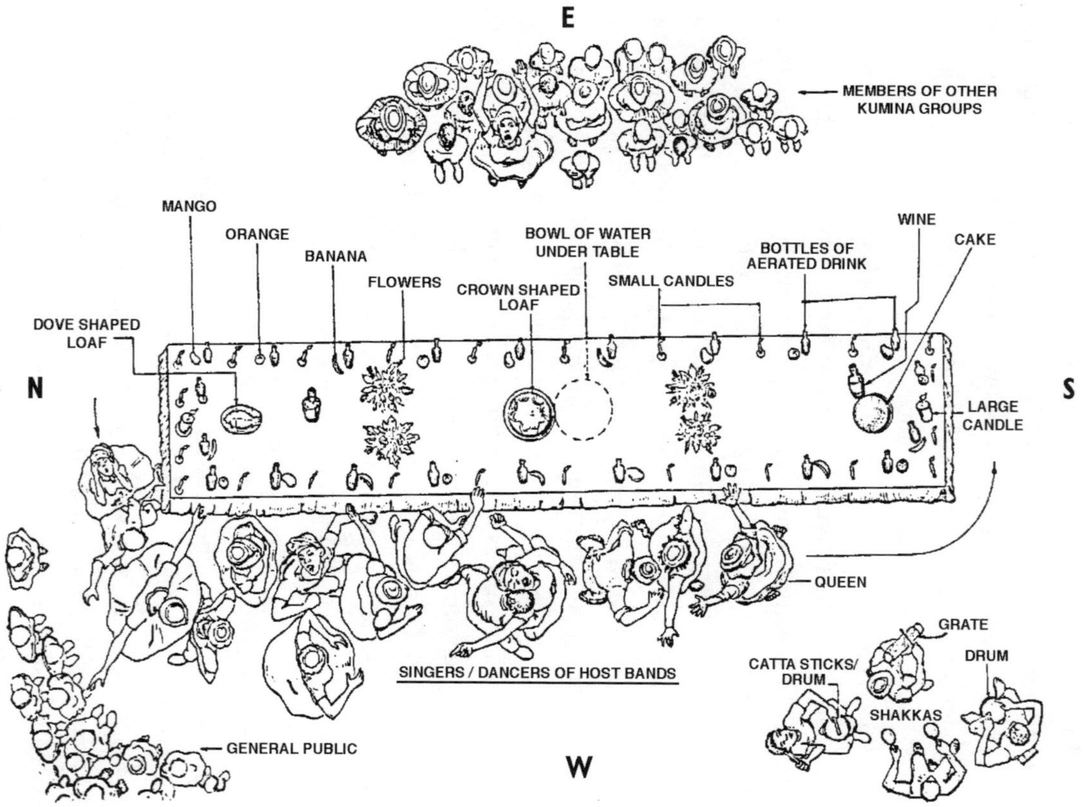
E
MEMBERS OF OTHER
KUMINA GROUPS
MANGO
ORANGE
BANANA
FLOWERS
CROWN SHAPED
LOAF
BOWL OF WATER
UNDER TABLE
SMALL CANDLES
BOTTLES OF
AERATED DRINK
WINE
CAKE
DOVE SHAPED
LOAF
N
S
LARGE
CANDLE
QUEEN
GRATE
DRUM
CATTA STICKS/
DRUM
SHAKKAS
SINGERS / DANCERS OF HOST BANDS
GENERAL PUBLIC
W

Kumina setting

Final preparations are made mainly by members of each of the participating bands on the appointed day, under the watchful eye and strict orders of the leader. The drums are put in place to the south-west of the table and consecrated with white proof rum. The drummers then drink some and pour a little into their cupped hands to wipe over their hands and faces. The bottle is placed on the ground between the drums. The drummers usually begin to warm up in the early evening while guests and visiting Kumina devotees arrive. Later, the host bands filter into the area raising and joining in songs, supported by the drummers and people playing percussion instruments like shakkas (maracas), tambourines and graters, and improvising with bottles, sticks or anything on which a rhythm can be played. Last to arrive is the leader, sometimes accompanied by the Kumina mother or master of ceremonies.

Intoning of the Kumina prayer, sung in call and response style and accompanied by drums and percussion, signals the official start of the ceremony. The leader "salos" to the drums with a bow or curtsy and slow waving of the hand, then leads the bands round the table in an anti-clockwise direction.

Kumina members say that their prayer is in the "African" language. This language has, in many cases, been proven to be Kongo based, but to date no linguist has identified any such links in the prayer. Carter [1986] says "in that its words are not from the pidgin, the Prayer defied all attempts at translation". Bunseki, in fact, could make nothing of it, saying that "It is probably something in the secret language of invocation (bindokila) of priests, like the use of Latin in the Catholic Church."

After the prayer, activities proceed in a way that is predictable as far as the overall sequence of events is concerned, yet unpredictable in detail, since there can be many variables and unforeseen happenings.

The important thread running through all Kumina ceremonies is the use of bilah/baila songs at the early stages of the ceremony, mainly to attract the spirits. When the leader or queen decides that there is enough spirit activity, baila give way to "Country" songs.

It is during the Country songs that the spirits usually appear. Whenever they are addressed a "salo" is made and a libation poured. Rum is placed in the mouth and blown into the air, poured on the drum head or on to the earth or both, to appease the spirits. The Country songs must then be used, since they contain the language understood by the ancestors. Possession can then take place. It should be noted that the spraying of rum from the mouth is also one of the ways of removing possessing spirits from devotees. Others include passing fire in the form of lighted matches or small lighted kerosene lamps around the head of the possessed person. Long Kumina trance states are discouraged unless for a very special cause. At rituals, people are brought out of trances by being placed between the drums or by fire. During spirit possession, devotees may accomplish amazing feats such as eating broken glass, walking through fire without being harmed and climbing trees backwards.

The later stage of the ceremony, when interaction with the spirits and the sacrifice takes place, is the most important and meaningful execution of the ceremony or ritual. The sacrifice can be a goat, chicken or dove and before its death it is symbolically invested with the inharmonious condition that the bands is seeking to correct. It is usually fed a little rum and taken around the ceremonial enclosure before being slaughtered by the leader or the queen, depending on who is in charge of the blood sacrifice. The whole head is removed, often with one blow of the cutlass. Cult members then dip their fingers into the blood of the slain offering and touch their foreheads and those of special friends. At this point, the table is broken.

The ancestral and other spirits have to be symbolically fed at the ceremony, a little removed from public view. It must be remembered that, in cultist thought, the dead continue to be part of their earthly families, and have feelings and urges as do humans, even though they are not visible to everyone. They do not seem to eat, yet food must nevertheless be given to them. Involving them in ordinary, everyday life processes is a way of remembering one's ancestors. Cooking salt-free food for the spirits is possibly an African retention, as many African people believe that the eating of salt contributes to a loss of spiritual vitality, a view which surfaces throughout the African diaspora in the New World. The living must not eat this food that has been prepared for the spirits. After the ceremony, it is buried in order to prevent the disastrous repercussions that could result. For this, devotees are led by the queen/leader in a candlelight procession to the appointed place.

After the procession returns, the rest of the animal, with the exception of a hind leg, is cooked. It is later served with rice to the assembled company. The hind leg is given to someone whom the Kumina people wish to honour as a special friend.

By this time the company will have thinned out and the music and dance activities all but ceased. When the last candle burns out, the drums are removed and put away for the next ritual, ceremony or celebration.

Songs

Two types of songs are used at Kumina ceremonies: Country songs and baila songs. Country songs are used for the more sacred sections of the rituals where communication with the spirits is sought and achieved, and are primarily for attracting, entertaining and appeasing the spirits. They are linked to the ancestral homeland through their language texts. Scholars of Kongo have verified that the African language used in Kumina is Kongo/Kikongo based [Carter 1986].

Country Song (spelt phonetically as heard). See sample translation below:

Oh . . . yee
Kinimba (1) Wenda (2)
Nkoyo ko meka *Nzambi* (3)
Zonge nimbala
Yakala (4) ndombe (5)
Koyo ko meka *Nzambi*
Ye ko meka kuna yande woya *ndomba*
Kuya ko meka Kwenda

Kumina usage		Kongo or Kikongo	
[Carter 1986; Bilby and Bunseki 1983; Seaga 1956]			
1. nimba or kiniba	spirit	Kiniumba	a spirit
2. wenda	come	wenda	go
3. Nzambi	King Zambi Great God	Nzambi a mpungo	God Almighty
4. yakala	man	nganga nkisi yakala	male ritual or herbal specialist
5. ndoma	girl	nduma	young woman

Country songs invoke and entertain spirits attracted earlier, and encourage them to participate in the dancing by taking over or mounting the bodies of devotees. They are then available for advice and assistance in matters relating to the ceremony. Country songs continue through the blood sacrifice and the feeding of the spirits until after the breaking of the table when spirit activity subsides. At that point, baila songs are again sung until dawn, when the gathering finally disperses. Baila song texts are in Creole, the main language of communication of the Jamaican people. These songs are used for the most part in the early stages of the ritual before serious communication with the spirits begins, or on recreational occasions. They are also more Western in style melodically and structurally, with less intricate accompanying drum rhythms.

One of the baila songs is "Cyan Fine no Money oh", already mentioned in chapter 3 in connection with traditional music and song becoming part of the National Festival of Arts. Here it shows how the song would be sung at the end of a Kumina ceremony.

Cyan fine (cannot find) no money oh (solo/call)
Cyan fine no money oh (chorus/response)
Have i' have i' no want i' (solo/call)
Cyan fine no money oh (chorus/response)
Want i' want i' cyan get i' oh (solo/call)
Cyan fine no money oh (chorus/response)

Kumina songs may have long, well-developed melodies as in the following example, but it is more usual for them to have short, repetitive motives (see p. 232, "Cha Cha") that may be improvised or elaborated upon. Song melodies sometimes are built on two to seven note scales and modes and use cadential formulae that are not usually found in Western music. Many melodies tend to show a typical West African feature, that of proceeding in a downward direction.

Bad Madanlah

Wonda weh me do you (how I've offended you) mek me name a ring (x3)

Ratta tear up me clothes an' me cyan go dung deh (can't go there)

Bad madanlah (mother-in-law) oh (x2)

Bad madanlah oh sidung an' tell 'tory (gossips)

Bad madanlah oh (x2)

Bad madanlah oh sidung an tell 'tory

Cha Cha Chimmi Yah

Cha cha chimmi ya (see me here) chimmi yah chimmi yah

These words are repeated several times with interjections such as "one day dah light" (at dawn), "doh de doh doh doh".

Kumina song performance is usually in group unison or antiphonal unison style. Harmony may result from the use of the customary overlapping call/response design, with the chorus answer beginning while the soloist is still singing or the soloist beginning before the chorus is finished. As well, some songs may be performed in a free contrapuntal style that can span three octaves.

The vocal tone used in Kumina singing is usually high pitched, loud and forceful. However, as in sub-Saharan Africa, special effects such as falsetto, guttural sounds, humming, grunting, whispering, and the interjection of words and untranslated syllables may be added to the songs.

The difference in status of people gathered for a Kumina meeting of any kind is quite clear. Participants at Kumina events are, in order of importance,

1. Queen/Leader
2. Drummers and percussionists
3. Singers and dancers
4. Members of other Kumina bands
5. Guests
6. General public

The first two categories participate fully in the ceremony. Most of the singers and dancers participate fully, but singers who are not conversant with the African language cannot do so. Some members of other Kumina bands who know the African language and Country songs are also aware that there are points at which it is not appropriate for them to join in. The guests and general public are considered outsiders or, in Kumina language, "mundongo". Of Kongo derivation [Schuler 1980: 69–70] it means outsider. Kongo mundongo = stranger, slave [Carter 1986].

At ceremonies there are grades of mundongo. Some are invited to join in certain activities, dancing in the circle early in the proceedings, singing baila songs and choruses of Country ones, for example. Other mundongo are expected to remain on the periphery throughout, apart, perhaps, from contributing to costs by lighting a candle and dropping a coin.

A baila song which alerts those in the know that an outsider is intruding beyond his or her limits is:

> *Tell mundongo fe tan (stay) one side (aside)*
> *Mundongo gal, you fe tan one side.*

On hearing this, Kumina people combine to put an end to the situation that elicited the song. They always succeed, and without embarrassing the person in question.

When a Maroon spirit, by chance, visits a Kumina performance, it is considered a good sign. As soon as one is recognized, a special song is sung:

> *Oh Maroon gahn oh*
> *Fare thee well oh*
> *Maroon gahn oh*
> *Maroon lef him pot a fire (leaves hurriedly)*
> *Maroon gahn a Hayfield road*
> *Maroon gahn oh Maroon gahn.*

Dancing

Kumina dances serve various functions. These can be divided into two main groupings:

1. Primarily social, as in ceremonies relating to marriage, welcoming a baby or raising funds for individual or community needs.
2. Religious, as a means of achieving trance states in ceremonies and rituals honouring the dead, or invoking help and guidance from or through ancestral spirits. On such occasions only a few may achieve trance states or become possessed.

Others in the Kumina circle dance to the rhythm of the Kbandu drums and assist in attracting gods and spirits. The rhythm is reproduced by the feet, while the florid and improvisatory patterns of the playing cyas drum impel movement of other parts of the body – head, shoulders, arms, hips. It also conveys to the dancers whether to proceed in the circular line singly or facing, as partner, one who is immediately in front or behind, or to spin and break before once more proceeding in single file, anti-clockwise.

The enthusiasm and stamina with which the singers use their voices and the way in which they respond to the drums greatly influence the drummers. This interaction is crucial, and at a very successful ceremony the tension and excitement build up until it is virtually impossible for even the most casual observer or timid outsider not to be drawn into the action. They cannot, unless invited by the queen to do so, join the circle, but physical response to the music and general atmosphere is welcomed by the queen and members of the bands.

Visitors who are attending merely to observe, and having no deep convictions concerning Kumina, have been known to find themselves carried away – making sudden jerking movements at intervals or breaking into abandoned twirls ending with characteristic breaking. These involuntary movements are often followed by a period of stillness.

The leader or queen is always on the alert and constantly aware of what is happening. If necessary, she herself or a member of her bands at her direction, will place herself in readiness to protect anyone in or out of the circle who might fall or be flung to the ground by a possessing spirit. Kumina people are not allowed to stay long in trance states during a ceremony. Depending on the nature of the possession as recognized by the queen or the other experienced cultists, one in trance must be brought back quickly.

At their ceremonies, Kumina dancers move in a circle round the ritual table and/or the drums in an anti-clockwise direction. They travel with a shuffling, hip-swaying motion in which sudden breaks for twirling or extemporised interaction between pairs of dancers are signalled by the playing cyas drum. Usually Kumina dancers are upright, spine erect and pelvis moving backwards and forwards, but there are instances when the traditional Jamaican movement pattern of left to right rotations of the pelvis is used rather than the customary backward and forward Kumina movement. The feet are for the most part flat on the ground and are used to propel the body along in a gliding, earth-hugging step. There may be a variation here too, for one foot may be on half-point instead of both being flat on the ground.

At times in the ritual, dancers curtsey (salo) to the drum, as a mark of respect and reverence to the spirit that is at the moment communicating through the drum. The salo usually occurs when the Country songs are being used, although it may be done at other times.

Costuming plays a minor role in Kumina, as in most Jamaican traditional ceremonies and celebrations, Bruckins and Christmas Masquerades being notable exceptions. It can be presumed that this is because slaves and plantation labourers, till the early twentieth century, were either paid nothing or abysmally low wages. They could not think in terms of anything but the bare essentials of living, and largely depended on charity for anything beyond rough working clothes. Christmas was the time to expect gifts of hand-me-downs or, for a fortunate few, custom-made clothes. A Jonkunnu Christmas procession song in chapter 5, *Christmus a come – me wan me lama* (fancy things) reminds us of this.

Kumina dancers wear clothes that show respect for the occasion and allow their type of movements.

The male leader or master of ceremonies often wears a loose-fitting skirt. This is done at the practical level for unhindered movement and, symbolically, to identify that the male is the helpmate/wife of King Zambi. The queen usually appears with a glittering crown on her head.

The queen as leader agrees with the role of "woman" in certain areas of postemancipation Jamaican life [Kerr 1963]. It is an accepted fact that she has been the head of the family and the breadwinner in the absence of fathers who often desert families or must seek employment far from home. This has been characteristic of plantation and other such seasonal

Queenie dancing with a glass of water on her head

Kumina dance positions

labourers. Most teachers, health and social workers are women, and in recent years, several important posts in the public and private sectors have been filled by women. In many cases, however, the legal and financial status of these women is not on a par with their male counterparts. The problems of Jamaica's non-convertible currency in the context of international financial developments during the 1970s motivated humble higglers/peddlers (mainly women) to seek solutions which took them from the streets of Jamaica to centres of commerce in the Caribbean, Latin and North America. They have become a very visible and affluent part of the society and, as a secondary development, now create employment opportunities.

Until recently, Kumina dancers danced barefooted. This facilitated the characteristic earth hugging foot movements, with the more skilful dancers visibly using their toes to propel them along. Nowadays, soft-soled shoes are often worn. Heads and arms are covered by devotees out of respect for their ancestral spirits and many guests do the same. Clothes are loose in order to allow free movement, especially during twirling. I have never seen dancing female participants wearing trousers, though members of the audience are quite free to do so.

As the older generation of Kumina devotees fades from active participation, only a few youngsters join with any spiritual involvement or deep commitment. It is a pleasure to see them performing the subtle, liquid movements of their forebears with no thought of audience appeal.

At another level, scores of young people learn the dancing, songs and drumming for theatrical and festival involvement. Standards of authenticity and artistry vary, but all must be free to interpret and recreate their own heritage. The Kumina people approve of some of the new developments and performers. Others they call "mundongo" with a curl of the lips, but even they cannot stem the tide of change.

Kumina drummer

Instruments

Drums dominate Kumina ceremonies of all types. It is their rhythms which, by egging on the singers and dancers, create conditions that attract spirits to these events, and make their success possible.

The performance style is therefore highly significant. If rhythmic patterns are not compelling to both living and dead members of the families, or if there is any unexpected interruption in the flow of sounds and their build-up, the spirits will not appear. Certain drum rhythms are reputed to call specific spirits. If these spirits are needed to serve the purpose of the duty, ceremony or ritual, the lead drummer must know which rhythm to play, and when.

Two kinds of drums are central to the music of all Kumina plays, ceremonies and rituals:

1. The Kbandu, which is about fourteen to fifteen inches in diameter and twenty inches long.
2. The playing cyas, which is a smaller version of the Kbandu.

Note that "banda" in Kikongo means a "type of drum; rhythm; meter" and that cyas in Kikongo is the name of a sensa drum [Brathwaite 1978: 54]. These drums may be made from kegs, from hollowed coconut, breadfruit or cedar logs, or from a length of the hollow trumpet tree trunk. They are headed at one end with the skin of a ritually sacrificed goat.

Kumina drums-two Kbandu and two playing cyas (smaller)

Goatskin for making Kumina drum

Ashes being applied to goatskin to loosen hair

Scraping hairs off goatskin with bottle

Log being hollowed for Kumina drum

Testing newly made Kumina drum

Finishing touches in making a drum

*Elijah Alexander consecrating
a new drum-head with rum*

A Kumina elder told me in my early days of field research that the skins used for making the drums had to be from goats of different sexes. The kbandu, being deeper toned, was considered male and was headed by the skin of a female goat, the higher pitched playing cyas, being female, headed by the skin of a ram. God, he explained, produces life on earth by the fusion of male and female. For success in efforts hinging on the use of life and life forces, the sexual partnership initiated by King Nzambi himself must be respected and included, hence the attention to the sex of each drum and the complementary use of the other sex for its skin.

Efforts to elicit confirmation of the above have constantly failed. It could be secret information or a tradition no longer respected. I doubt the latter as much as I doubt that my elderly informant deceived me. I also fervently hope that I am not guilty of divulging secret information which would have been given in confidence.

The skin is attached to the drum by nails driven through a band of wood or wyss (vine) which circles the drum head. Before the drums are made, libations are poured to appease the spirits of the wood and of the skin. When completed they are consecrated with libations of rum and sugared water. The drum is tuned by hitting the band of wood or wyss

in a downward direction to tighten the skin, and rum is rubbed or blown onto it for both fine tuning and ritual purposes.

The Kbandu maintains the basic ostinato rhythm

which is said to be favoured by King Zambi. The playing cyas provides the more complicated and melodic rhythms.

The drummers sit astride the drums and use the heel of the right foot, fingers, and different parts of their hands to produce the many possible sounds. Fingers may be grouped together or separated. The pitch and the quality of the sound are altered by the player pressing the heel against the drum head (heeling). In the case of the Kbandu, heeling is done on alternate beats, but playing cyas drummers heel the drum head to change pitch at will or for special effects. The cyas rhythms are the ones used to call or charm the spirits in general or specifically.

There are usually two Kbandu and two playing cyas used at large ceremonies. Two or more Kbandu drums can be used simultaneously since the rhythm is constant. The ostinato rhythm of this drum provides steady support for the complex playing cyas patterns. These cannot be duplicated. Only one playing cyas is used, although the other may play the Kbandu rhythm. The simultaneous use of two playing cyas drums would present difficulties in terms of communication with the spirits, since each, even with rhythms pleasing to a particular spirit, would be improvising in a distinctive style. The resulting confusion of sound would seriously hamper the dancing and singing and snarl the lines of communication. Rhythms for specific spirits are not shared with outsiders, and trusted ones are expected to respect this, even when the information is occasionally given. Note that even Dixon, the master drummer, served a long period of apprenticeship before being allowed to "mount" the playing cyas.

Drum rhythms for the early part of the ceremony differ considerably from those used in the Country (African language) songs, when there is increasing spirit participation. These rhythms intensify, and the tempo quickens when the spirits are summoned, climaxing just before the sacrifice. It is this crescendo of rhythmic sounds accompanying lengthy presentation of Country songs that often brings on trance state.

Since Kumina discourages lengthy trance states, less intense drumming and slower tempos are used to control devotees after the trance state occurs. According to Queenie Kennedy, prolonged Myal can lead to serious mental disorders.

Two catta ticks (sticks) beaten against the side of the Kbandu help to build up rhythmic excitement (with a pattern played ostinato).

The playing of these sticks is considered important by the leader, drummers and dancers/singers who will halt proceedings and voice displeasure if there is the slightest discrepancy between the "catta" and the Kbandu.

Other small percussion instruments of indefinite pitch may be used: shakkas made of dried gourds with seeds or small pebbles inside, scrapers of grooved wood a grater or metal over which a nail or similar metal article is drawn. Sticks struck together and many other forms of improvised percussion may complement the main instruments.

Kumina drummers are invariably lusty singers and proficient dancers. They must also have experienced possession. Wide and deep knowledge of Kumina songs and language is imperative since the drummers need to respond quickly and accurately to the musical and ritual instructions of the queen or leader. Several players can interchange in playing the Kbandu, shakka, scraper and similar instruments, but the number of experienced playing cyas drummers is small. Apart from the skills already mentioned, it takes considerable time for the drummer to understand and cope with the many spirits, friendly and otherwise, that visit during a Kumina ceremony. Elijah Dixon, one of Jamaica's finest and most famous drummers, states that he played the Kbandu for six years before being allowed to mount a playing cyas.

Their drums are highly respected by Kumina people, and skilled drummers enjoy great prestige in the community. Outstanding drummers of bygone days are remembered with veneration, and youngsters who show promise and interest are given every encouragement. It is always hoped that such talent indicates that an ancestor is ready to pass on his expertise to another generation.

Contemporary master drummers are careful to use their knowledge and technical prowess freely and for good, only. Nothing less is worthy of their gift from Nzambi.

Kumina Language

Honouring ancestral spirits and communicating with them are prime functions of Kumina. It is therefore essential for serious devotees to understand and speak the language of the Nkugu or ancestral spirits. Referred to by Kumina people as the African language, it has been identified as mainly Kongolese with some Kimbundu. Laura Tanna [1982], in a *Sunday Gleaner* article, stated:

> Twenty-eight years ago (1954) in Trench Town, Edward Seaga interviewed Cyrus Wallace, better known as 'Baba C.' and from their conversations collected several tape recordings about the customs and language of Kumina. Few people are more qualified to discuss Kumina and the Kikongo language as it exists in Jamaica than seventy-four-year-old Baba C. for he learned it in St Thomas as a boy of ten from Mother Bartlett. Sixty-four years ago she was already an old woman, which means the knowledge Baba C. gained from her goes back at least 120 years.

Wallace quotes Mother Bartlett as saying that his grandfather's language was "kongo", and hers "mumbaka". He remembers her telling him that the Kikongo word for rum is *malavu*. In 1977, Dr Igor Kopytoff, a visitor to the island, was struck by the sprinkling of Kongolese words in Queenie Kennedy's speech, and her ability to translate them. He pointed out, however, that malavu which she translated as "rum", in Kikongo means "palm wine", the African equivalent of rum. Dr Hazel Carter, reader in Bantu languages, suggested that "mumbaka" may be a name from kimbandu, a dialect close to Kikongo.

African words from Edward Seaga's field papers were sent to the School of Oriental and African Studies (SOAS) at London University and identified by a scholar there as being Kikongo. Three of these papers were resubmitted to the SOAS in 1982. Hazel Carter identified forty-seven words spoken by Baba C. (Wallace) as being recognizably Kikongo words. She writes:

> From the fact that some of them include long vowels, and that the form for 'male' is yakala, I would place the original homeland of the people in the southern part of the Kongo speaking area, in Angola, around San Salvador . . . further north, the form is 'bakala [Carter 1986].

Tanna states that Carter found that apart from differences in vowel length, some words used in Jamaica "are almost unchanged from modern

Kikongo". Examples cited included:

Ngomad	rum
Ndzaambi amphuungu	God (of the highest)
muuntu	person
mwaana	child, baby
ngulu	pig
dya	cat
leka	lie down
mungwa	salt

In words such as boolo, bread, and bizi, meat, which in Kikongo would be mmboolo and mmbizi, the initial nasals have been removed.

Carter found that there were grammatical changes, for example, maalu, the plural, instead of kuulu, the singular, for foot: mwiin, "drink" which is in fact "having drunk". Some words have taken on new meanings in Jamaica. For example:

Baba C's Kongo

Ngaang awoka	god
yakala	boy
yaaya	old lady
malembe	How do you do?

Modern Kikongo

Mgaang awwuka	healing doctor
yakala	male, man, husband
yaaya	mother
maleembe	kindness, gentleness

Baba C's speech tone is close to modern Kikongo, but he uses Jamaican inflections in some words, rising on the last syllable. Hazel Carter states:

> To date almost 300 words have been recorded, and the language operates something like a pidgin, with invariable forms, all grammatical apparatus

being supplied by Jamaican Creole. That is, the Kumina 'pidgin' does not operate as a fully functional language, but is a rather small set of vocabulary items and phrases, morphologically invariable. In some ways, however, it is typical of pidgins generally. For instance, there is no systematic pattern of derivation from one form for a particular category. The typical pidgin tends to derive verbs from one form, usually the infinitive, of the base language, but Kumina verbs are derived from many diverse Kongo morphological forms. The word *bawenda* 'they went' in Koongo is used for 'go' (also 'come'), alongside the infinitive-derived *dwenda*; *iwiidi*, the perfect stem of the verb *fwa*, 'die' in Koongo, is used for 'die', 'dead' or 'kill', though some speakers do use the infinitive-derived *fwa* . . . there is very little stability, Community-wise, in the Kumina vocabulary. The numbers of speakers is very small, but it is not uncommon to find five or six variants of a word; in addition to *bawenda* and *kweenda*, there are also *wenda* and *waenda*: . . . The words for 'goat' and 'cow' have become confused so that the word for 'goat' appears as *iombo, koombo, komba, konve, koonvi, ngoombo* and *goombe (Koongo nkhoombo* 'goat', *ngoombe* 'cow'). Kumina speakers have however been very creative in combining words to form compounds – quite unknown in the original languages, such as *saambi baazu* (God fire for 'sun') and *kombo biizi* for 'goat meat' (cf *Koongo mbizi ankhoombo*) [Carter 1986].

The following specimen illustrating the use of Kumina pidgin is taken from "An Interview with Queenie, the Kumina Queen, Imogene Kennedy", by Maureen Warner-Lewis and Monica Schuler (Creole words are interspersed with the African):

Wen yu goin to have dina nou, *se yetuwayet* children! weenda kuna yaandi! a gwain sita nguma – *tala yo maiso bifo yu sita nguma* . . . Sapuoz a waan to beg yu somtim nou – me se yuz *mudongo nkeenti* – yuz not an Afrikan laik os bikoz yu kaan spik the langwij – yu se *modongo nkeent, weenda!*

Translated by Queenie Kennedy, it reads:

When you are going to have a 'dinner' (Kumina ceremony), now, you say, '*Friends*, children! come to me! I'm going to *beat the drum* – look you eyes before you beat the drum' . . . Suppose I want to ask you for something now – I say 'You are an *outsider woman!* – you're not an African like us because you don't speak the language' – you say, '*Outsider woman! come!*'

Carter finds that in spite of the variations, Kumina pidgin is common to all "bands", but that when calling spirits different bands do not understand each other's language.

Beverley Hall-Alleyne, a Jamaican linguist specializing in African languages and Caribbean Creole, points out, "the Kumina lexicon shows certain differences from the original Kongo". She cites examples of final vowels and initial nasals being dropped, extension of meanings and confusion of source items. Yet she finds much that is recognizably Kikongo.

The lexicon on which Hall-Alleyne bases her comment was compiled by Kenneth Bilby and Fu-Kian Kia Bunseki. Bilby collected several interviews during field research in Jamaica. The Kikongo links were identified by Bunseki, a Congolese anthropologist, and in many cases cross-checked with the Appendix to the *Dictionary and Grammar of the Kongo Language* and the *Dictionaire Kikongo Francais*. Bilby also utilized data collected by Dr Joseph Moore during field work in Jamaica in the 1950s.

Edward Kamau Brathwaite in "Kumina: The Spirit of African Survival in Jamaica" [1978] worked from the tapes of the interview conducted by Maureen Warner-Lewis and Monica Schuler with Mrs Queenie Kennedy in 1971. Using his transcription of the tapes, he obtained "significant comments from Bunseki". This commentary, Brathwaite declares, "if nothing else, indicates the accuracy of Miss Queenie's oral and memorial rendition". Bunseki, who is Congolese, recognized not only Kikongo words, but knowledge of Congolese cosmology in Queenie's utterances.

The evidence presented here is more than enough to prove that Kumina devotees are indeed linked linguistically through their "African" language to Kongolese ancestry. It is easy to understand why they are adamant that anyone wishing to participate fully in rituals for contacting ancestral spirits must be conversant with their "African language".

In addition, as Bilby and Bunseki [1983] say regarding Kumina language in practice, ". . . the lexical items collected continue to live and to change . . . most important, these 'Country' words continue to carry a semantic load shared by those who use them, and to serve a significant communicative function; in a sense, they may be said to form part of a 'second language' spoken by a diffused, though quite visible, network of individuals dispersed over a wide area of eastern Jamaica."

Country	English	Kikongo	English
	Queenie		Bilby and Bunseki
Bimbambi	Food reaped by ancestors in Africa	Kimbambi Dimbambi	Large bean that grows on a vine
Bimbi	Heavy	Nabimbi	Very dense
Bandu	Larger Kumina drum	Banda	A type of drum rhythm: meter
Buta	Friend, man	Mbuta	Term of address for one who is older e.g. Chief, Headman, etc.
Bwa	Dog	Mm-bwa	Dog
Dia	To eat	Dia	To eat
Gangga Nkisi Yakala	Obeah man	Nganga Nikisi a Yakala medicine	Male ritual specialist in curing and herbal
Jimbu	Money	Mzimbu Njimbu	Money, beads Valuables

Country	English	Kikongo	English
Kandal	Cloth worn round the waist: cloth used to wrap parts of corpse before burial	Kandalala	A very long measure of cloth; dead; stretched out and exposed to the air in order to be dried out (said of corpse)
Kento	Woman	Knento	Woman
King Zambi	Great God	Nzambia Mpungo	God Almighty: the principle of the most powerful vitality
		Kinzambi	Divinity, Godhead

Queenie		Kongo Language	
Sikaanga	Beat the drum	Sika Ngoma	Beat drum
Kuyu-Nkuyu	Spirit	Nk-Kuyu	Spirit
Malavu	Rum	Malavu	Palm wine
Matoto	Earth, stone, grave	Nttoto	Earth
Mbele or Beele	Knife, cutlass	Mmbeele	Knife
Boolo	Bread, flour, rice	Mgoolo	Bread, cake, biscuits
Kuunga	Talk, sing, dance	Nkuunga	Song
Zambi-Baazu	Sun, Moon	Nzambi Baazu	God, fire

The following texts are two variants of the same song as performed by different groups. The drummer's general translation is consistent with that of the scholarly team, Bunseki and Bilby, supporting the use of the participants' translation.

1. Queenie, in Waterloo

Banyaku Banyaku Banyaku Bele
Sikangga Guma
Sikangga Guma
O Nama
Beti Balulu
Banyaku (x3) Bele
Sikangga Guma (x2)

According to Bertram Kelly (Kumina master drummer) it says "Our friends gone and we must play the drums good."

2. Singer from Arcadia

Banyaku (x3) Bele (Wele)
Sika Kumu (Kumu Siko)
Banyaku (Ba) Yau Konde
Oh – Nama
Beti Balulu
Mu (ku) Yaku Bele (Wele)
Sika Kumu (Kuma Siko)
Banyaku (Ba) Yaku Bele (Wele)

According to Bunseki and Bilby, "Wele" should be "bele" in order to agree properly with the plural form "banyaku" (singular – wanguku); these are older forms of the word, not commonly used today. The modern usage is "wayaku/bayaku".

Your colleagues (x3) have just gone
Play the rhythm
Your colleagues (x2) went hunting
Oh – follow
Those who are being raised
Your colleague has gone
Play the rhythm
Your colleagues (x2) have just gone.

9

Queenie Kennedy:
Her Life

I mogene "Queenie" Kennedy's precise age is shrouded in mystery. Ask her and she turns to her husband, brother, or adopted son and repeats the question.

Warner-Lewis, in an article based on a 1971 interview [1977: 57], states, "Miss Queenie is now in her mid-40s and lives with her husband and children in a yard in lower Kingston." Place this beside Tanna [1982], who tells of the joint leadership of Queenie and Cyrus Wallace "in the 1930s", and one realizes that there is a discrepancy. The first puts her year of birth in the mid 1920s, the second eleven to fifteen years earlier, since she would hardly have become an active Kumina queen in her early teens.

The point is, however, that chronological or physical age was of absolutely no interest or importance to Queenie. It is not age but her ability to carry out the functions of Kumina queen that matters. Confident of having been appointed leader for life by ancestral spirits, her prime intent is to carry out the pertinent duties and responsibilities of this charge: a charge that ends when she joins her ancestors at whatever age she might then be.

Queenie saw her life as a journey marked by milestones. The road was sometimes rough, sometimes smooth, sometimes precipitous; but always purposeful as it led to the fulfilment of her commission to abide by the values of her ancestors; to do the will of her gods, ancestral and other spirits; to interpret their messages for those lacking the psychic insight to do so, and to be the conduit of spiritual healing, causing health and harmony to flow into earthly affairs and conditions.

The milestones in Queenie's life varied. In one instance she described them according to her homes: (1) Dalvey in St Thomas where she was born to a "nation" removed by only two or three generations from its African homeland and where she was called to lead Kumina; (2) Kingston to which she was drawn by the very practical and active interest of a young student of sociology; and (3) Waterloo in St Catherine, to which political upheavals and urban change caused her to relocate. At another time Queenie expressed her milestones in relation to events: her childhood visits to forbidden Kumina happenings, her call to service at the root of the cotton tree, followed by a crowded schedule of Kumina duties, marriage and raising a family. She included her participation in national, regional and international festivals, workshops and seminars in this interpretation of her life.

Although Queenie Kennedy never mentioned age or placed events in particular years, the sequence was always chronological. In this account, facts from many sources are used to trace the life story of this remarkable woman. It will take us from her quiet beginning in a small Jamaican village to theatrical and educational presentations, in person and by electronic media, on both sides of the Atlantic. The chief sources are interviews and conversations with Mrs Kennedy herself, her husband, and her master drummers, one of whom is her brother.

Early Life

Imogene Kennedy was born in Dalvey in eastern Jamaica, some time in the first two decades of this century. She knew neither the day nor the year of her birth. She had no recollection of her father, who died when she was young. Of her mother, Imogene told many tales, some of which will be related here.

Her warmest memories are of her grandmother. Growing up in a typical Jamaican situation in which the mother supports the whole family, Imogene was often left in the care of her grandparents. Until she went to school, most of her waking hours were spent with them. There was little mention of school life, no anecdotes about teachers and classmates. Perhaps her attendance was irregular and perhaps short-lived. The school day was long and boring compared with the hours spent with her grandmother who told her many entertaining stories.

Her grandmother spoke of Africa, the huge country which was home to her. She and many others had been lured by music into the hands of slave catchers. They were well out to sea when another ship forced the slavers to turn back. It was all very frightening, but they were powerless participants in the drama. Eventually, they were put off on a little island but did not get a chance to settle, since agents persuaded them to better themselves by "signing up" as workers for plantations in the West Indies. They would be paid and at the end of their "contract" could return to Africa. It was wonderful to look forward to seeing their homeland again.

When they landed in Jamaica, things were very unsettled. Life was hard for them, but even harder for the ex-slaves and their children. Some church members and even a few planters were on the side of the little people, but the government and most of the estate owners were very much against them. There were even some black people, who "fought their own colour". Although she heard it was Maroons who helped to capture runaway slaves and, later, rebellious plantation workers, she was also told of their long, courageous and essentially successful struggle against the British. She thought that was marvellous.

The new arrivals, having come by sea, were nicknamed "salt-water bungos", and made to feel very different. Yet their sympathies were with the "sufferers", especially as they had no other homeland; no Africa to welcome them back. There were serious clashes, especially when a man named Bogle led a march to the Morant Bay court house (1865). It was a bad time. Canefields were set on fire, but in the end the big man won. Bogle and a lot of other people were hanged. Many were captured and shot.

Such stories made a deep impression on the little girl. She also learnt about tata mbenji, "a little ole man from Africa" [Lewin interview 1969; Brathwaite 1978: 53, 54] who "go roun' with a basket". In Kikongo "nytetye mbinza" is "a type of very small bird" and "ntete, basket" [Bilby and Bunseki 1983: 35–36]. The Kongolese anthropologist Bunseki, commenting on the Warner-Lewis/Schuler taped interview said: " 'Benze' is a clan: 'tata' means father. 'Tatimbeenj' (Tata m'beenze) means: 'I belong to the clan Benze.' Benze is actually the first name of this clan, whose totem or symbol is the basket. Note that Miss Queenie said, 'He juss go round wid him basket' " [Brathwaite 1978: 53].

Note too the symbolic importance of the basket in Ogotommeli's account of the plan of the world system [Griaule 1965: 31–34, 41]. Grandma told Imogene that tata mbenzi was their very special provider and judge. He had everything they needed in his basket, but he also had punishments there for evil-doers. He liked walking around in the market watching. One minute you would see him, and the next he would vanish. Old immigrants used to put gifts of foodstuff in his basket in order to please him. To this day, no member of succeeding generations has seen him, but "he could still be aroun'."

Imogene's grandmother told her "a whole heap of story", and taught her some of the African language. Carter [1986: 6] in commenting on Kumina refers to this language as "African":

> . . . It is rather the remnant or remnants of languages, closely related, and apparently dominated by Kongon, spoken by the 'late arrivants', used principally for communication within family or groups of the same linguistic background, gradually decaying into a secret, a ritual code.

Her grandmother's death made an important difference to Imogene's life. Having joined their ancestors, she was now seen by the little girl as one of the "ole arrivants" and a strong link with the spirit world.

Imogene's peers could not understand why she preferred to be alone. They sometimes sought her out to make her play with them, but she did not enjoy herself. When her spirit was "uplifted" she had to be alone. She became more successful at slipping away to the bushes, to sit by herself, often on graves. Sometimes "brown people" were sitting there and she would turn back.

At night the drums drew Imogene to the Kumina yard next door. It was the home of Man Parker. He and his father, Ole Parker, are among the most highly respected forebears of the Kumina nation, famous for their deep knowledge of ancestral values and practices. Their names are frequently mentioned with near reverence by present-day Kumina people. Ole Parker came from Africa, so in life was a link between the new and the ancestral homelands. At death he became an even more significant intermediary between the generations, those on earth and those in the spirit world. A sixty-year-old woman had vivid memories of Man Parker as a forceful and dynamic Kumina leader in St Thomas up to forty years ago. He was constantly consulted on personal and communal matters when human understanding and aid fell short. His followers kept him busy.

Imogene's mother, an ardent Baptist, disapproved of Man Parker's activities. She considered it neighbourly, however, to visit him, and even sometimes to watch Kumina ceremonies. She let Imogene accompany her. This caused problems because the child always contrived to be out of sight when her mother was ready to leave.

> When the drums sweet me, I couldn't leave to go home. By the time I realize it mus' be late, is morning already. The door would lock and nobody would open it, all I knock an knock. One night I jus decide to res' meself 'gains the mortar in the kitchen. I nevva know I doze off till I wake and see a big figure, white from head to foot, lookin' at me from the corner [Lewin interview 1969].

The figure turned out to be an uncle draped in a sheet, trying to scare her out of repeating her escapade. It did not work.

The drums continued to draw Imogene to Man Parker's yard. Locked doors and corporal punishment did not succeed in deterring her. She recalls, with a chuckle, stealing out of bed, slipping out of the house and through the fence, too excited to worry about the consequences of her escapade.

She told of a later experience when she and teenage friends stole away to a distant Kumina meeting. She knew that when she returned home she would be locked out and beaten in the morning:

I make up me mine to take me punishment. The playing cyas have as much things [great power] in it. It carry as much in the music, sending the message all roun'. Even if you deh [are] far, you know well something a gwan [is happening]. Feelings take you. Any wheh you deh [anywhere you are] you haffi [have to] move, man. Because it draw you direck [affects you immediately]. Any wheh you is an you hear it, you know to leave an' go. One time when we get to a certain place, we los' [lost]. It is buryin' groun' [cemetery]; is night, an' we haffi sidung [had to sit] a de buryin' groun' wheh we deh [where we were] an listen fe the drum. An when the big drum start, an you think a ya so i' deh [it is here] a de echo come over [it was only the echo]. An me say, we mus' tek time now an listen for the playing cyas to answer the kbandu. An so we listen, and take time fine we way. But anytime de drum stop, you haffi stop too. So we res' till it start again, and we falla [follow] the soun' until we fine de direct spot weh it deh. Remember, is night, but de playing cyas carry you go any wheh you fe [are to] go.

Imogene was by now seriously interested in Kumina. She felt the presence of her grandparents' spirits, and was never lonely or afraid. This set her at odds with young people in her age group who sought each other's company, and were often afraid of the dark.

The following story was frequently told by Mrs Kennedy. Several researchers, local and visiting, have recorded it on tape. It is given in a paraphrased form for easier comprehension.

One day a fine some lilies, seven lilies, an' a plant the lilies them in a row. An' one Sunday mornin' when a wake, a see all the lilies them blow. The seven lilies them blow. An' a fine meself leave an go dung to a gully, an a pick up some coconut in the gully bottom, an wen a look a si a big cotton tree, an a jus fall right down . . . at the cotton tree root. An' is twenty-one days I doan eat neider drink nothin at all. The cotton tree like it hollow inside, an is inside there I is: an some ole time African grave near to the tree an' they is tomb . . . An' a lay down in the cotton tree, and a night time a see like little candle light up the cotton tree. An' like a sleepin', dozin', and a hear like a little voice talkin to me, but is spirit talking to me an' say "Now you is a nice little chile, an I gwine get you right up now into the African worl'. You have good brains so we goin' teach you." "Swikkidi, swikkidi lango", that is sugar an' water, an then them teach me the prayer which say,

Kwali kwali, non den de
Beli kuluma kisoolaya
Pam Iakaya
Len legele
Luwi zakwe ndakwe so
Belam mpe Mbanbele

which is the Our Father prayer in the African language. Them carry me on, but a fall fass asleep, an when a wake again dem learn me. "Malavu", that rum, an "Nini so so lango", that is pure water [Kongo nl-laangu, water: Carter 1986: 6].

Them rest me at that, till daylight come. An a sit dung at the tree root, an a see me mother an all the res' o' children them come roun' cause nobody know where I am. An' them cryin' cause them cyaan fine me. An a watching them, but a cyan talk becaw me tongue stiff into me haad an get heavy. So a cyan talk, an a cyan eat. A only sit dung an' look. An a fine a start to sing "Yaaaay . . . Changeli mbala, yabala mdumba Koya kus mdumba . . . Ayee . . . Nima wenda koyo mpe nzonge, Zonge mbala yabula ndombe, Koya ke meka nzonge." An' dem res' me at that. An a next voice come an say,

Ohhh
Madda Margaret gba Kongo
Yerri, yerri Kongo
Nikkita Nikkita Kongo
Yerri, yerri Kongo

(Ohhh

Mother Margaret bawl Kongo

Alas, alas Kongo

Spirits, spirits of Kongo

Alas, alas Kongo.) [Schuler 1980: 740]

An' them res' me at that. An' when it reach six o' clock I still there . . .
An' one time when a look a see a black puss circle the cotton tree, three
time, and him cry say miaow an then a doan see him again.

An' a was there till night come dung an a hear a voice say to me,

Keinto, ye tu wa yetu (woman we are who we are).

Kwenda wa yande sika ya ngoma (go where they are beating the
drums).

[Schuler 1980: 75]

An' a jump out a me sleep for a was dozin', but when a hear the voice a
jump an' say "When?" but him doan say nothin more to me till long time
more when a travellin an dozin', travellin an dozin', him say to me say,
"Aw right Keep on travel till you days is ended."

Well, a keep comin up, comin up, comin up. But me mother still cyan
fine me an she frettin. An' a have a uncle, an she sen an call him, say how
she cyan fine me. An' he tell her doan fret, for if I get the African drums,
dem, I will come out so he will come an' relieve me.

Well they get the drums, an' they buil' a booth, an' them buil' a dress,
an they come roun', an after days they take me out, an they buil' the African
dance. An' after they buil' the African dance, gradually I start to come out,
an I go back home.

An' a man name Man Parker have a African dance in Dalvey, an a leave
me mother in the night to look pon the dance. An when a go there a jus
stan up an fol' me hans so, an everybody dancin, dancin . . . I still stan up
fol' me hans, an like a feel me body jus going to lif' (rise up) . . . A girl jump
an hol' me in mi neck an a drop (I fell). An' after a drop, a jus gone. Is the
Myal hol' me, an I start to dance: an I dancin Kumina now. A do me twenty-
one days at the cotton tree root, an I come out a African Queen.

Queenie Kennedy's Spiritual Experience in a Broader Perspective

The in-depth study referred to earlier by Warner-Lewis [1977] gives useful insights into Queenie Kennedy's life and initial spiritual experience at the root of a cotton tree near her home.

Reminding us that the silk cotton tree is the traditional home of spirits in Africa and the West Indies, Warner-Lewis points out that the young Imogene's location within the hollow base of the tree savours of a return to the womb, which is at the same time a journey into the tomb. The graves of the dead mentors surround the tree so that Miss Queenie (Imogene) enters the world of the dead in order to return with the secret word of life.

The tree root is significant too because it is the nodal point of contact between the nether world and the habitation of those in the flesh. Fixed in the earth, which for African minds carries profound significance as sustainer of life and abode of the dead, the tree draws life through the root. Being in constant contact with this important symbol, the tree becomes central to the procurement of knowledge and truth.

Warner-Lewis notes that in primal mythology, the secret of life is often found through a descent into the world under the surface of the earth. She also calls attention to the African as well as the universal nature of both Mrs Kennedy's symbolism and her religious retreat. This withdrawal phenomenon is universally symptomatic of profound religious disturbance or concentration. Several parallels for this exist. In Hebraic culture, men with a religious vocation wandered off into deserts to commune with the celestial. Jesus and St John the Baptist were such men. Hindu ascetics opt out of ordinary social life and by living alone and travelling about the towns and countryside, achieve that solitude necessary for mystic concentration and release from ordinary mortal concerns. Similarly, Buddhist monks retire into monasteries or choose the way of the pilgrim.

The tree has always played a significant role in religious experience being the vehicle of suffering and/or of wisdom. This has been so at least in the case of Germanic, African, Hebrew and Asiatic religions and it is either while hanging on a tree or seated under one that man enters the spiritual domain. It is interesting to note that in Asia the banyan tree carries the same sacred aura as the silk cotton does in Africa and the West Indies. The Buddha, like Miss Queenie, left his home one day and while seated under a banyan tree, received his enlightenment. There, he first experienced Nirvana: the reconciliation of man's spirit with that of the supreme being [Warner-Lewis 1977: 64, 65].

Like the Buddha, a life of visionary experience was predicted for Miss Queenie. Her seclusion and spiritual communion at the cotton tree root unlocked this dimension of psychic potential and she was promised by the unseen that this gift would always be hers.

Imogene had been chosen to do the work of the spirits for the rest of her life. She realized this, and so did the members, old and young, of the Kumina nation. Her new status was recognized, her prestige assured.

Elizabeth Spence of St Thomas, another contemporary Kumina Queen, reported that her spiritual calling was also effected during a period of isolation [Lewin interview 1969; Schuler 1980]. She slipped away from home one night to attend a Kumina event near Morant Bay. The drums impelled her to dance, soon after which she was knocked violently to the ground by a possessing spirit. This was her first experience of Myal. She remained in this state for four days and four nights, neither eating, drinking nor able to get up. When she came "back to herself", she saw "many different things". Her surroundings were lush and green. The "ole arrivants" came and taught her the African language and a lot of spiritual wisdom.

The story of the life of Emily, a South African ngoma, as told by her husband, also shows marked similarities with the Jamaican experiences, though it was "from her first day in the world (that) her miraculous powers became apparent". On the day of her birth, a pestilence that had plagued her people's cattle disappeared, and "cattle became well again as suddenly as they had been afflicted" [Sachs 1947: 194].

Nor was she like other girls. She refused to do any work; she brooded often for hours; she scarcely associated with her companions; sometimes she would disappear for days; once she disappeared for a week . . . One night she felt a choking feeling as though fire were burning inside her. She left the hut and went to the river. For seven days she stayed under the water with the little people. These people were spirits, and Emily talked to them for seven days. A one-eyed woman led her among them, and at the end of that time, gave her two bundles of roots, one white and one red. With the old woman behind her, Emily climbed up a black pole and out of the water. She came back to her home. For a long time after her return she was very ill. On her head and arms was white paint, which the one-eyed woman had put there. Through this sign the people knew that Emily was chosen by the spirits. Then a great nganga came to the Kraal. He took Emily under his care and taught her witchcraft and the use of medicines [Sachs 1947: 195].

A doctor then pierced her ears and put "medicine" in the incisions. Since then she had been able to hear the spirits talking. For a long time the people thought her mad.

Emily and her work were eventually accepted. Her husband added, "spirits come down to her every day. They stay with her and talk to her. If she becomes angry, however, the spirits go away." And he concluded, "When this happens, Emily loses her voice and feels like one dead." We shall later see Imogene, as Queenie a full-fledged Kumina leader, being struck dumb because the spirits were displeased.

Life in Kingston and St Catherine

Queenie Kennedy had no recollection of the year in which she moved from St Thomas to Kingston. The earliest mention of her in the new location is made by Tanna who, writing of Cyrus Wallace, states that he "became a Kumina leader in the 1930s after he moved to Kingston and met Imogene, 'Queenie Kennedy' " [Tanna 1982].

These two combined to lead a bands in which Elijah Alexander, Queenie's brother, was master drummer. He had been taught first to play the Kbandu by Man Parker in St Thomas. Six years later he was allowed to "mount the cyas". His stamina and skill at improvising rhythms had long been evident; his ability to keep a strong, steady catta tick going for long periods was repeatedly demonstrated.

As we have seen, the cyas drummer is crucial to the success of a bands. He must not only be conversant with information about spirit activity and rhythm requirements but he must also learn the African language and interpret immediately. There are no short cuts to gaining this body of knowledge. Mistakes at this level will confuse singers, dancers and other knowledgeable participants, and threaten the success of any ritual or ceremony. "If you don't play the drum good, an' know what you doing, not a thing happen: not a spirit come, whole night. But that never happen to me yet" [Lewin interview 1966]. Elijah became an excellent playing cyas drummer.

People in Queenie's neighbourhood noticed how adept she was at solving problems. They soon started to take their troubles to her. She remembered people trekking in and out of her yard day after day. Her dogs gave the first warning, and then as the visitors neared her room, the pigeons fluttered and cooed, telling her that, once again, her services were required. There were family friction and domestic disputes; conflict in the community and mischief-making; straying spouses and loss of jobs; pending court cases, sudden illness and creeping depression.

Queenie advised and admonished, anointed and ministered. Sometimes this was not enough, and she asked Baba C. to help her with a ritual: drums, singing, dancing and invocations. Each success led to more requests, concerning, for example, frequent accidents on a building site, or a group stranded many miles from home through poor leadership. In the latter case, Queenie used Kumina music and dancing to raise funds to buy food and provide money to pay for seats in buses or market trucks. Gradually all the members could return home, but a few chose to stay and assist their benefactor.

The difference in attitudes to Kumina and its uses became increasingly evident, as Queenie and Baba C. worked together. He saw it as a religious ritual mainly for private use, and was very selective in giving interviews and passing on information. Though also selective, Queenie was far more open in her attitude. She seemed eager to explain, teach and dispel ignorance and suspicion regarding this cult, which to her was also an effective tool for social change and community solidarity. For Queenie, Kumina was far more than a private religious ritual. After drifting apart for many months, the two leaders made a clean break.

This had its advantages for Queenie. She was more autonomous, could grow according to her own inclinations and develop the distinctive style of leadership which had earned her widespread admiration and respect.

At this period in Queenie's life, she met and married Clinton Kennedy, a mundungo. Asked how her Kumina nation viewed this, she said they had no objection. In the old days some of the elders would have disapproved, since they considered that Kongo marrying Kongo strengthened the nation, and any other liaison weakened it. It was, however, presumed that anyone marrying into the nation knew and had a high regard for its history and heritage. Anything else spelt disaster, even if the "Kongo" spouse was not a Kumina devotee.

Fortunately Clinton and Imogene respected each other's religious convictions, Christian and Kumina. Their wedding reflected this. There was one at a church on the Wednesday, followed by a reception for "the big shot people who no wan go a Kumina" and merriment at her yard where Kumina had started from the Monday before. "Dancing, singing an' dinner. An the day me a go married me buil' a table like wah you see me set up here all de while." This was the culmination of two days' invocation, chanting, drumming and dancing to gain both the approval and the blessings of the ancestral spirits. On the wedding day, two goats and six chickens were killed and cooked for the guests. Drinks flowed freely at both locations. Following the church ceremony, the couple went to the "big" yard. "We cut cake and parson an everybody eat an drink and feel good; the soun' system start an who fe dance, dance and reggae-up themself. Then, we say awright, watch me now, 'Who ah go home wit me?' An you see when me reach home a yard, that time drum dem a bark, you know. An when you go roun' deh go look, in deh dark you know. An me no bother take off me clothes. As me come outta the car with the veil back-a-me, me just make three circle an salo to the drum."

Mrs Kennedy explained that the three circles made at the entrance to the yard and the salo to the drums, were very significant. Marrying in Church was mainly for her husband's sake, he being a practising Christian. There was no conflict for Queenie, since she and other Kumina cultists recognize the Christ spirit, and its unfailing power for good. It was, however, necessary for her to dance into the Kumina yard and greet her ancestral spirits by salo-ing to the drums.

They danced, sang, drummed and made merry all that night. Some persons went into Myal, but all the signs were good. The couple could rest assured that the deceased arrivants and other spirits approved and blessed them. They also knew that they had the support of the contemporary nation. A week of feasting ensued. "So," commented Queenie, "when me married, is Kumina me married into. I have to live good and obey the rules."

An incident after a Kumina duty in St Thomas underlined how important it was for the rules to be obeyed. One of the dancers fell to the ground in what people saw as Myal. They were preparing to place her between the drums and pass fire around her head to bring her back to normal. However, a doctor in the audience insisted that the dancer had hit her head and was unconscious: she should be moved quickly and carefully for him to take her to hospital. After much argument, the people reluctantly complied. When the doctor left, the session soon came to an end.

The dancer died the next day.

Distressed at the news, the doctor returned to the village to apologize for having interfered. For the people, the question was not how, but why the woman had died, so no blame was attached to him. She had been living with another villager's husband. They were convinced that for this, disapproving spirits had struck her.

In Kumina, the approval of the unseen, but ever watchful, world is more important than that of human beings. Anyone, even Mrs Kennedy, could lose spiritual gifts, be struck with illness or be disabled, were they to offend the spirits or in any way fall short of Kumina rules/principles.

Queenie often spoke in front of her husband of his roving eye, adding that she pulls him back whenever she feels that their marriage is threatened. Otherwise, since she would take drastic action if he were to get really out of hand, she could not be sure of using methods of which her ancestors would approve. Prevention was therefore better than cure. Signs of Kennedy's straying were taken even more seriously by Queenie's drummers. One, Elijah, being her brother, caused serious family problems. His open antagonism to his brother-in-law tended to increase and prolong tensions long after Queenie would have wished to settle matters amicably. His sister's attitude puzzled Elijah, and even caused him to leave her Kumina compound and live elsewhere for many months; a serious step for him to take, as Master Drummer, without her approval. Such action made it difficult for Queenie to balance the roles of queen, wife and sister. However, she succeeded in re-establishing harmony in the home and bringing her brother back into the fold. It should be noted that, regardless of his whereabouts and his attitude to his brother-in-law, Elijah never withdrew his services as Master Drummer from his sister and Kumina leader.

What is important is that Queenie conducted herself in keeping with ancestral "rules" concerning marriage and family life.

The only child born to Queenie is a middle-aged daughter with a family of her own. They live in another part of the island, but attend Kumina duties, participating in the preparations and in the singing and the dancing. The Kennedys have cared for "about seven children", some from babyhood, others from infancy. They wish this aspect of their lives to remain private since they wish the children to be regarded as their very own, and also to see themselves as such. One son is well known to guests at Kumina and to visiting scholars since he grew up during the years when Queenie was involved with many public Kumina duties, field researchers and media specialists. He was a quiet, home-loving boy with serious interest in his school work. As a student, he maintained creditable standards in academic studies, extra curricular activities and deportment and is now doing well. Queenie, though a loving mother, was the disciplinarian, her husband always supporting her stand. Nevertheless, he could be depended on to pour oil on troubled waters and dry the tears.

While she was living in Kingston, Queenie kept fairly good health apart from one serious bout of "spirit sickness". This came upon her because she was present when a man slashed the head of a consecrated Kumina drum, a serious violation of Kumina principles. It caused her to get a "bad bounce" (psychic shock). The incident occurred one evening, and by next morning her "tongue was heavy" and she could not speak. She remained dumb for twenty-one days. In an interview with Hazel Ramsay in 1986, she mentioned that she also wandered about, not always conscious of where she was or what she was doing. Members of her bands took turns to shadow and protect her. On one occasion she was snatched from the path of an oncoming train as she stood on the line, neither seeing nor hearing its approach.

Her bands tried to help her with music and dancing but failed. A friend from the University College Hospital of the West Indies brought doctors to treat her, but that too failed. It was therefore decided that a healing duty be held for her. The requirements were provided by her student friend, and on the night of the duty, Queenie was "delivered" from her sickness, and spoke.

Scholarly Interest, National and International Exposure

The student friend was Edward Seaga. As a sociology student, he had been preparing a study on religious cults in Jamaica. With the help of the Para-Psychology Foundations Inc. of New York and scholars such as M.G. Smith and Harold Courlander, he was later able, in 1956, to share some of his findings through an Ethnic Folkways Library disc and pamphlet. These were the first major publications to include Kumina music and information on its instruments, language, beliefs and ceremonies.

Queenie had contributed significantly to these. She tells of travelling in an open-backed truck from Kingston to St Mary to perform a Kumina duty when she and her bands noticed a car that seemed to be following them at a discreet distance. Eventually when it crossed the river at the same fording that the truck had used, they knew that it was no coincidence. At their destination, a young man came out of the car and stood a short distance from the clearing where preparations had been made for the Kumina event. Queenie went over to him and asked, "Can I help you, sir?" He explained his interest and sought permission to observe the proceedings. She invited him to draw nearer.

That was the beginning of an association which developed from scholarly interest, to participation and lifelong friendship. It was also to lead to Kumina being brought to public attention, initially through the National Festival of Arts and then through the development of wider interest in the cult. This trend was enhanced by theatrical interpretations, especially that presented by Jamaica's National Dance Theatre Company.

Kumina, and Queenie in particular, became great attractions not only at Independence Festivals from 1963 onwards but also at national events and private functions across Jamaica. These led to participation in international events, including the 1971 Joint Conference of the International Folk Music Council (now the International Council for Traditional Music) and the Inter-American Council on Ethnomusicology (CIDEM), the 1975 American Festival of Folklife in Washington DC, the Caribbean Festival of Arts (Carifesta) in 1976 in Jamaica, and in Barbados in 1981, the Commonwealth Institute Focus on the Caribbean (Ancestral Voices) in London in 1986, and the Edinburgh Festival of the same year.

Queenie always held her audiences spellbound with her commanding vocal style, exciting dancing and confident and informative responses to the questions that flooded across the footlights. She was even more impressive in intimate settings, such as a lawn in Kensington Gardens, London, or the garden of a friend, a professor or a diplomat. Contact with "Mother Clay" also increased her vitality.

Kumina began to be seen on television in the 1960s. This and public performances subsequently attracted the attention of several scholars, particularly Africans and Africanists, to what was manifestly a strong link with Jamaica's African past. These scholars included Chief Fela Sowande of Nigeria, Klaus Wachsmann, Hugh and Andrew Tracey of South Africa, Kwabena Nketia of Ghana, John Akar of Sierra Leone, Igor and Barbara Kopytoff, James Early, Hazel Carter, Kenneth Bilby, K. Kria Bunseki of Zaire, Jack Daniel and John Blacking.

Monica Schuler of Guyana did field research from which, in 1980, she produced an in-depth sociohistorical study of the Central Africans who came to Jamaica as indentured labourers in the mid-nineteenth century, bringing customs and beliefs which developed into Kumina. Edward Brathwaite and Maureen Warner-Lewis of the University of the West Indies also wrote stimulating and informative papers based on the life and work of Queenie Kennedy in 1977 and 1978, respectively. These and Hazel Carter's essays on the linguistic aspects of Kumina, as well as comments by Martha Beckwith and Frederic Cassidy, have provided useful source material. Joseph Moore, Donald Hogg, Leonard Barrett and several others have also published works dealing with Kumina or mentioning aspects of it.

In most of these, Queenie Kennedy is mentioned by name. Even when she is not quoted or referred to, it is safe to assume that she and her work contributed to the study. Queenie Kennedy's openness regarding her cult and her calling was consistent in spite of the strong disapproval of many members of the Kumina nation, and exploitation by some of the "mundungo" with whom she has shared her priceless knowledge.

New Homes, New Problems Solved

The Kennedys moved house in the later 1960s. Still in Western Kingston, the new yard at first seemed cramped and unsuitable for Queenie's work, but their vision of this new setting must have gone far beyond what my eyes could see. In less than a year, it had been transformed and was described by Maureen Warner-Lewis after her interview in 1971 as follows:

> Miss Queenie is now in her mid-40s and lives with her husband and children in a yard in lower Kingston. You enter the yard from a wide unpaved roadway, pushing at a large zinc door that opens on to a square fenced-off compound. To the left, there is a piece of open ground shaded by a tree. The earth everywhere is swept clean. Deeper in the yard stand the houses, wooden, neat in size and appearance. You need to bypass some three or four before you reach Miss Queenie's little home, tucked away in

a corner of the enclosure and itself fenced off from the other residences. The gurgling of Miss Queenie's doves announces to anyone who has visited doctor-priests anywhere in the Caribbean that you have arrived at your destination, for you had set out to interview a queen of a Kumina 'bands'. In such a context, you may be sure that the shrubs and vines around the front of the little home have more than decorative value. For in African religion, healing is accomplished by spiritual means, and herbs are one of the agents of cure. The doves too play a part in effecting not only physical cure but also the psychic restoration of balance between man and the spirit world since they are meant for sacrifice – blood sacrifice. By virtue of the life-sustaining quality of blood, it forms the most eloquent symbol of that self-denial, that renunciation which man intends to signify when he makes offerings to the spirits.

Queenie's activities continued to develop along the lines established at her previous home: private and public Kumina duties, interviews and specially arranged sessions for scholars, students and media programmes. Queenie was by this time a national figure. She had won several gold and other medals for Traditional Dancing in Festival events, received citations and certificates from academic institutions and civic organizations at home and abroad, which earned her country's respect and recognition. It also attracted violent verbal attacks from some Christian groups who had become aware of the deeper levels of Kumina through the media and considered it to be devil worship, the blood sacrifice, a heathen practice quite unworthy of twentieth century Jamaica. Queenie was little less than disdainful of the criticism. "What about Jesus?" she asked. "Don't he shed his blood and don't them say them drink it every Sunday? An' what 'bout the whole heap of cow and pig and goat them kill to eat. We use one goat, or two dove or two chicken for a cleansing, an' to help all them too." Queenie's perception of the blood sacrifice is reflected in Mutwa [1966: 286]: "Go, oh honourable goat . . . Go straight to hell and take all our sins with you . . . and leave us in peace and happiness."

Other problems began to create difficulties for Queenie, her family and her work. Political divisiveness grew alarmingly during the 1970s.

273

Crowded, rundown areas of Kingston, like the one in which the Kennedys lived, became particularly restless and discordant. There were outbreaks of violence. Many of those who could not move to more peaceful neighbourhoods tried to protect themselves by being tight-lipped and neutral. Queenie would do neither. She claimed to be defending not a person or a political party, but "the right way". This provoked serious hostility from a small but vehement group towards her, her work and all who continued to associate with her. Although Queenie was not intimidated, her work suffered. The situation was solved when in 1975 the decision was made to level her part of Kingston for urban development.

A few weeks before Queenie and a group of Kumina musicians and dancers, including Mr Kennedy, were to leave for the American Festival of Folklife in Washington DC, the Kennedys found a plot of land almost twenty miles away in the village of Waterloo in St Catherine. They at once removed their belongings and the materials from which their rooms were made to this location. Family, friends and members of the Kumina bands worked assiduously to clear the new site and erect enough living accommodation to keep them and their belongings safe. Two separate rooms were built; one for Mr and Mrs Kennedy, their "son" and the person who would look after him during his parents' absence in the USA, the other for her Master Drummers, Elijah Alexander, and Bertram Kelly.

The plot of land was spacious, but very rocky. The men made a sturdy fence of wooden posts, lumber and zinc. The dogs would live under the Kennedy house, the doves in the coops that had been brought from Kingston. Their son was responsible enough to find his way to and from school in Kingston, until better arrangements could be made.

When the Kennedys left for the USA, their minds were at ease. All would be well at home until they returned. The Kumina bands was a great success at the Festival in Washington. Queenie, as usual, electrified the audience, and was invited to lead her group and participate in performances in other cities.

On returning to Jamaica, Queenie set about picking up the pieces of her life as wife, mother and Kumina queen. This did not take long, although she was at first viewed with suspicion by her new neighbours.

Even Queenie was surprised at how quickly a path was beaten to her door by friends and associates from the old days, visitors from abroad, representatives of national and international media and other organizations soliciting her help and participation in various programmes and events. Queenie was delighted. She was busy, but not too busy to prepare for a duty to have her new home blessed by the ancestral gods and spirits.

This was a big and joyous affair. Guests and friends arrived from Kingston and beyond. Kumina devotees from St Thomas, Portland and Kingston converged on the clearing within the Kennedy's rocky yard. Members of Queenie's bands, scattered by the relocation of their leader, were early on the scene, a few having taken up residence days in advance in order to prepare for the duty. A notable participant was Queenie's uncle who had helped to "deliver" her after her sojourn at the cotton tree root in St Thomas many years before.

The duty must have been very successful for Queenie and her family had a good life in Waterloo. Money and this world's goods were sometimes in short supply, but that is not the relevant measure of success in Queenie's world. Her work prospered, her marriage stabilized, her older "children" were making their way in life, the younger ones improved in health and social adjustment. Her services were constantly in demand at deep as well as academic and entertainment levels. Her neighbourhood had accepted her, the children loved her and the nation honoured her with the Order of Distinction, one of its highest awards, for outstanding service in the area of heritage protection, so crucial to a young nation.

10

Queenie: Her Teachings and Her Work

In Queenie's world, she owned nothing. She was specially chosen to be a channel through which the spirits, in turn, are agents of King Nzambi, the supreme God. Her talents and physical needs were all provided to enable her to carry out her commission. Failure to do so earned her swift and unpleasant punishment. She explained that one is punished not for but by one's actions or inertia, as the case may be. Those who know better should, therefore, even for their own sakes only, do better. It is also incumbent on them to help those who wish to improve themselves. Sharing knowledge, wisdom and expertise is one sure way of doing this.

For this reason, Queenie believed that questions asked about Kumina should be answered, as long as ancestral secrets are not divulged; that songs, drumming and dances should be taught even if their full significance is not explained; that customs and beliefs that have proved their worth through many generations should be passed on.

Fortunately for hundreds of scholars, students and people who were simply asking to see the quality of their own and other lives improve, Queenie was an excellent communicator and dynamic teacher. But for Queenie Kennedy, words were not enough. Beliefs must underpin one's lifestyle, and talents become instruments of peace, harmony and healing.

Most of the information in this chapter which deals with Queenie's beliefs, teaching and work has been gleaned from interviews I conducted with her from 1966, complemented by the work of Hazel Ramsay-McLune since 1971.

Birth, Life on Earth and Death

Queenie saw existence on earth as but one phase of an ongoing and endless life. We enter it through birth and leave at death. At that time, one part of the spirit returns to the world of King Nzambi (and spirits at peace), while the other either remains in the grave or wanders restlessly about, sometimes even doing mischief. While on earth, the human being is preparing not only to join the ancestors and enter King Nzambi's world, but also to be able to return and share knowledge and experience gained on earth with those still struggling with human problems. This happens through possession or by spirits "mounting" human beings whose minds and bodies are made receptive with the help of, for instance, music and dancing.

Such beliefs give rise to many customs, ceremonies and rituals relating to birth, life on earth and death.

A new baby is considered a precious gift to the Kumina nation, and should be properly welcomed when nine days old. Family and friends celebrate the birth with dancing and a feast. It is a happy, light-hearted affair, at which no one goes into Myal. Speeches and invocations are made, gifts are presented to mother and child, and chickens or doves sacrificed on their behalf.

Naming the baby used to be entirely a Kumina affair, but nowadays children are usually christened and named in a church. Even so, for the child to thrive it should be named on the advice of an ancestor. It must be noted that in Queenie's world view, the baby comes through and not from its parents, who provide only the physical home for the life which is spirit. The infant arrives with its own history and its own name. These are known to the ancestral spirits who pass the information to a close relative or specially appointed "choosing" man or woman in a dream or flash of inspiration. Ignoring ancestral advice and using the "wrong" name can cause confusion and even illness. To counteract and cure this condition, the spirits must be placated with music, dancing, a feast and, at times, even a sacrifice, and the use of the "right" name.

According to Queenie, life on earth is intended by the supreme god to be peaceful and harmonious. Human beings through ignorance and sin defeat King Nzambi's purpose, thereby causing problems which manifest themselves in "all kinds of sickness", physical, mental and spiritual, strife in families, communities and the wider world, diseases in plants and animals, and disasters in the world of nature.

She told of "ole arrivants" who could influence the weather, like Manuka, the rain-maker. He is remembered in a Country song the words of which are not shared with mundungos. We heard the name Manuka and the word "lango" and recalled that the spirits at the cotton tree taught Queenie that "soso lango" means pure water.

Everyone is given a talent which should be used for the benefit of all. Some, like Queenie, are specially endowed. She was a healer: one in a succession that leads back to the ancestral home, since some who came as indentured labourers were "medicine men". But they all depend on the help of their ancestral spirits, called by the playing cyas drum, and by King Nzambi whose rhythm the Kbandu plays to effect the cures, whatever the ills might be.

The greater the gift, the greater is the responsibility. Watching Queenie as she prepared for a duty, one realized how seriously she took every little detail: the colour of flowers, candles and cloth; the position of the water; the food and drinks to be arranged on the table; the containers for moncy donated as each candle was lit; the absolute cleanliness of the setting and everything to be used. She checked on the special loaves; the glass which she would later fill with water and balance on her head as she danced; the rum to consecrate the drums, wipe over the faces and hands of the drummers, pour as libation to the earth spirits and blow to the spirits of the air and the sky gods. She tested the strength of the table, made of lengths of board resting on wooden supports so that it could be dismantled easily once the food and drinks had been given to the participants and guests. Until then, it had to be strong enough to withstand a bounce or two, should a possessed dancer move too suddenly to be restrained. Queenie's friends and members of her bands assisted with the preparations by fetching and carrying, sweeping, cleaning and washing, but Queenie always kept a stern eye on everything. As other Kumina devotees, guests and members of the public arrived, Queenie became less visible. It was time to prepare herself not only physically by a thorough cleansing, but also mentally and spiritually. The success of the duty would depend on how she conducted and guided the activities, seen and unseen, for the next twelve hours.

The quality of life on earth depends on the harmony maintained with other forms of life, particularly with those beyond the grave. The mission of persons like Queenie is to liaise between the visible world of human beings and the invisible but very real one of the departed spirits. Such persons must help to maintain the harmony on which health and happiness depend, or re-establish it when human limitations and ignorance disturb or destroy it.

Death, being a gateway to another phase of life and a means of rejoining ancestors, is an occasion for celebration rather than sadness. Those who die must be given a proper farewell and burial, or their spirits cannot rest. They might then return to punish or annoy those who had neglected them, with illness and other problems. It is better to avoid having to placate the spirits of the departed with special duties by giving the dead a proper burial and a tombing a year or so later.

The corpse of a Kumina devotee is supposed to be bathed, anointed and wrapped in a cloth called a "kandala" or, in older terms, a "makutu ku". Burial may be Christian, but there should also be a ceremony called a Mourning Table or Memorial Dance to ensure the proper departure of the spirit of the dead to the world of King Nzambi. Black and white predominate in clothing, candles and decorations, since black is the symbol of physical death and white of rebirth into the world of ancestral spirits.

Departed members of the Kumina nation sometimes bestow their special gift to someone left on earth. Queenie was given her distinctive style of dancing by Mother Margaret, whose movements older devotees recognized in Queenie after her initiation at the cotton tree. Mother Margaret also used to dance with a glass of water on her head. At duties, Queenie waited until her benefactress approved before performing this feat.

Queenie, who knew and admired Mother Margaret, but was not related to her, had no idea that she would have inherited her skill. When she danced like her benefactress, Queenie also knew that Mother Margaret was also ready to help and advise her, and made herself receptive, either without actually going into a trance or by doing so for only a short time. Help could, therefore, be offered by spirits of the Kumina nation and not necessarily by those of ancestors. It is wise, however, to keep on good terms with elders in life and after death, since their spirits remain close to earthly ties.

The final responsibility to the dead is the tombing. The drums are played at each end of the grave, and the dancers' feet used to actually ram the earth smooth and solid (mash dung the grave), thus finally laying to rest the spirit below. No more will it then wander and/or annoy the human family.

It is important to continue to "feed the dead". Libations are poured, and food is prepared for them (without salt) at every Kumina event, private as well as public. They do not, of course, consume these provisions, but the offerings and the symbol of remembrance and respect please the spirits and keep the vital lines of communication open between the ancestors and their family still in the flesh. This food is buried when and where no non-cultist can see it.

Drumming, singing and dancing are crucial agents of this communication, which in Kumina thought is essential to the well-being of all life on earth.

Queenie as Healer

In order to look at this aspect of Queenie and her work in the world of Kumina, it is necessary to examine the whole belief system regarding health and disease.

In the Kumina world, disease is, as the word says, dis-ease. It exists at many different levels. First, within the individual, manifesting itself physically, mentally or psychically. Then between individuals as in families, and outward through communities to the wider world, causing discord and conflict of varying degrees of gravity. There can also be disease in animals, plants and other levels of nature, or between them and human beings. This is evident in puny and unproductive animals, drought, flood, blight, infestation by pests and failure of crops.

When disease is patently physical, the services of a medical doctor are sought. Queenie, the healer, had no qualms about referring problems which she saw as belonging to a clinic or hospital. She herself was treated by doctors and had been a hospital patient. She usually saw psychic, spiritual and mental problems as being within the realm of dis-ease that could be addressed by Kumina rituals and ceremonies.

Overall, however, whether it be social, physical, psychic, spiritual or mental, it is stressed in Kumina that the cause and not the manifestation of disease is what has to be examined. If the cause is spiritual, then the resulting condition must be dealt with at that level. Any sort of disease can be caused by people offending their ancestral and other spirits or by being attacked by spiritual entities that are directed towards them by persons intent on harming the person or community in question. In situations like this, a healer like Queenie seeks to solve the problem and gets to work. She also sensed people's "spirits" and, if they were uncooperative she behaved accordingly.

When asked how she started to heal, Queenie said, "Is because of the dancing and the singing why I get that; because in the dancing and singing, I get more uplifted and that time I see more gifts coming to me."

Queenie explained that prior to that, she had not considered what she was doing to be actually healing. She could see when things were wrong and put them right. During the twenty-one day period of possession in Kingston, Queenie had wandered about compulsively. At that time, she was conscious of the need to gain more understanding, and in order to do so she had to be possessed and disciplined by the spirits.

Her first real experience of "healing" was in Kingston. It grew out of an incident when she solved a young man's problem in a way that astonished everyone. This man had claimed that someone had stolen a towel which he had taken to the meeting in question. He asked that it be returned. There was no response. Said Queenie, "I spin, a just spin right where a girl was, and when ah spin and go there ah said, 'Anybody who tek the towel, han' it up to me please', an' ah spin back." A little time passed. Nothing happened so she danced again to this girl. At that time she found that she knew that the girl was sitting on the towel though there was no evidence, so she raised the girl's dress exposing the lost article. Pulling it from the girl, she handed it to the man.

Some days later, this same young man brought a woman who had a very putrid sore on her foot. She was in a lot of pain and crying. As a means of testing their confidence in her and ensuring the husband's approval, Queenie asked that the woman return with her husband on Sunday. She then explained to the husband that if he wanted her to work on his wife's foot he would have to leave her for a time. The husband agreed. Queenie stated that she did not then know how she would deal with the situation, so she sat and meditated. After a time, it was as if she heard a voice telling her what to do: "Get a coconut shell, burn it and crush it into powder, then find a bitter cassava and grate it." She was also told to get some olive oil and to take leaves of the chigganut plant and boil them to bathe the foot. She carried out these instructions exactly as told, mixing the cassava with the powdered burnt coconut shell, then adding some olive oil. This she spread on the foot daily for four days. On the fifth day, maggots began to work their way out of the sore. As they came up, she put them into a bottle. When no more maggots came out of the sore, she found that she had thirty in the bottle. At this point, the sore began to run a thin trickle of watery blood. She put ice on it. She treated the foot in this way until it started to heal. The woman was by now feeling much better so it was time to have a Thanksgiving Duty.

Husband and wife provided her with all the necessary food, drink, candles and flowers. At dusk on the appointed day, family, friends and visitors began to gather. Soon the drummers and other percussionists began to play. Kumina folk who had been helping with preparations were gradually joined by others coming from St Thomas and many parts of Kingston. It became a joyous occasion. Queenie, as usual, began the real duty with the prayer "Kwali" which the spirits had taught her at the cotton tree root in St Thomas. Many songs "came" to her that night in addition to others learnt through the years at other leaders' Kumina events. For Queenie there was no question of her composing a song since all Kumina music is passed to the receptive cultist by the spirits. There was little possession on that occasion, but the whole area throbbed with happy drumming and singing. When the table was broken at midnight, many partook.

After this, the woman sent other people to Queenie. They in turn sent others and so her reputation spread. According to Queenie, "I don't have no advertisement. Is jus' my success."

What are the requirements for healing? First, the healer must analyse the situation and know the cause. The manifestation of the underlying reasons may be varied, yet many physical problems respond to the same herb, often with the addition of honey and/or olive oil. It is the administering of it and the surrounding ritual that make the difference. Cleansing is also very important. Queenie had to cleanse herself thoroughly with a bath of soap and water and sometimes also anoint herself with oil and certain carbonated beverages. She and her husband must be living clean lives and keeping their dealings above board. There must be no extramarital affairs and the people and atmosphere surrounding them must be as peaceful and orderly as possible. Water is usually adequate for personal cleansing but blood is sometimes needed. Blood is far more purifying than water and it might also at times be considered advisable for the healer to make a blood sacrifice before directing her attention to the situation to be dealt with.

In all Kumina ceremonies, the blowing of rum is important. Rum must be rubbed into the drum-heads for tuning and, more importantly, to make them attract friendly spirits. It must be poured onto the ground to appease ground spirits, in the air for the spirits of the air and on the person needing to be healed. The special help that Kumina can give arises from its ability to attract and invoke the assistance of ancestral and other spirits. This is done by the duty, which varies according to what is being sought.

The drums are vital. While the Kbandu maintains the steady tu-tum, tu-tum, tu-tum, tu-tum rhythm associated with King Nzambi, the Supreme God, the playing cyas has to weave rhythms that attract the specific spirits being invoked. The spirit that will help with a social situation may not be the one to be involved in a health problem. It is important for the cyas drummer to know what rhythm will attract a particular entity. This is one reason that playing cyas drummers are few whereas there can be many Kbandu players. Queenie's playing cyas drummer was her brother Elijah who had been taught by Man Parker, who had also taught her some of the language and later ritually released her from that period of withdrawal and possession at the root of the cotton tree.

Dancing and singing are essential. They help to attract the spirits during baila songs and, later, to communicate with them in Country songs which use "African language". The interplay and mutual motivation between drummers and dancers and singers is crucial in building up the right atmosphere for the spirit activity necessary to deal with whatever situation is being addressed.

Queenie pointed out that drums are not always used for healing and that many healings take place at private ceremonies. The drums, however, are always brought into play after the healing, when there must be a Thanksgiving for deliverance from the disease. If the drums are not played properly, or if wrong rhythms are played, "You can't," in Queenie's own words, "focus to the dance, you just drop back. But when the right drumming play, you get into the right state. You see, when you sick, you can't get better? So a say, a going to try the drum. Then I will buy me little candle and whatsoever necessary to set up a duty to try for deliverance an see if I can get through."

"Then Queenie, can the drum help you to get the other person better?"

"Yes! Sometimes when it reach all midnight, you tek the sick person out to the drum and if the person can't get up, you spread a sheet on the ground and you put her to lie down. An' you put one a the drum at him head, and one at him foot, and then you start to sing now and pray for him in the language. An' if that person can't turn when it touch certain hours, whether from twelve o'clock to one o'clock, any time that spirit operate pon him, him just shiver, you understand? Any time that drum start to play, yu know is den the spirit them going start to come in and move around you and then focus on that individual who lay down on the ground sick. And then you go now and rest you hand on that person from him head to him stomach and you talk now to the spirits, understand? And you talk in the language, and you ask God for the deliverance at that same time with the drum. And the drummer now, him sit down and him penetrate what you is saying and him is on the drum now and moving up with it with what you speaking for the sick. So this drum matching what I asking the Almighty for, and then you will see that person turn. And after him turn, you can able to help him now and make him sit. And after him sit down, the drummer still playin', you get a little olive oil and you sap him, from head come down. And the foot dem will weak, and you sap him, and you try to help him get up and after you help him and him get up you start to salo with him. That is, dance wid him. After you dance wid him, dance wid him for a little time, you see, you let him go and after you let him go now, you watch him and him start to move him feet them, you understand? But you have to watch him, to hinder him from drap and him start move him feet them and you go on gradually with him. Meantime now you have the rum blowing on him. You understand? But you just burst two bottle of aerated water over him head mek it come down on him."

"Then Queenie, do you always manage to help the person in one time or maybe two?"

"You have to have, say, two and you come out move around him for a little time, you understand? By now him not so bad and him come and lay down a little and by day to light a morning, him feel little more better, then him can able to move. I understand because dat happen to meself, that I can able to move around a little and then go and use the aerated water, the olive oil and bath meself."

"Why aerated water, Queenie?"

"Well, dat tek away plenty destruction. That's why the white aerated water good, you not to jus' drink it so. It move a lot of destruction that was on me, understand? And then now, you use it with the olive oil and you bath yourself. When you rub down youself, souse you foot them and then you move along that time talking to God sincere."

"You talking in the language all this time, Queenie?"

"Yes, is the language you mus' use, understand? You see you talking in the language and yu saying yu prayers in the language."

"Then Queenie, when you have something like that, can other people help you?"

"Yes, other people can come to help, but sometimes them is helping, and sometimes them is helping you down (hindering), I know when I did dumb, people come to help me and then give me salt which them shouldn't do. That time my mouth stop and them giving me salt and salt not to touch me at that time. I just have to make sign and ask for little water, take up me mug and wash out me mouth, you understand?"

"Yes, Queenie. Then the singing, does that help you too?"

"Yes. You see, after the drumming start and somebody start to sing with me, it help me more, because that dullness and that weakness that I have, the singing help me up, you understand? To make me revive more, and if I helping a person, the singing help that person too. So you see, the music itself is a direct powerful thing. It has power in itself to help you along and while I sing, the drum them following right along. Most time a have to sing the whole journey through. I have to sing and that drum have to follow behind."

The following incidents and stories illustrate different facets of health, illness and healing, as seen through the eyes of Queenie and her Kumina people.

Sharing Knowledge and Experience

It was in the late sixties that Queenie became very special to the Jamaican Folk Singers, the group of friends who had come together in 1967 as a result of field research into Jamaica's musical heritage. Although the group was made up of people working and living in Kingston, all had started life in various rural areas. Some had come from quite small villages and had considered themselves knowledgeable about the island's folklore. The research proved how little they had known. It therefore seemed useful and desirable to share and exchange the knowledge that members brought from different parts of the island, first among themselves and then with whoever else so desired.

One of the most exciting sounds that had come out of the field research was that of Kumina: the modal scales, vocal timbre, singing sometimes in unison or at others with the predominance of perfect intervals, very wide vocal gaps and, of course, exciting drum and percussion rhythms. The songs had been introduced by tapes given to the research project by Edward Seaga, who had made them during his sociological studies of Jamaican cults. Realizing the importance of the music and the desirability of having further work done in that area, he had kept the tapes, waiting for an opportunity to pass them on to someone who would work seriously on them and explore the music further.

Queenie was very dynamic and full of confidence, once she was in her own setting. The Jamaican Folk Singers therefore visited her as often as possible at her home base. Whenever she told them of a ritual or ceremony, they made every effort to attend. Eventually they wished to try singing some of her songs and to learn the drumming. She helped them to acquire drums from Kumina drum makers and worked hard for the singers to retain the quality and integrity of the music, even while changing its context.

When Queenie attended a performance by the Jamaican Folk Singers, her first comment, with a chuckle, was, "You trying." Eventually, she reached the stage of wishing to perform with the Singers. They regarded this as a great compliment and welcomed her. There was also an occasion on which, after a performance in a large theatre, a short oral message was received. "Queenie says to come to the yard after the show." The Folk Singers complied. There they found in progress a ritual designed to bless the work they were doing. This made them confident. After that, many performances included Kumina.

On one of her visits to the Folk Singers, Queenie noticed that one of the drums was splitting. She said that it should never again be used. "Why, Queenie?" "It use at a ritual and must not use for entertainment. It splitting, and same way anybody who straddle it will break down." The Singers obeyed.

Queenie had previously told me that my fears about using the drums were groundless. She assured me that the ancestral spirits knew what we were trying to do. Even if we erred, they would not punish us as they would in the same circumstances chastise her, simply because we knew no better. She did. Punishment varied according to circumstances. The same error need not attract the same punishment.

Drumming: "A Gift From God"

In 1973, the Jamaican Folk Singers were due to leave for England for a series of concerts at the request of the Jamaicans who had emigrated there. Through their High Commission, they had asked that we go and raise their spirits in their new and sometimes unfriendly homeland. On the Friday night before the Monday when we were due to leave, the main drummer, who was also a tenor, brought the disappointing news that his company could no longer allow him to be absent from work so he would be unable to go with us. This posed a serious problem. My daughter suggested that we ask Queenie to let one of her drummers go instead. I took her advice. and she herself went to make the request. She called her master drummer, Elijah, and instructed him to prepare to leave for England two days later. A casual labourer, he had been out of work for over two years. His fine personality meant that his lack of formal education and inexperience with etiquette did not matter to us.

Elijah was an inspiration to the rest of the group in the way he prepared himself backstage. An hour or so before the performance, while the rest of us were busy from place to place, he would be seen sitting quietly, eyes closed, or staring intently into space with his head resting on his hands as if in another world. We avoided disturbing him, but when it was necessary to speak with him, we often had to call his name many times before he would respond. He would not allow himself to be jolted.

His performance was electric. It drew warm praise from the English press, with the *Daily Telegraph* singling him out for special mention. This brought home to the rest of us the tragedy of having this brilliant keeper of our culture living from hand to mouth. When he did work, his tasks were hard on his hands and endangered his playing of Kumina drums. We decided that on returning to Jamaica we would spare no effort to get him suitable work. This was harder than envisaged, since there was not much else that he could do. Eventually, the idea came to me that he could teach drumming to the many people who had begun to be interested in this once despised instrument.

I visited him in the crowded run-down area of Kingston where he then shared yard space with Queenie, her family and Kumina adherents. Yes, he would be happy to come. We agreed on Wednesday at three o'clock at my house. People who were approached were overjoyed and arrived in good time on the appointed day. Our drummer did not come. I apologized and promised to see when next he would keep the appointment and let them know. Another journey to his home, another promise that he would come on Wednesday next, three o'clock at my house. Once more we all gathered and waited. Once again we dispersed, disappointed and more despondent than before but still hoping that another meeting could be arranged.

On my third visit to Elijah I told him that I knew there must be something wrong. "Come clean with me, Elijah, tell me what it is." He lowered his head and looked upwards through the corners of his eyes. "Teacher, the drumming is a gift from God, and I can't sell it." Most prospective pupils would not accept his services free of cost.

Elijah could not accept payment for the lessons but subsequently he helped with workshops and in many other ways. However, from then on, I knew that I should never equate his drumming with monetary gain. This, he later told me, would have exposed him to getting "lick" (punished). It would have offended the spirits and they would have had to punish him with illness or loss of speech, some social problem or even death. It was a risk he could not take. Fortunately it was acceptable to slip him some money, suggesting that he get a skin for his drum, buy something for the children or take a taxi home.

Cases and Conditions Cured by Queenie

1. Disquiet in the community

As in all crowded run-down areas of cities, squabbles and tensions arose between residents in Kingston slums. Queenie's neighbourhood was no exception. She, however, could not allow herself to live in a continuously unsettled atmosphere. It would make her ill and weaken her ability to heal. So whenever discord began to be felt, she had to do something about it. She would arrange a duty to invoke the help of ancestral and other spirits in uncovering and working on the root causes of the discord. In her own words, "To make the people behave themselves and live in peace."

The candles, water, aerated drinks, wine, special loaves of bread, flowers and food items would be acquired. The colours blue and green for peace were much in evidence, with the usual white for purity. One such duty that I attended was very successful. It became even more exciting when one of the chief gossips and trouble-makers came by, apparently intending to remain aloof, a little distrustful and negative. Queenie was quick to notice her presence: "She not working with us." She immediately changed the tempo of the drumming, blew more rum, broke bottles of aerated water and sprayed it north, south, east and west. The dancing grew to fever pitch. There were several possessions that night. Later, residents claimed that life in the neighbourhood was much calmer after that night.

2. A mentally ill teenager

In the mid 1970s, a teenage girl suffering from severe mental illness was taken to Queenie by her mother. Her doctor had recommended hospitalization but she could not face this for her child and wanted to see if something else could work. Queenie said, "Leave her, I will see what I can do." She did not divulge details of her diagnosis but the girl stayed with her for many days, during which there were private rituals to relieve her of the spiritual curses that had been laid on her. In Queenie's words "she get a strike, a hard strike", and she had to work tirelessly to rid her of it.

The girl was seen by outsiders on the night when the duty was held to seek spiritual advice. After leaving the gathering for a quarter of an hour or so, Queenie returned with the child, leading her by the hand slowly. She was put to sit at the head of the table, candles were lit and the music, drumming and singing seemed to become more intense as Queenie laid her hands on the child's head and sang many songs in the "African" language.

After a considerable time, Queenie told the child to stand. This she did. Queenie then encouraged her to dance, holding her by both hands and taking her in an anti-clockwise direction around the table, she herself dancing backwards.

The child became increasingly involved in the dancing and Queenie let her go from time to time, always keeping a very close watch on her. After the child danced a few circuits of the table by herself, she was taken back to the little house from which she had been brought a couple of hours beforehand. It was not possible to make any serious judgement of her state, having not known how ill she had been, but it certainly seemed to us that the child was genuinely more in control of herself when she left the duty than when she had arrived. Subsequently, Queenie informed us that she had improved sufficiently to be sent home, and there had been no relapse.

3. Self-diagnosis

In 1976, it became increasingly clear that Queenie was suffering from thyroid malfunction. Her throat was swelling and she was very excitable. A doctor, shortly to emigrate, offered to examine her and, if necessary, operate. Queenie, would have none of it. She wanted to check it with the spirits first. In accordance with her usual methods, she "made contact with the spirits" and returned with the news that she had neglected them the previous New Year's Eve, by not offering them a large enough duty. That was the cause of the problem.

Ten years later, Queenie had to admit that there was something wrong with her glands. She was confident that the condition had affected her heart, resulting in palpitations when she overexerted herself and causing her high blood pressure problems. It was interesting to note that having placated the spirits she was no longer afraid of what might happen to her because of the problem. She felt that it was just a simple physical matter which could be dealt with by medical doctors and their remedies. Accordingly, she often consulted a doctor and carefully followed his instructions.

4. Social unrest

During the 1970s, Jamaica underwent severe partisan political upheaval. The society became very polarized and there was much violence. This disturbed Queenie greatly and, in keeping with her beliefs, she decided to ask her ancestors to assist her in bringing "peace to the land".

She therefore held a very special, large duty. There were extremely intense prayers and offerings of aerated drinks to the four corners of the earth, as well as sacrifices of both a goat and a chicken. She herself went into Myal and complained that she and others would need to endure great suffering to "come through". She assured us that a lot of the violence and many of the problems were caused not by what seemed to be the reason, that is, political antagonisms, but by "wicked heartedness". She stated quite confidently that as long as people did not search and cleanse themselves, the violence would continue.

5. Serving her time

Queenie had once witnessed the desecration and defilement of Kumina drums. This was a very serious matter. As it happened, she did not see how she could do anything about it, but was punished and struck dumb. In her own words, as quoted by Warner Lewis [1977]:

A went to me bed de night
An' when a went to me bed an' wake de mornin'
A fine me tongue heavy
An' when a decide to talk a couldn' talk

A feel a did get a bounce

A get a terrible bounce.

You see a man cut de drum an' den a get a bounce,

Spirit.

An' a get dumb an' come home

An' a was dere an' couldn' talk.

She relates that after serving her time, she felt that she could ask the spirits' forgiveness and help in restoring her speech. She was low in funds, however, and also feeling rather isolated and threatened because of the enemies who had exploited her situation and spoken out against her. There was also the possibility, she said, of her being poisoned by people motivated by jealousy and encouraged by her silence. She appealed to a highly placed friend for assistance with providing an animal for sacrifice, various food provisions, drinks and candles. These were as usual forthcoming.

Queenie informed me that she had a "hard journey" on that occasion, but eventually "came through" after the four cardinal points had been honoured and a lot of rum blown on the drums to invite spirits that would help her. She danced particularly energetically hoping that the spirit whose dancing she had inherited, would come to her aid. After the blood sacrifice and the breaking of the table, there was a period of tension and stillness. Everyone, including herself, hoped and felt confident that she would receive her speech, but no one could be sure. There was an air of expectant optimism. Queenie was sweating and exhausted. She retired to her room, leaving the assembled company. Some were quiet, some drifted away. The drums continued to play. Those who cared, sang and danced, more gently now as the candles which had been removed from the Table and set on the ground near the drums burned lower and lower. As dawn crept up, the drums were silent.

Next morning Queenie was able to speak.

6. Earth enriched by the drums

When Queenie moved to her home in Waterloo in 1975, the site was mainly rocks. It became a veritable Garden of Eden. In 1987, Queenie took me by the hand "to show me something". It was a little circular section in the barren yard beaten hard by much dancing. This plot, about three feet in diameter, was like an oasis. In it, plants were growing in profusion, blooming and succulent. There was even a healthy gourd vine growing upwards. Beaming, Queenie watched me as I said, "This is wonderful. How is it so lush?" She chuckled, "Is here the drums usual play. The spirits love the spot and give it plenty life."

7. A secret formula

When Queenie was asked how many children she had, she would pause. She knew she had given birth to only one, a daughter, but had to count how many she had "raised". Her husband helped her. It was seven.

In 1985, a baby, very fretful, undernourished and apparently with a hearing defect, was left on Queenie's doorstep. As usual, she took the child in. According to Queenie, he was also a little mentally retarded, but she felt that it was because of some curse that had been put on him. She decided to keep the child and try to release him from the curse. She has never divulged the methods that she used, apart from saying that she and her husband "try hard with him". They gave him nourishing food and a lot of loving attention.

Two years later, the child was a sturdy toddler. He was unable to form any words, but was healthy, quite well-adjusted socially, and responsive to the drums. Queenie hoped that his hearing would return and, with that, his ability to speak would develop. However, his parents took him home at this time and she heard no more of him.

Also in 1985, Queenie's husband brought me a message. She needed to speak with me. Was it urgent? He did not think so, but she "well wanted to see me". At my first opportunity therefore, I made space for Queenie. She seemed to be in a state of suppressed excitement. "What is it Queenie?" The messengers had visited and told her that she must feed the people. "Which people?" The old people at the Golden Age Home. This was the new home for the aged that had replaced the dreadfully run-down Eventide Home when it was destroyed in a disastrous and tragic fire. The new compound with its clusters of pleasant cottages was spacious, with room for beautifying the surroundings and, if necessary, adding new cottages. Business and private organizations were encouraged to adopt a cottage or a cluster and provide furnishings, appliances, food and general services. Government gave financial assistance and put a permanent staff in place. It was to this home that Queenie referred. She wished me to find out how many people were in one cluster and obtain permission for her to visit them, taking lunch for that group. A date was set. Queenie and her bands set to work, buying rice, a goat, bread, seasoning, everything needed to feed fifty people. They cooked through the night.

The Memory Bank provided transportation for Queenie and her team. When they arrived, there were speeches of appreciation from the administration but, more moving, from the inmates themselves who were overcome at the thought of someone who was obviously of very modest means even thinking of doing something of this magnitude for them. Queenie was asked to bless the food. She lifted up her voice in thanksgiving to God for the opportunity to be of service, then moved into her chant and the Kumina Prayer. The air was electric. She and her bands members served a rich soup, curried goat, rice, bread, and a fruit drink to the inmates who were more than satisfied and also enjoyed the special camaraderie. Some months later, Queenie repeated the exercise.

It was much later that she told me how all this had come about. Someone who viewed her as an obeah woman had approached her with a request to hurt someone against whom he bore a grudge. Queenie refused. "I only help people," she said. "Then help me," said the man. Queenie tried to persuade him to let her cleanse him of the grudge he was bearing. She explained that if she directed evil towards anyone it would return to her. The man was not convinced. He left money for her to go to work, and refused to take it back.

That was the money Queenie had used to feed the people. The man had provided a service of which he was not even aware but which she asserted would nevertheless cause him to be blessed.

Queenie as Leader

Queenie and her husband both believed that her ability to heal resulted primarily from her knowledge and use of music, dance and "African" language. Her recognition and capacity to operate as a cult and community leader grew out of this. Queenie herself has said that she was chosen to be the leader of Kumina in Jamaica by the Prime Minister of the day, Sir Alexander Bustamante. However, harking back to her own words, "I have no advertisement for my healing, just my success", it seems to me that she is the leader because she has proved her ability to lead.

First she became leader of her Kumina bands. The members recognized her as the most knowledgeable person regarding cosmology, language, use of songs, drums, rhythms and movements to entertain the spirits and attract their help in solving problems. From this her leadership spread outwards into the community.

As healer, Queenie dealt not only with the diseases of individuals, but also with social ills. Tensions and hostilities in the neighbourhood and beyond were conditions towards which she successfully directed her energies. Her ability to resolve conflicts and make people agree was acknowledged and respected.

Three major factors contributing to Queenie's elevation to leadership were:

(1) Her work as healer/therapist not only among the Kumina "nation" but also to people beyond it. In a small country like Jamaica, the news of her ability to heal many different types of illness travelled far and fast along the still efficient "bush telegraph". Her success generated confidence and enhanced her ability to lead.

(2) Her competence and absolute authority at rituals and ceremonies which identified her as someone with tremendous drive and power to lead.

(3) Characteristics of her life which set her on a pedestal.

In her home parish, St Thomas, she was recognized as someone special after her twenty-one days of withdrawal and preparation which set her apart. She now had powers. She was fluent in the "African" language, danced as had the late revered Mother Maragaret, even balancing a glass of water on her head. When she moved to Kingston, she joined forces with Cyrus Wallace, a very highly respected Kumina leader based there. They added to each other's prestige.

In Kingston, Kumina was not well or widely known, but in the neighbourhood in which it was practised, Queenie's authority was even more marked. With the coming of the Jamaica Festival of Arts, her special qualities became known beyond the Kumina areas. Her spectacular dancing and singing, her ability to guide and control a group of persons simply by the power of her personality and inner strength, made a deep impression on those who saw her perform in person as well as on the media.

All these elements were building her reputation, not simply as a dancer and an expert on Kumina, but as a leader. Persons wishing to have information on the cult, its activities, the interpretation of movements, translation of songs, the reason for the use of certain rhythms and symbolic acts, were confident that they could be informed and instructed by Queenie. If she chose not to divulge any matter, this had to be accepted. Normally, in Jamaica, people who have had a formal education and belong to the middle or upper classes would expect someone like Queenie, with little formal education and of humbler social standing, to look up to them and be ready to please them. Yet in the case of Queenie, it was the other way around.

When Queenie came to Kingston, those who had accepted her leadership in St Thomas still did so. If she was officiating at a duty in Kingston or if they themselves had a problem, they still turned to her. The political upheavals of the 1970s forced her out of Kingston, and she re-settled well off the beaten track in Waterloo in St Catherine, west of Kingston, so that she was moving further and further away from St Thomas in the East, the centre of Kumina, and from people who accepted her as Queen and foremost exponent of their cult. But even when she left physically her spiritual position had not changed: she had simply added

Kingston to her domain. If there was an important ceremony or ritual in

St Thomas, Kingston or St Catherine, different groups converged. Queenie was often specially invited to participate, with her drummers and members of her bands. Similarly, she invited drummers and other important members of Kumina bands from St Thomas and Kingston to assist with duties in her new home.

A brief look at membership of the Kumina cult shows that most members were:

(A) Self-employed: small farmers, traders in their own farm produce; or their family members;
(B) Casual labourers or junior staff in the private and public sectors

The (A) members are rooted to the area in which they live and own property but can choose to travel to and attend, even overnight, events away from home. Once they decide to participate in Kumina events, they are usually very loyal and dedicated members. Those under (B) are less independent and self-sufficient. Unless very dedicated, their involvement may be less sustained and more liable to fluctuations since their livelihood largely depends on their employers, who would probably not accept their absences from work. In addition, persons who work in the public or private sectors may be cautious about belonging to a cult group in case they lose the social mobility desirable in a work situation or the approval of peers who may belong to disapproving groups such as the Evangelicals or Pentecostals.

In St Thomas, Kumina was an integral part of the social fabric, generally known and attracting a lot of support. In Kingston, Queenie Kennedy had built up respect for her remarkable competence and talent in leading Kumina ceremonies as well as for her leadership in the communities in which she lived. In her new neighbourhood, the situation was different. When she moved with her household to the two houses at Waterloo she found that, although she was supreme on their own premises, those living in the neighbourhood were suspicious and hostile, especially those who were members of the Pentecostal church. Some looked upon her as an obeah woman and dealer in witchcraft. They considered it their Christian duty openly to disapprove of her. Queenie was not upset. She said that she would give them time, knowing that, eventually, they would understand and change their attitude.

The disapproval did, however, affect her and her Kumina activities in that some of those who had been supporters and who had even taken part in ceremonies began to drift away. They did not want to risk losing friendships or work. Gradually, it became evident that nothing sinister was happening behind the high zinc fence surrounding the Kennedy homestead. The villagers saw that the children gravitated towards Queenie and that she helped them. She put on Kumina "plays" to enliven their holidays and to raise funds to buy books and other school supplies for them. If they were hungry or ill they would go to her. It became evident that Queenie was doing good. The open hostility began to subside and she began to be called not Queenie, but Goddie, a term of respect and affection. That they chose to call her by this commonly used abbreviation for godmother rather than "Queenie" indicates that they saw her as a caring woman, rather than as a cult leader.

The power of Queenie's personality, the effect of the drums, singing and rhythms on even those who wished to remain aloof, caused concern and even alarm in people who considered themselves above associating with her and her "pagan practices". Queenie did not allow attitudes to affect her activities. In fact, at some of her duties, she was very outspoken in her discourses. She knew of people's suspicions, that some were trying to work against her and were discouraging their children from associating with her. She also emphasized that she was doing good work – God's work, adding, "Whom God love, no man curse." She was still being visited by admirers and people who needed her help, advice or healing and she was also visited by well-known and respected members of the wider Jamaican society. Nevertheless, she was not yet as busy as she would have liked to be. It was difficult for her to wait patiently for her services to be sought. She filled her time with homemaking and gardening, bringing life to the barren earth.

Waning Physical Powers

Queenie gradually became noticeably less sturdy. At the Kumina ceremony on New Year's Eve, 1986, she danced for no more than ten minutes at any one time. Years before she would have danced all night, with energy that seemed never to flag. Her lack of stamina was due partly to health problems which caused her to become noticeably out of breath after short periods of energetic dancing. It was very difficult for Queenie to change her intense and dynamic style of movement. When the drums played, her response was instant, her involvement total.

Fortunately, 1987 saw a marked improvement in her physical condition, thanks to the constant care of an admiring doctor. As far as her mental and spiritual strength and her capacity to heal were concerned, Queenie then was potent as ever, still enjoying public confidence. Having raised seven children, and been busy in Kumina for decades, Queenie was once again bringing up children left in her care.

These added responsibilities did not perturb her, though she and her very supportive husband were by no means affluent; she managed well on her husband's modest salary, augmented by donations and presents. "I have to help the poor," she said. "I am poor too, but that is what the Messengers say I am to do." She, therefore, expected God to provide or to show her how to provide for herself and anyone who needrd it. She declared that her faith had never failed her. Even when food and money had been very short, she and her family never went hungry. Somehow, something always turned up.

Ordinary folk would find the uncertainty of funds worrying; not Queenie. Her husband helped her to throw a "partner", but this was set aside for specific uses. Some cash came from grateful people whom she had healed. She could not, however, make any specific charge for her healing work. Equating the gift from God and her ancestral spirits with personal gain would be a very serious offence.

Thrift and Resourcefulness

One of Queenie's great assets was her resourcefulness. She saved and, for instance, if someone gave her money to buy a goat for a sacrifice, she tried to get one that would have kids before the event. When the kids arrived, she cared for them, kept one for a future feast and sold the other. When she danced with the glass balanced on her hand, people would drop coins into it and, at duties, when one lit a candle, one made a donation, and so on. Queenie emphasized that this money could not be spent on her household or herself; it had to be used "for the good of the people". To this end, when there was cash in hand, she would buy and store away staple foods which would then be available when anyone seemed hungry or asked her for food. They never left empty-handed.

Queenie also saved for duties. She was obliged to have one at the end of the year. Another was sometimes held to honour our slave ancestors on July 31 and to celebrate Emancipation Day at dawn on August 1. Certain supplies were needed for the duty and at least one animal or bird for the sacrifice. Close friends helped, though Queenie rarely itemized her needs. The duty was essentially her responsibility and she shouldered it squarely. One, however, was always conscious of Queenie's strong faith that help would be forthcoming and that her friends would become the hands through which God and friendly spirits provided for her. So helping her was not seen as simply a human act, but as spirit working through a human being.

It must be remembered, too, that in Queenie's world view, it is dangerous to ignore traditional ancestral rites. To neglect them is to risk being "bounced" or "licked" with illness, social problems, or, as happened to her, being struck dumb. In extreme cases, even a life might be lost. When, in human frailty, people ignore spiritual duties, there has to be a ritual to make restitution and re-establish harmony that will counteract the resulting punishment and bring back again healthy conditions of one type or another. Spirits have been shown working for good and through human beings. They can also cause mischievous or destructive behaviour. People in Myal states sometimes act violently. One man would bite when he got into the spirit. Nobody blamed him. They would try to tie his mouth so that he did not hurt other people who were also expected to keep out of his way. In the Kumina belief system, such a man is not seen to be himself biting, but an evil spirit working through him. The same attitude is evident when someone in Myal tries to hit people. The use of drums and fire eventually resolves such situations. Queenie would direct this and had a few strong persons in reserve, ready to moderate violent behaviour until ritual means succeeded.

Queenie herself unquestioningly carried out the instructions of the spirit messengers, the Nkuyu. It is from them that she derived the strength to carry out their commands. They never failed her, and she was confident that they never would.

Queenie Kennedy's prime concern was to recognize or identify her successor and pass on "the knowledge an' the language". She had tried to teach various adults, "but they cyan take it more than so, an' the children too young and modern". Youngsters were learning to play the drums and to dance, but no one was ready for instruction in language and cosmology. Queenie continued to look and to try, but she knew that should she die without having identified a successor the matter would be in the capable hands of the ancestral spirits.

11

Conclusion

To collect and study Jamaican folk music, its surrounding lore and underlying beliefs as an insider had advantages, but also some serious disadvantages. Among the benefits were the ability to understand the local speech styles and innuendoes as well as the body language and, in return, to be understood; to have access to the background knowledge absorbed and stored since birth by those growing up in a Jamaican rural village; contact with a wide variety of people; knowledge of a childhood spent in a sugar plantation area where stories about slavery were often told and where old traditions lived among the peasantry; the early realization that although colour was sometimes considered and used as an important yardstick, in the minds of country-bred Jamaicans such as myself, in fact, the majority, it was an unnatural and imposed gauge.

Among the disadvantages have been the difficulty in being objective when dealing with situations that involved or mirrored those of close family and friends, and that affected people whose past I shared and whose lives were inextricably entangled with mine; coming to terms with situations in which information that ought to have been passed on had been given in confidence which must be honoured; and the inability to record on tape certain events because of being made a participant and/or assistant to the convenors.

As the work progressed, the picture became more complex. Impressions and information sometimes flowed in from different directions before they could be properly sorted out. Questions often arose faster than they could be answered. Poor communications and mushrooming schedules aggravated the problems. Conditions in any one cult seemed to have as many exceptions as rules, more unpredictables than probabilities. Between cults themselves, the differences were even greater. Contacts with ancestral and interested spirits, as Blacking notes, were made in a variety of ways, depending on the person, the occasion and the cult. The drum/song/dance combination worked in Kumina and Maroon situations, for instance, while in Ettu the call was made by means of a song given to each member by an elder before death. Dreams were important sources of information through links beteen the mortal and the spirit worlds for Ettu, Tambo, Maroon, Kumina and Revival people. Rastafarians sought wisdom by "reasoning", and meditation with the aid of chanting, drumming and the smoking of "the weed" (marijuana) without any reference to a spirit world intermediate to Jah (God). In spite of very obvious differences in performance-style and interpretations, however, each cult was relating in its own way to certain generally held beliefs.

Cultists made their own decisions with regard to exposing their material and activities. Some were quite convinced that they should not, and would not, allow themselves to be involved, if at all, to more than a very limited extent. Others, such as Kapo, Queenie and certain Maroon leaders, shared generously yet had very definite points beyond which they would not go. Expert in changing the course of an event in a moment, should they become uneasy or decide that they ought to pull back, they had effective codes for internal communication always in place for instant use. Fears regarding the presentation of cult material at Festivals and for stage performances were largely groundless. The leaders were themselves very aware of the dangers and were always vigilant.

It is important to note that the heritage under discussion is still living and changing. This study makes no claim to be complete or perfect. It is an attempt to organize and pass on information seen by the author as important even in its unfinished state, much of which may all too soon be unavailable. It can be a useful beginning to many other studies, an aid to Jamaican self-discovery and to greater human understanding on a wider scale.

In carrying out research, there is the temptation to organize one's data and impress informants in order to produce a coherent and systematic structural analysis of social relations, belief systems and musical styles. One also wishes to show that one's informants are organized, rational beings and that performances of folk music are systematic and are subjected to critical analysis by participants. Nevertheless, to organize and control the data for the sake of coherent presentation can distort the reality of flexibility and adaptation to context in performance, which are so important to the participants. If Queenie, for example, seemed to contradict herself on different occasions, it was not that she did not know her own mind or could not be coherent and systematic, or that she was right on one occasion and wrong on others: it was rather that each situation required a different creative, adaptive response.

It must be noted that although some historians claim that "Cumina . . . existed in Jamaica at least as early as 1730", there is far more evidence that Kumina was brought to Jamaica between 1841 and 1865 by labourers who came from Central Africa. Many present-day devotees are, therefore, now only three generations away from the African practices and beliefs brought here. Even when they recognize Jesus Christ as "a powerful good spirit", they do not accept Christian forms of worship. Other Jamaican cults are either African/Christian syntheses, as in Revival and Rastafarian, the latter adhering to the Ethiopian Orthodox Church, or their followers are willing to be members of Christian churches, as in Ettu, Maroon, Tambo, Goombeh, and Nago. Kumina is, therefore, one of the purest traditional African non-Christian retentions in Jamaica.

Kumina people arrived in Jamaica at a time of great dissatisfaction and unrest among the freed slaves and their offspring. This discontent ultimately led to the Morant Bay "Rebellion" of 1865 which was harshly suppressed and the leaders and hundreds of followers hanged. Maroons, bound by their long-standing treaty with the British, were used to track down the rebels. Despite these traumatic beginnings, the Maroons, Kumina and other strong knots of "African" manifestations have "held strain" and continued to influence the lives of many people. As a result of the desire to seek solutions within themselves, Jamaicans have evolved dynamic ideologies reflecting an African and Christian symbiosis.

Queenie was, in many respects, like traditional African healers or ritual experts who are also skilled musicians and for whom healing and community work are inseparable. There were (and are) in sub-Saharan African societies with many patterns of related and contrasting skills associated with music, dance, healing, and leadership. There is the healer who is "taken" by a guiding spirit and the healer who learns a craft by apprenticeship. In some societies, neither role is associated specifically with musical skills. In others, such as the Venda, leadership in the spirit-possession cult and expertise in leading and performing the dance and music of initiation are associated with the practice of particular medical skills, but not with the more general practice of divination. Elsewhere, as among the Nsenga of Eastern Zambia, the most important musician in a gathering of healers is a master drummer who is not himself a healer. Amongst the Shona of Zimbabwe, highly skilled performance on the mbira is inseparable from leadership and influence as a spirit medium.

What is not clear in most reports from Africa and elsewhere is: Which came first: the musical skill or the gift of healing? Queenie stated in interviews with both Lewin [1969] and Ramsay (in 1986) that expertise in music and dancing preceded her ability to heal. In a taped discussion with Jean Snyder-Burt (1985), Queenie said:

> Now you see music, when I hear music, you know, it just make me feel happy . . . An' the soun' of the right music no care [no matter] how me down [how depressed I am]. An' sometimes me alone sit down . . . an me jus' penetrate pon [concentrate upon] me music . . . An' who know it an' who can penetrate it an' who can live up to it, because is not everybody can live up to music. Music is the key of Africa.

It is also clear that her skills and public acceptance as a leader were a consequence of her abilities both as a musician and healer.

In the belief of Kumina groups, neither musical excellence nor healing can be entirely learnt: they are gifts of the spirit. Since Queenie's skills in music and a passion for it preceded the discovery of healing and other powers, her career is an example of an individual whose social actions are a consequence of artistic practice, especially since one of the main duties of every Kumina Queen at every event is to choose the songs, lead the singing and dancing and, when necessary, guide and conduct the drumming. Her musical activities can be described as generating social situations rather than reflecting them.

As Brathwaite comments:

> Miss Queenie, in Western Kingston, Jamaica . . . In her yard there is healing, there is advice, there is sound and music, dance: there is psychological and physical examination, there is prayer. She's a politician, economist for self and household, yard and her community, priestess: all in one.
>
> And she has the power of Nommo: spirit, force, and memory of the Word. It is she who remembers and restores the past [Brathwaite 1978: 47].

She also demonstrated herself to be the heritage protector not ordained by any government, nation or set of scholars. Seeing with an all-encompassing world-view, she taught us how to understand ourselves and our beginnings as a people.

Queenie, because of her charisma and the popularity of the music and dancing far beyond Kumina and other circles of traditional beliefs and practices, became one of the island's most visible social leaders but not the only one; Brother Brown and Kapo quickly come to mind. Count Ossie was another. Although they belonged to three cults that consider themselves to be very different, Kumina, Rastafarian and Revival, their styles of leadership were strikingly similar. Each, on pain of death, had to be true to the God/gods and spirits to which allegiance is due. People of peace, they did not hesitate to "fight" fearlessly for principles and precepts in which they believed; they led with confidence and conviction, but did not drag or push; acutely aware of their power, they never used it to dominate; they were not intimidated by personalities, no matter how important these might be in the temporal world, yet they did not confront and were "as wise as serpents and gentle as doves"; they were not daunted by problems and difficult situations since they saw them as temporary and man-made. They knew that God's will must eventually be done.

This approach to life rejects the norms of modern living and has its roots in African traditional thought, as many other universal peasant philosophies have in their own traditions. Examples are the tendency to see time as a circular development rather than a linear progression; traditional games that stress cooperation and communal camaraderie rather than the glory of the individual victor; belief in the oneness of life that flows from one source through all creation and the cosmic plan being one of harmony among all things; the strong feeling that communication between the physical/visible and the spiritual/non-visible is the basis of religious practice and must be actively maintained at all times, not only on days of worship. Through all of this, people like Queenie consider that the laws of God contribute to overall harmony, in contrast to the destructiveness of man-made laws/systems such as slavery. Land, for example, was viewed by the colonial powers and early landowners as something to be exploited or raped, while for Queenie and her followers, land is a holy, communal possession; "Mother Clay", as she called it.

This view of Queenie may not seem unique compared to other folk research. What is new, however, is that it is being recognized and incorporated into national, everyday consciousness in a developing country.

> Now that the real treasure, to end our misery and trials, is never far away:
> it is not to be sought in any region; it lies buried in the innermost recess of
> our own home, that is to say, our own being. And it lies behind the stove,
> the life-and-warmth-giving centre of the structure of our existence, our
> heart of hearts if we could only dig. But there is the odd and persistent

fact that it is only after a faithful journey to a distant region, a foreign country, a strange land, that the meaning of the inner voice that is to guide our quest can be revealed to us. And together with this odd and persistent fact, there goes another, namely, that the one who reveals to us the meaning of our cryptic inner message must be a stranger, of another creed and a foreign race [Jewish parable cited in Zimmer 1946].

For many years, most research into traditional cultures in developing countries was carried out by foreigners who had the resources and skills. Indigenous researchers were still unsure of the worth of their own cultures and, subconsciously, even held them in low esteem. In the 1960s and 1970s, nationalism and other factors stimulated an interest in indigenous research in some developing countries, but it was still executed with methods of collection, storage and analysis, often in a foreign library or information centre and unrelated to local needs. Today, there is a need to rationalize research by applying it for urgent solutions to problems and for formulating policies in national development.

Reluctance to try solutions that appear to be simple has had a long history. In the Old Testament, 2 Kings 5: i–xvi, Naaman, a captain in the service of the King of Syria, was "a great man with his master, and honourable . . . a mighty man of valour". He was also a leper. Told of the possibility of being cured by the prophet of Israel, he set off with a letter from his master to the King of Israel and gifts of gold, silver and clothing. The letter, asking the King of Israel to "recover [Naaman] of his leprosy" annoyed him, until Elisha asked for Naaman to come to him. Arriving at the prophet's door, the captain received a message: "Go and wash in Jordan seven times and thy flesh shall come again to thee, and thou shalt be clean." Naaman was "wroth" and left "in a rage". He was advised by his servants, no doubt simple folk, that since he would have carried out difficult directions, he should comply with Elisha's simple instructions. Naaman accepted this advice and was healed. Elisha, like Queenie and other Jamaican traditional healers, would accept no recompense. It is assumed by the very terminology that "developing" countries should look to the "developed" ones for solutions. Yet a man of the calibre of Yehudi Menuhin states:

> In our technological age we have come to believe that safety lies in control, in mastery over man as well as nature. Admittedly, this has brought us certain advantages, but can we claim advances when, as our many wars in this century confirm, we still pillage and kill without purpose: We fail because man is neither at peace with himself, nor has he mastery over himself; therefore, he seeks mastery over others [Menuhin and Davis 1979: 3].

The time is ripe for a reappraisal: to see people of Queenie's ilk as nodes in a network that can buoy people up; to initiate a rethinking that must stimulate deeper digging into traditional cultures, with emphasis on the value of folk perceptions of the world rather than the grand designs of ethnocentric academic analysis. Examination of the world-view and philosophies of individuals like Queenie can improve and increase national resources by understanding the nature of the source. Thus, new social groups and nations can achieve a more informed and sympathetic grasp of their own backgrounds and behaviour, as well as the behaviour of others. Through understanding better the creativity of individuals and the richness of their own heritage, they can, perhaps, also learn to appreciate better similar situations in other countries, provided that there is not some international competition for cultural superiority.

In the long run, we always return from the cosmic abstract to individuals like Queenie. Back to the microcosm, those who seem to have a wider, more all-encompassing view of the world: people like Queenie and my mother who, despite their limited experience in space and formal education, could deal with every situation in their own world and understand other worlds in principle. Theirs is the mastery of the culture, and theirs the mission to disseminate what would otherwise be shrouded in a "shameful" past.

So from their small bodies emanate strength and a message, a deep sense of being. These could even now be used to reach through their circle of influence, to the community, the country and, eventually, the world. Reinforced by an innate knowledge of another consciousness, Queenie continues, despite upheavals in Jamaica and the wider world, to be a symbol of something beyond the present and the immediate. She helps to remind us too, of the centre of peace and harmony that is within and available to each one of us: to show us that Jamaica's upheavals and eruptions of violence are short and temporary because even the most sophisticated has a "Queenie" side. Beneath the surface, regardless of appearance, the pervading materialism and craving after foreign "gods", our roots are buried deep in Jamaican soil. Our spirits live at the root of the mighty cotton tree.

References

Barnett, Sheila. 1979. "Jonkonnu: Pitchy Patchy". *Jamaica Journal* 43: 18–32.

Barrett, Leonardo. 1976. *The Sun and the Drum: African Roots in Jamaican Folk Tradition*. Kingston: Sangster's.

Baxter, Ivy. 1970. *The Arts of an Island: The Development of the Culture and the Folk and Creative Arts in Jamaica, 1494–1962*. New Jersey: Scarecrow Press.

Beckwith, Martha. 1928. *Jamaica Folk-Lore*. New York: American Folk-Lore Society.

Beckwith, Martha. 1929. *Black Roadways. A Study of Jamaican Folk Life*. New York: Negro Universities Press.

Berliner, P. 1976. "Music and spirit possession at a Shona Bira". *African Music* 5: 130–138.

Bilby, K. and F. K. Bunseki. 1983. "Kumina: a Kongo-based tradition in the New World". *Les Cahiers du CEDAF* 8: 1–114.

Black, Clinton. 1958. *History of Jamaica*. London and Glasgow: Collins.

Blacking, John. 1955. "Some notes on a theory of African rhythm advanced by Erick von Hornbostel". *African Music* 1, no. 2: 12–20.

Blacking, John. 1970. *Process and Product in Human Society*. Johannesburg: Witwatersrand University Press.

Blacking, John. 1984. *The Aesthetic in Education*. Oxford: Pergamon Press.

Blacking, John. 1985. "The context of Venda possession". *Yearbook for Traditional Music*, Vol. 17.

Bleby, Henry. 1853. *Death Struggles of Slavery. Being a Narrative of Facts and Incidents which Occurred in a British Colony*. London: Hamilton Adams & Co.

Bonner, Tony. 1974. "Blue Mountains expedition: exploratory excavations at Nanny Town by the Scientific Exploration Society". *Jamaican Journal* 8, nos. 2 and 3: 46–50.

Brathwaite, E. K. 1978. "Kumina: the spirit of African survival in Jamaica". *Jamaica Journal* 42: 45-63.

Brandon, William. 1961. *The American Heritage Book of Indians*. New York: American Heritage Publishing.

Broadwood, Lucy. 1907. "English airs and motifs in Jamaica". In *Jamaica Song and Story*, by Walter Jekyll. London: Folk-Lore Society, London University.

Carter, Hazel. 1970. "Consonant reinforcement and Kongo morphology". *African Studies* 11: 113–146.

Carter, Hazel. 1974. "Negative structure in the syntactic tone-phrasing system of Kongo". *Bulletin of SOAS* 38, no. 1: 29–50.

Carter, Hazel. 1986. "Language and music of Kumina". *ACIJ Newsletter* 12: 3–12.

Cassidy, F. G. 1961. *Jamaican Talk: Three Hundred Years of English Language in Jamaica*. London: Macmillan.

Cassidy, F. G. and R. B. Le Page. [1967] 1980. *Dictionary of Jamaican English*. Cambridge: Cambridge University Press.

Clarke, Edith. 1966. *My Mother Who Fathered Me: A Study of Family in Three Jamaican Communities*. London: Allen and Unwin.

Clerk, Astley. 1975. "The music and musical instruments of Jamaica". *Jamaica Journal* 9, nos. 2 and 3: 59–67.

Cundall, F. 1915. *Historic Jamaica*. London: West Indian Committee for Institute of Jamaica.

Dalby, David. 1971. "Ashanti survivals in the language and traditions of the Windward Maroons of Jamaica". *African Language Studies*, no. 12: 31–35.

Dallas, R. R. 1803. *History of the Maroons*, Vols. 1 & 2. London: Longman and Rees.

Dougherty, Richard. 1973. *Rediscovering the Land of Look Behind*. Miami: Miami Herald Publishing.

Dridzo, A. D. 1971. *Jamaica Maroon*. Moscow: The Academy of Sciences of the USSR, Institute of Ethnography.

Duerden, J. E. 1897. "Aboriginal Indian remains in Jamaica". *Journal of the Institute of Jamaica* 2: 43.

Dunham, Katherine. 1946. *Journey to Accompong*. New York: Henry Bolt and Co.

Eaton, George. 1975. *Alexander Bustamante and Modern Jamaica*. Kingston: Kingston Publishers.

Edwards, Bryan. [1807] 1974. *The History: Civil and Commercial of the British Colonies in the West Indies*. London: Stockdale.

Edwards, Bryan. 1976. *Observation on the Disposition, Character, Manners and Habits of Life of the Maroons*. London: Stockdale.

Epstein, Dina J. [1981]. *Sinful Tunes and Spirituals: Black Folk Music of the Civil War*. Urbana: University of Illinois Press.

Fewkes, J. W. 1907. "The Aborigines of Puerto Rico and neighbouring islands". *Twenty-fifth Annual Report of the Bureau of American Ethnology*, 199.

Firth, Raymond. 1958. *Human Types*. New York and Toronto: The New American Library.

Garvey, Amy Jacques. 1963. *Garvey and Garveyism*. Kingston: Collier Books.

Gilbert, Pia and Aileene Lockhart. 1961. *Music for the Modern Dance*. Iowa: Wm. C. Brown.

Gordon, Diane. 1981. "The Jamaican Buru masquerade in the socio-cultural context of Bowens". The Queen's University of Belfast, unpublished study.

Griaule, M. 1965. *Conversations with Ogotemmeli*. Oxford: Oxford University Press

Grove, Charles. 1947. *Grove's Dictionary of Music and Musicians*. New York: Macmillan.

Hall-Alleyne, Beverley. 1982. "Asante Kotoko: the Maroons in Jamaica". *ACIJ Newsletter* 7: 3–40.

Hall-Alleyne, Beverley. 1984. "The evolution of African language in Jamaica". *ACIJ Research Review* 1: 21–46.

Hamilton, J. C. 1980. *The Maroons of Jamaica and Nova Scotia*. Toronto: The Copp, Clark Co.

Harcourt-Smith, Simon. 1966. *The Maroons of Jamaica*. London: History Today.

Harris, C. L. G. 1977. "The Maroons of Moore Town: a colonel speaks". Unpublished.

Hart, Richard. 1971. "The Maroon treaties: letter to the editor". *Jamaica Journal* 5, no. 2: 2.

Henriques, Fernando. 1953. *Family and Colour in Jamaica*. London: Eyre and Spottiswoode.

Herskovitz, M. J. 1941. *The Myth of the Negro Past*. Boston: Beacon Press.

Higginson, Thomas W. 1969. *Black Rebellion: A Selection from Travellers and Outlaws.* New York: Arno Press and New York Times.

Hill, Frank. 1943. "Political development". In *Ian Fleming Introduces Jamaica*, edited by Morris Cargill. London: André Deutsch.

Hogg, D. W. 1960. *The Convince Cult in Jamaica.* New Haven: University Publications.

Hogg, D. W. 1961. "Magic and 'science' in Jamaica". *Caribbean Studies* 1: 1–5.

Hornbostel, E. M. 1928. "African Negro music". *Africa* 1, no. 1: 52.

Hurston, Z. N. 1939. *Voodoo Gods: An Inquiry into Native Myths and Magic in Jamaica and Haiti.* London: Dent.

Jacobs, H. P. 1965. "Dialect, magic and religion". In *Ian Fleming Introduces Jamaica*, edited by Morris Cargill. London: André Deutsch.

Jekyll, Walter. 1907. *Jamaica Song and Story.* London: Folk-Lore Society, London University.

Joyce, T. A. 1907. "Pre-historical antiquities from the Antilles, in the British Museum". *Journal of the Royal Anthropological Institute of Great Britain and Ireland* 37: 404–407.

Jung, C. G. 1967. *Seven Sermons to the Dead.* London: Stuart and Watkins.

Karpeles, Maud. 1967. *Cecil Sharp: His Life and Work.* London: Routledge and Kegan Paul.

Kerr, Madeline. 1963. *Personality and Conflict in Jamaica.* London: Collins.

Kopytoff, Barbara K. 1975. "The Maroons of Jamaica: an ethno-historical study of incomplete politics 1655–1905". Thesis, University of Pennsylvania.

Kopytoff, Barbara K. 1976. "The development of Jamaican Maroon ethnicity". *Caribbean Quarterly* 22: 35–50.

Kopytoff, Barbara K. 1976. "Jamaican Maroon political organisation: the effects of the treaties. *Social and Economic Studies* 25: 87–104.

Kopytoff, Barbara K. 1978. "The early political development of Jamaican Maroon societies". *William and Mary Quarterly* 35: 287–307.

Kuper, Adam. 1976. *Changing Jamaica.* London: Routledge and Kegan Paul.

Laman, Karl. 1953–1968. *The Kongo: Studia Ethnographica*, 1–4. Uppsala.

Lekis, Lisa. 1960. *Dancing Gods.* New York: Scarecrow Press.

Leslie, Charles. 1739. *A New and Exact Account of Jamaica.* Edinburgh: Fleming.

Leslie, Charles. 1740. *A New History of Jamaica.* London: Hodges.

Lewin, Olive. 1967–1987. "Choral arrangements of 240 Jamaican folk songs". Unpublished.

Lewin, Olive. 1967. "Jamaica folk music". *Caribbean Quarterly* 14, nos. 1 and 2: 49–56.

Lewin, Olive. 1969. "Jamaican folk mass". Unpublished.

Lewin, Olive. 1970a. *Some Jamaican Folk Songs*. Kingston: Oxford Publishers.

Lewin, Olive. 1970b. "Twelve Jamaican songs for piano". Unpublished.

Lewin, Olive. 1971. "Jamaica's folk music". *Yearbook of the International Folk Music Council*, 15–22.

Lewin, Olive. 1973. *Forty Folk Songs of Jamaica*. Washington, DC: Organization of American States.

Lewin, Olive. 1974a. "Jamaican songs for voice, clarinet and piano". Unpublished.

Lewin, Olive. 1974b. "Four Jamaican songs for guitar". Unpublished.

Lewin, Olive. 1974c. "Folk music research in Jamaica". *Black Communication*. New York: Speech Communication Association, 121–35.

Lewin, Olive. 1974d. *Brown Girl in De Ring*. Oxford: Oxford University Press.

Lewin, Olive. 1975a. "Mass media for development: required research in the Caribbean". *Caribbean Studies* 14, no. 4: 143–149.

Lewin, Olive. 1975b. *Alle, Alle, Alle*. Oxford: Oxford University Press.

Lewin, Olive. 1975c. *Beeny Bud*. Oxford: Oxford University Press.

Lewin, Olive. 1975d. *Dandy Shandy*. Oxford: Oxford University Press.

Lewin, Olive. 1976a. *El Estudio de la Musica Folkloric de Jamaica*. Havana: Casa de las Americas.

Lewin, Olive. 1976b. "Jamaican songs for solo voice with piano/guitar accompaniment". Unpublished.

Lewin, Olive. 1978. "Music for 'maskarade': a Jamaican historical drama". Unpublished.

Lewin, Olive. 1980. "Jamaica". In *The New Grove Dictionary of Music and Musicians*, edited by Hanley Sadie. London: Macmillan.

Lewin, Olive. 1982. "Musical life of Jamaica in the 19th century". *Die Musikkulturen Latein Amerikas in 19 Jahrhundert*. Regensburg: Gustav Bosse Verlag, 277–297.

Lewin, Olive. N. d. "An old man dies, a book is lost". In *Jamaica Folk Art*. Kingston: Institute of Jamaica.

Lewin, Olive. 1986. "The research into Jamaica's heritage began as a national undertaking in 1966". *Anuario Musical* 39–40, 1–15. Barcelona: Instituto do Musicologia del CSIC, Barcelona.

Long, Edward. 1774. *The History of Jamaica*. London: Lowndes, 1–3.

Loven, S. 1935. *Origins of the Tainan Culture*. Goteberg: Elanders Bodtryckeri Aktiebolag.

Martin, Leann. 1973. "Maroon identity: processes of persistence in Maroon Town". PhD dissertation, University of California, Riverside.

Mensah, Atta. 1980. "Music south of the Sahara". *Music of Many Cultures: An Introduction*, 172–188.

Menuhin, Y., and Curtis Davis. 1979. *The Music of Man*. Toronto: Methuen.

Merriam, Alan P. 1982. *African Music in Perspective*. New York: Garland Publishing.

Moore, Joseph G. 1953. "Religion of Jamaican Negroes: a study of Afro-Jamaican acculturation". PhD dissertation, Northwestern University.

Moore, Joseph G. 1965. *Religious Syncretism in Jamaica*. Reprinted from *Practical Anthropology*.

Murray, Tom. 1953. *Folk Songs of Jamaica*. Oxford: Oxford University Press.

Mutwa, Credo. 1966. *Indaba My Children*. Great Britain: Stanmore.

Myers, C. S. 1907. "Traces of African melody in Jamaica". In *Jamaica Song and Story*, by Walter Jekyll. London: Folk-Lore Society, London University.

Nettleford, Rex 1985. *Dance Jamaica. Cultural Definition and Artistic Discovery, The National Dance Theatre Company of Jamaica, 1962–1983*. New York: Grove Press.

Nketia, J. H. Kwabena. 1974. *The Music of Africa*. New York: Norton & Co.

Oppenheimer, E. P. 1917. *As a Man Lives*. London: Ward, Lock & Co.

Patterson, H. O. 1973. *The Sociology of Slavery: An Analysis of the Origins, Development and Structure of Negro Slave Society in Jamaica*. Kingston: Sangster's Book Store Jamaica in association with Granada Publishing.

Reckord, Mary. 1969. "The slave rebellion of 1831". *Jamaica Journal* 3, no. 2: 25–31.

Robinson, Carey. 1969. *The Fighting Maroons of Jamaica*. Kingston: William Collins and Sangster.

Roth, H. L. 1887. "The Aborigines of Hispaniola". *Journal of the Anthropological Institute of Great Britain and Ireland* 16: 269.

Rouget, Gilbert. 1985. *Music and Trance. A Theory of the Relations between Music and Possession*. Chicago: University of Chicago Press.

Rouse, I. 1948. "The Arawak". In *Handbook of South American Indians,* edited by J. H. Stewart, vol. 4, 554.

Sachs, Wulf. 1947. *Black Anger*. New York: Greenwood Press.

Scott, Clarissa Stewart. 1968. *Cultural Stability in the Maroon Village of Moore Town Jamaica*. Boca Raton, Florida: Florida Atlantic University.

Scholes, P. A. 1941. *Oxford Companion to Music*. Oxford: Oxford University Press.

Schuler, Monica. 1980. *Alas, Alas, Kongo: A Social History of Indentured African Immigration into Jamaica, 1841–1865*. Baltimore and London: Johns Hopkins University Press.

Schweitzer, Albert. 1949. *The Philosophy of Civilization*. New York: Macmillan.

Seaga, Edward. 1956. "Folk music of Jamaica". Introduction and notes to *Ethnic Folkways* LP no. 453. New York: Ethnic Folkways.

Seaga, Edward. 1969. "Revival cults in Jamaica: notes towards a sociology of religion". *Jamaica Journal* 3, no. 2: 3–13.

Senior, Olive. 1983. *A–Z of Jamaican Heritage*. Kingston: Heineman.

Smith, M. G. 1965. *The Plural Society in the West Indies*. Berkeley: University of California Press.

Sowande, Fela. 1970. "The role of music in traditional African society". Paper presented at African Music: Meeting in Yrounde, Cameroon.

Sowande, Fela. 1974. "The quest of an African world view: the utilization of African discourse". In *Black Communication: Dimensions of Research and Instruction*, 67–117. New York: Speech Communication Association.

Spence, Lewis. 1941. *Myth and Ritual in Dance, Game and Rhyme*. London: Watts.

Tanna, Laura. 1982. "Kumina: the Kongo connection". *Sunday Gleaner Magazine*, 1–3.

Tanna, Laura, and Hazel Ramsey. 1987. "Dinki Mini". *Jamaica Journal* 20: 2.

Thompson, I. E. 1938. "The Maroons of Moore Town". *Anthropological Series of the Boston College of Graduate School*, 472–480.

Tuelon, Alan. 1973. "Nanny, Maroon chieftainess". *Caribbean Quarterly* 19, no. 4: 20–27.

Waddell, H. M. 1963. *Twenty-Nine Years in the West Indies and Central Africa. A Review of Missionary Adventures 1929–1958*. London: Frank Kass and Co.

Warner-Lewis, Maureen. 1977. "The Nkuyu: spirit messenger of the Kumina". *Savacou* 3: 57–82.

Wedenoja, W. A. 1978. "Religion and adaptation in rural Jamaica". PhD dissertation, University of California, San Diego.

Williams, Joseph J. 1934. *Psychic Phenomena of Jamaica*. New York: Dial Press.

Williams, Joseph J. 1938. *The Maroons of Jamaica*. Chestnut Hill, Massachusetts: Boston College.

Williams, Stephanie E. 1985. "On folk music as the basis of a Jamaican primary school music programme". MA thesis, Faculty of Music, McGill University.

Wright, Philip. 1970. "War, peace with the Maroons 1730–1739". *Caribbean Quarterly* 16, no. 1.

Zimmer, Heinrich. 1946. "Myths and symbols in Indian art and civilization". *Bollington Series* 4: 219–221.

Index